# GEORGIA HERITAGE

## Treasured Recipes

Published By
The National Society
of
The Colonial Dames of America
in the State of Georgia
1979

The National Society of Colonial Dames of America in the State of Georgia, extends grateful appreciation to its members who contributed the recipes for this book. Regrettably, we were unable to incorporate all of the recipes due to the lack of space.

Georgia Ferguson
Cookbook Chairman

Headquarters of the National Society of the Colonial
Dames of America in the State of Georgia is:
The Andrew Low House
329 Abercorn Street
Savannah, Georgia
Water Color Illustrations by Mrs. Jack M. Passailaigue.

Printed in the United States of America
**Wimmer Brothers Fine Printing & Lithography**
Memphis, Tennessee 38118
*"Cookbooks of Distinction"* ™

# Committee

Mrs. Lonnie D. Ferguson, *Chairman*
Mrs. Jack Passailaigue, *Illustrations*

Mrs. Albert S. Britt, Jr.
Mrs. Hilliard Burt
Mrs. Bon Durham
Mrs. Sewell Brumby
Mrs. William Farinholt
Mrs. Arnold Barrett
Mrs. Gordon MacGregor
Mrs. Forman Dismukes
Mrs. Sara A. Tyler
Mrs. Nathaniel Hardin
Mrs. James Treadwell
Mrs. Dan M. Hicky
Mrs. Dillon Winship
Mrs. Walter Williams
Mrs. Arthur Simkins

Mrs. Jack Smith
Mrs. James D. Maddox
Mrs. Lloyd Summer
Mrs. Shelby Myrick, Jr.
Mrs. Jack Bracey
Mrs. L.S. Flowers
Mrs. Felton Davis
Mrs. John Shields, Jr.
Mrs. Sam N. Roberts
Mrs. Roscoe Fleetwood
Mrs. Frank Turpin, Jr.
Mrs. Lucian Daniel
Mrs. E.P. McCollum
Mrs. Robert Clark

# President's Statement

Preservation and appreciation of the tangible heritage of the Past, for the betterment and enrichment of life in the Present, has been a guiding policy of the National Society of the Colonial Dames of America in the State of Georgia since its founding in 1893.

Since 1928 one of the Society's most important projects has been the preservation and maintenance of the impressive classical house on Lafayette Square in Savannah, which was built in 1848 for the prominent English cotton factor, Andrew Low. Though it was acquired solely as Headquarters for the Georgia Colonial Dames, its role has greatly widened in the past half century. For many years now it has been open to the public, and is one of the most admired historic houses in the area.

Proceeds from the sale of this book will be used to help maintain the Andrew Low House and its furnishings in the style of a family home in the flourishing port of Savannah during the 1840's.

Alice H. Daily, President

# Table of Contents

# FOREWORD

Not long ago a young Georgia bride sagely remarked that anyone could cook who was able to read. What a far cry from that not too distant past when many, if not the majority, of cooks in our kitchens not only couldn't read, but needed only a list of ingredients and a few sketchy instructions, to turn out the most delectable dishes!

This cookbook is a blend of the old and the new. Many of the recipes, from treasured collections handed down from mother to daughter for generations, give a nostalgic glimpse of earlier days. However, for the modern housewife who must combine other roles with that of cook in her many-faceted, busy life, we have added definite instructions, and paraphrased some of the delightful original wording.

Our recipes come from all over Georgia—"from the mountains to the sea", from our largest cities and our quiet countryside. Some originated in other states, and some were brought from foreign lands.

Variety, color, and zest are musts for a successful menu. May the experienced, as well as the new cook, find all three in good measure in these pages.

# Beverages

Mary F. Passailaigue

# BANANA PUNCH

4 packages presweetened
  lemonade mix (2 quarts per
  package) *OR* lemon-lime
  Kool-aid
2 large cans (1 quart, 14
  ounces) pineapple juice

2 12-ounce cans frozen orange
  juice
1 small can (6 ounces) lemonade,
  frozen
6 ripe bananas
5 cups sugar (or to taste)

Slice bananas for garnishment. Combine all other ingredients. Reserve enough punch for a small ice ring to chill punch, if desired. Makes 3 gallons.
**Mrs. R. E. Champion, Jr. (Mary Barrett)**
**Albany**

# WATERMELON PUNCH

5 cups watermelon juice
2 33-ounce bottles of Sprite
1 cup orange juice

½ cup lemon juice
melon balls

Mix and chill. Serves 25 to 30.
**Mrs. Robert Shepherd (Bailey Alexander)**
**Monticello, Florida**

# SANGRIA

½ gallon dry red wine
1 can (6 ounces) frozen orange
  juice
juice of 4 lemons

grated rind of 4 lemons
¾ to 1 cup of sugar (to taste)
1½ cups of brandy or bourbon
1 can fruit cocktail

Mix in pitcher diluting just before serving with ⅓ to ½ amount of soda water.
**Mrs. T. Miesse Baumgardner (Lauretta King)**
**Brunswick**

# REFRESHING PUNCH

3 cups sugar
6 quarts water
1 46-ounce can unsweetened
    pineapple juice

3 cups bottled lemon juice
2 46-ounce cans unsweetened
    orange juice
3 quarts ginger ale

Mix sugar and water to simple syrup. Add other ingredients except ginger ale. Pour over block of ice in punch bowl—one gallon of the mixture and one quart of ginger ale. Stir and serve. Yield: 3 gallons.

**Mrs. John Groover Kennedy (Connie Austin)**
**Savannah**

# MOCHA PUNCH

1 small jar instant coffee
1 can Hershey chocolate
3 quarts milk

1 pint boiling water
2 pints of vanilla ice cream

Dissolve coffee in boiling water. Add other ingredients. It will serve 36 cups.

**Mrs. Gordon MacGregor (Mary Bacon Bland)**
**Brunswick**

# PUNCH FOR ONE HUNDRED

2 dozen lemons, squeezed
5 cups of sugar
2 gallons of water
2 tablespoons vanilla

1 tablespoon of almond extract
2 large cans of frozen orange juice
2 large cans of pineapple juice

Dissolve sugar in water and mix with other ingredients. Make ice molds with mint leaves. A Bundt pan is ideal for molding the ice.

**Mrs. Edward Harrison Mixson (Katherine Hudson Oglesby)**
**Valdosta**

# ICED COFFEE PUNCH

6 quarts chilled coffee*
6 cups half and half
½ cup Hershey's cocoa

1¾ cups sugar
6 quarts vanilla ice cream

*To make instant coffee, put 2 tablespoons plus 1 teaspoon instant coffee in 1 quart boiling water.

Mix the first four ingredients and chill in refrigerator. When ready to serve, set out vanilla ice cream to soften and place in punch in punch bowl, cutting ice cream in small pieces so that it will meld with the coffee. Keep adding ice cream as needed to keep punch cold. Fills 78 punch cups or 39 eight-ounce glasses.

**Mrs. Sam Noble Roberts (Mary Stanton)**
**Atlanta**

# BACK PORCH PEACH SOUP

2 pints half & half
4 tablespoons sugar
6 teaspoons nutmeg
4 teaspoons cinnamon

5 tablespoons Amaretto
2 tablespoons peach liqueur
6 large peaches (skinned)

Whip half-and-half for 3 minutes. In Cuisinart mix all ingredients until peaches are liquified. Garnish with mint sprigs. Serves 4.

**Mrs. D. Williams Crawford (Diane Williams)**
**Baltimore, Maryland**

# MAMA'S EGGNOG

12 eggs, separated
12 tablespoons sugar (1 cup)

1 pint whipping cream
24 tablespoons bourbon

Beat egg yellows. Put half the sugar in the egg whites and beat until stiff. Slowly put remaining sugar in egg yolks, then add whiskey slowly while beating. Whip the cream and fold in the egg whites. Serves 12.

**Mrs. Jack C. Hughston (Sarah Hardaway)**
**Columbus**

# EGGNOG

| | |
|---|---|
| 12 eggs | 10 ounces bourbon |
| 12 ounces heavy cream | 1 ounce Jamaica rum |
| 12 teaspoons sugar | 1 ounce cognac |

Beat egg yolks until light, adding the sugar gradually. Add liquor. Refrigerate over night. Fold in stiffly beaten egg whites and cream. If too thick, milk can be added.

**Mrs. Howard Morrison (Mary Lane)**
**Savannah**
**Recipe of Mrs. Mills B. Lane (Mary Comer)**

# EGGNOG FOR FIFTY PEOPLE

| | |
|---|---|
| 5 dozen eggs, separated | 2 quarts bourbon |
| 1 quart rum | 2 pounds sugar |
| 2 quarts cream, whipped | 3 quarts milk |

Beat egg yolks until light. Beat in sugar. Beat in bourbon and rum slowly, so the egg yolks do not curdle. Refrigerate for several hours. Fold in milk and whipped cream when ready to serve.

**Mrs. Thomas McKey Tillman, Sr. (Louise Phinizy)**
**Athens**

# BLOODY MARYS FOR A CROWD

| | |
|---|---|
| 1 46-ounce can V-8 juice | 2 tablespoons Worcestershire |
| 1 46-ounce can tomato juice | 2 teaspoons salt |
| 6 cups vodka | 1 teaspoon seasoned salt |
| 1 cup lemon juice | |

Mix together and serve over ice. Serves 20.

**Mrs. Shelby Myrick Jr. (Alice Barrow)**
**Savannah**

# LEMON SYLLABUB

1 cup sugar
1 quart heavy cream or half
    milk and half cream

2 cups good white wine or sherry
juice of 6 lemons

Place all ingredients in a deep bowl, stir well. Place syllabub churn in bowl and slowly pump dasher to produce a light froth. As the froth accumulates, skim off with a spoon into tall serving glasses or goblets. Continue to churn until mixture is used. Sprinkle each serving with grated lemon or nutmeg. Serves 8-10. This recipe may also be used for dessert when made thick and served in parfait glasses or it may be made with part milk and served as a sauce over trifle or fresh fruit.

Syllabub is traditionally a holiday drink and in the south is often served at Christmas parties and family gatherings. This recipe comes from a collection published by my great-great-grandmother in 1866 in Columbus, Georgia.

**Mrs. Flewellyn Plant Murphy (Valeria McCullough)**
**Macon**

# RUM LIME SLUSH

1 6-ounce can frozen limeade
6 ounces light rum

6 ounces water

Mix all in a blender and serve in chilled julep cups.

**Mrs. Samuel Wasden Wood (Maude Talmadge)**
**Athens**

# SYLLABUB

2 cups cream (whipping)
1 cup sherry

½ cup sugar
1 cup milk, fresh as it easily curdles

Mix ingredients lightly and put in deep bowl. Put churn in and move plunger rapidly up and down. As foam accumulates on top skim off with large spoon and put directly in compote. Delicious served over wine jelly.

**Mrs. Edward Vason Jones (Maria Martin)**
**Albany**

# ICED TEA

1 lemon
1 cup sugar

2 cups water
3 regular tea bags

Squeeze lemon, set juice aside. Bring to boil both lemon rind halves, sugar
and water. Add tea bags, cover and steep. Cool with tea bags and lemon
halves left in mixture. Strain, add lemon juice and enough cold water or ice
cubes to make ½ gallon.
**Mrs. Gardner Wright, Jr. (Jeanne Brown)**
**Rome**

# ICED TEA

1 can of frozen lemonade
6 cans water
2 ice cream scoops sugar

1 tablespoon instant tea
mint sprigs

Mix all ingredients together and serve over ice.
**Mrs. J. A. Sibley (Barbara Thayer)**
**Atlanta**

# INSTANT RUSSIAN TEA MIX

½ cup instant tea,
  unsweetened
2 cups Tang
1⅓ cups sugar

1 teaspoon cinnamon
½ teaspoon ground cloves
1 teaspoon dry lemon rind

Mix well. For individual cup of tea, add 2 teaspoons to 1 cup of boiling
water.
**Mrs. Albert Felton Jenkins, Jr. (Julie Richardson Green)**
**Atlanta**

# MINT TEA

2 cups sugar
½ cup water
grated rind of one orange

juice of 6 oranges
6 glasses of very strong tea
several sprays of mint

Boil the sugar, water and orange rind about 5 minutes. Remove from the fire and cool. Into the tea put the orange juice. Half fill the iced tea glasses with ice—add the tea and sweeten to taste with the mint syrup.

**Mrs. James D. Gould (Mary Frances Young)**
**Brunswick**

# MINT CUP
*(Serves 25-30)*

3 bunches of mint
6 large lemons—juiced
3 quarts ginger ale

1½ cups sugar
1½ cups water
block of ice

Crush leaves of mint. Add lemon juice, sugar and water. Refrigerate over night. Strain and right before serving add ginger ale. Pour in punch bowl. Add block of ice.

*Note:* Be sure *liquid* is put in punch bowl *first*—then add ice. This will save many tears and a broken punch bowl.

Spirits could be added but those who taste seem to think it already has.

**Mrs. Floyd T. Taylor, Jr. (Annie Lee Wilson)**
**Brunswick**

# HOT BUTTERED RUM

¾ cup of soft butter
1 cup brown sugar
1 teaspoon nutmeg
dash of salt

48 whole cloves
boiling water
rum
wax paper

Cream butter and brown sugar. Stir in nutmeg and salt. Pat mixture out between two pieces of wax paper to ¼ inch thick. Cut in one inch squares and top with a whole clove. (This makes about 48 squares.) Freeze on paper until hard. When frozen, store in freezer cartons in freezer.

To make a cup of hot buttered rum, place a frozen square in a prewarmed mug. Add 1 to 2 jiggers of boiling water to one jigger of rum. A hearty cold weather drink.

**Mrs. Irwin W. Stolz (Virginia Howard)**
**Jacksonville, Florida**

# Appetizers and Hors d'oeuvres

Mary F. Passailaigue

## CAVIAR EGG MOLD

8 eggs
1 small onion, minced
4 tablespoons butter

4 ounces sour cream
salt and pepper to taste
caviar

Chop hard-boiled eggs finely. Add butter, onion, salt and pepper and blend well. Place in mold and refrigerate several hours. Turn onto plate at serving time and cover with sour cream. Drip on caviar. Serve with crackers. Serves 12 to 14.

**Mrs. R. D. Heinitsh (Beulah Reeve)**
**Atlanta**

## BEAU MONDE DIP

1 pint mayonnaise
1 pint sour cream
3 tablespoons minced onion
3 tablespoons Beau Monde
   (Spice Islands)

3 tablespoons dill weed
3 tablespoons chopped parsley (6
   tablespoons if dried)

Mix ahead and refrigerate. Will keep 2 weeks. Good on potato chips or vegetables.

**Mrs. James Bowen (Frances Rylander)**
**Americus**

## DAVE'S CURRY DIP

1 cup mayonnaise
1 hard-boiled egg
1 teaspoon ginger
salt and pepper to taste

1 teaspoon curry powder
1 tablespoon minced onion
2 teaspoons lemon juice

Blend all ingredients until smooth. Place in glass container; cover and chill for at least four hours before serving. Use as a dip for pared vegetables.

**Mrs. William Wortham Farinholt (Katharine Woltz)**
**Atlanta**

# CAVIAR DIP

3 eggs, hard-boiled
2 tablespoons butter
1 to 2 tablespoons mayonnaise
salt
white pepper
1 teaspoon Dijon mustard

celery salt
3 spring onions
1 cup sour cream
2 2-ounce jars of Romanoff Caviar
   or Beluga Caviar (fresh)
1 box of melba rounds (2 dozen)

Make 3 eggs into egg salad using 1 teaspoon Dijon mustard, celery salt and white pepper to taste. Line shallow bowl with salad and cover with the chopped onion in a thin layer. 1 cup of sour cream as third layer on top of onions. Cover this with 2 jars of 2-ounces each of Romanoff Icelandic Lumpfish Caviar or fresh Beluga Caviar. Serve on buttered melba rounds.

**Mrs. W. O. Kinney, Jr. (Lillian Birdsey)**
**Atlanta**

# CAVIAR MOUSSE

¾ cup sour cream
¼ cup chopped onions
3 hard-boiled eggs, chopped
3 tablespoons mayonnaise
4 tablespoons lemon juice
1 2-ounce jar red caviar
½ teaspoon salt

½ teaspoon Lea & Perrins
¼ teaspoon Tabasco
¼ teaspoon white pepper
2 tablespoons plain gelatin
2 tablespoons vodka or hot
   water

Mix all the ingredients except gelatin and vodka and caviar in the blender. Add 2 tablespoons of gelatin that has been dissolved in 2 tablespoons of hot water or vodka. Fold in a 2 ounce jar of red caviar. Mold.

**Mrs. Lawrence M. Austin (Dede Harrison)**
**Savannah**

# KODIAK DILL

1 cup mayonnaise
1 tablespoon Beau Monde
   seasoning
2 tablespoons parsley flakes

1 tablespoon green onion flakes
1 tablespoon grated fresh onion
3 tablespoons dill weed
1 cup sour cream

Combine all ingredients and stir. Let set ½ hour before refrigerating. Will keep indefinitely. Can be used as a dip, but most tasty if placed on rye strips and run under broiler.

**Mrs. John Carroll (Martha Burney)**
**Covington**

# EGGS STUFFED WITH BACON

12 hard-boiled eggs
6 slices of bacon, fried crisp,
   and crumbled
3 tablespoons chopped chives

2 tablespoons soft butter
1½ tablespoons vinegar
4 to 5 tablespoons sour cream
salt and pepper to taste

Cut eggs in half lengthwise. Remove yolks and mash. Add to them bacon, chives, butter, vinegar, sour cream, salt and pepper. Fill egg halves and chill. Before serving decorate with tiny sprig of parsley. Serves 12.

**Mrs. Heywood Mason (Edith King)**
**Thomasville**

# BOURSIN

1 8-ounce package cream
   cheese
⅓ cup sour cream
¼ cup sweet butter

1 small clove garlic, minced
1 tablespoon chives
1 tablespoon parsley, chopped
salt and pepper to taste

In mixer or blender beat softened cream cheese and butter with sour cream. Add all other ingredients and mix well. Put in small mold and chill for at least 12 hours. Serve with crackers.

**Mrs. Buell Herzig (Caroline Shields)**
**Waycross**

# HOT CHEESE HORS D'OEUVRES

1 loaf party rye bread
1 cup grated sharp Cheddar
   cheese
1 cup grated Parmesan cheese

1 cup mayonnaise
1¼ tablespoons chopped onion
1 small can black olives, chopped

Mix last five ingredients together and spread on rye bread. Freeze on trays until hard. Wrap and put in freezer. When ready to serve, put under broiler a few minutes until cheese is bubbly.

**Mrs. John Phillips, Jr. (Aynn Kirtley)**
**Albany**

# BLUE VELVET MOUSSE

2 egg yolks
1 tablespoon gelatin
2 egg whites, stiffly beaten
8 ounces Roquefort cheese, or
   blue cheese

¼ cup light cream
¼ cup cold water
1 cup cream, whipped

Combine egg yolks and light cream in a saucepan. Mix thoroughly before heating. Cook over low heat until mixture coats spoon. Remove from heat immediately. Soften gelatin in cold water and dissolve over hot water. Add to egg and cream mixture. Sieve cheese. (Real Roquefort is better but blue cheese will be good.) Fold into gelatin mixture. Gently fold in the stiffly beaten egg whites and lastly the whipped cream. Pour into a 1-quart mold which has been lightly greased with salad oil. Set in the refrigerator to chill until firm. Unmold and serve with crackers.

This is also good served as a small spoonful on the top of fruit salad which has been marinated in a very light French dressing.

**Mrs. Wesley Turnell Hanson, Jr. (Marie McHatton)**
**Athens**

# WIGHT'S DELIGHT

1 8-ounce package cream
  cheese
creamed horseradish

⅓ of 10-ounce jar of blueberry
  preserves

Ice top of cream cheese with ⅛ to ¼-inch of horseradish. Drizzle blueberry preserves over top.

**Mrs. William McCollum (Carolyn Eidson)**
**Thomasville**

# CHEESE BISCUIT

1 pound sharp cheese
1 pound butter
½ teaspoon red pepper

½ teaspoon salt
1 tablespoon sugar
5-6 cups plain flour

Cream cheese and butter. Add remaining ingredients. Place in refrigerator for about an hour. Roll about ¼ inch thick and cut with small cutter. Bake at 275 degrees for about an hour or until biscuit is crunchy. Makes 95 small biscuits.

**Mrs. Charles Smith Hogg (Fred Singer Turpin)**
**Americus**

# LEFTOVER-CHEESE BALL

½ pound any cheese you have
  on hand OR ½ pound sharp
  Cheddar
2 packages (8 ounces each)
  cream cheese
1 small onion (shallot is best)

1 tablespoon Worcestershire
  sauce
¼ teaspoon celery salt
½ teaspoon salt
1 cup nuts

Grate cheese, combine with cream cheese (best to let it come to room temperature first), grated onion, Worcestershire sauce, salt and celery salt. Form into ball and roll in chopped nuts. Or it can be rolled in chopped parsley or blushed with paprika instead. Also it takes nicely to being formed into a roll and rolled in a mixture of paprika and chili powder.

**Mrs. C. P. Whiting (Louise Osborne)**
**Albany**

# CHEESE-ONION SPREAD FOR CRACKERS

8 ounces sharp Cheddar
   cheese
6 ounces cream cheese
½ teaspoon curry powder

¼ teaspoon salt
3 tablespoons sherry
10 ounces chutney
¼ cup finely chopped green onions

Blend everything except chutney and onions with electric beaters or with a food processor. Spread in a shallow dish and chill until firm. Spread chopped chutney on top and sprinkle onions on top of chutney.

**Mrs. Randolph Brooks (Polly Chisholm)**
**Savannah**

# CHEESE STRAWS

1 pound extra sharp cheese
1¾ cups plain flour
½ cup butter

1 teaspoon salt
½ teaspoon red pepper

Grate cheese. Soften butter. Put all ingredients in mixer and mix thoroughly. Put through cookie press. Bake at 350° until light brown—about 20 minutes. Makes about 100 cheese straws.

**Mrs. Henry D. Green (Fran Yates)**
**Brunswick**

# CHEESE COOKIES

1 pound grated sharp cheese
1 pound butter (do not
   substitute margarine)
3½ cups sifted flour

½ teaspoon salt
¼ teaspoon cayenne
1 cup chopped pecans

Soften butter and cheese. Cream with electric mixer, add flour sifted with salt and cayenne. Turn mixer on low and mix in flour for 1 minute. Add chopped nuts. Drop by ½ teaspoonful on ungreased cookie sheet. Cook in moderate oven about 20 minutes.

This recipe may be mixed ahead and frozen or cooked and frozen. Delicious hot as hors d'oeuvres.

**Mrs. Ralph Crutcher (Eleanor Henderson)**
**Savannah**

# CHEESE RINGS

1 pound sharp Cheddar cheese, grated
1 cup margarine
2 cups sifted all-purpose flour
1 tablespoon sugar
1 teaspoon salt
½ teaspoon red pepper
½ teaspoon paprika

Cream cheese and margarine. Add flour, sugar, salt, red pepper, and paprika. Mix until smooth. Put mixture into cookie press. Press out into rings or desired shape on ungreased cookie sheet. Bake 20-25 minutes in 300 degree oven.

**Mrs. Converse Ferrell (Jane Lumpkin)**
**Valdosta**

# CHEESE DAINTIES

¾ cup butter or margarine
1½ cups sharp cheese, grated
¼ cup Parmesan cheese
⅛ teaspoon red pepper
1 teaspoon salt
1½ cups flour

Cream butter and cheese together. Sift red pepper and salt with flour and add. Chill for ½ hour before rolling out. Cut with small biscuit cutter. Bake at 350 degrees for about 12 minutes. If you like, you can put half pecan on top.

**Mrs. Alfred Blackmar (Frances Dixon)**
**Columbus**

# CHEESE WAFERS

½ cup butter
½ cup margarine
2 cups flour
2 cups Rice Krispies
2 cups grated cheese
dash of sugar, salt
Tabasco—one drop
½ cup finely chopped pecans

Mix butter and flour together. Add grated cheese and Rice Krispies and nuts. Bake at 350° for 15 minutes.

**Mrs. Isaac M. Aiken (Alice Harrison)**
**Brunswick**

## CHUTNEY CHEESE BALL

2  3-ounce packages cream
   cheese
1 cup sharp grated Cheddar
   cheese
4 teaspoons sherry

½ teaspoon curry powder
¼ teaspoon salt
chopped chives
2 tablespoons chutney

Soften cheeses. Place cheeses, sherry, curry powder, and salt in mixer bowl or container of food processor. Blend well. Form into a patty. Top with chutney and sprinkle with chives. Surround with crackers.

**Mrs. H. H. McNeel (Patricia McCormick)**
**Marietta**

## BAKED CHEESE PUFFS

1 pound loaf of unsliced white
   bread, trimmed of crusts
¼ pound sharp Cheddar
   cheese, grated
salt and cayenne to taste

½ cup butter
3 ounces cream cheese
¼ teaspoon dry mustard
2 egg whites, stiffly beaten

Soften cream cheese and butter. Cut bread into 1-inch cubes. In a heavy saucepan, combine the butter, cream cheese, grated Cheddar cheese, mustard, salt and cayenne. Heat the mixture over low heat, stirring, until is just melted and the ingredients are well combined. Transfer the mixture to a bowl and fold in 2 egg whites, stiffly beaten. Dip the bread cubes into the cheese mixture to coat them, letting the excess drip back into the bowl, and put them on a buttered baking sheet. Chill them loosely covered with foil overnight. Bake the puffs in a preheated 400 degree oven for 8 to 10 minutes, or until they are golden. Serve immediately.

Makes about 70 puffs

**Mrs. L. Neill Bickerstaff (Sara Bussey)**
**Columbus**

# PINEAPPLE CHEESE BALL

1½ pounds sharp Cheddar
  cheese
½ pound Swiss cheese
8 ounces cream cheese
¼ pound blue cheese

¼ pound butter
½ cup apple juice
1 tablespoon Worcestershire
  sauce

Grate all cheeses and mix together. Add creamed butter and apple juice. Shape into a pineapple. With a wet teaspoon make texture like a pineapple. Decorate with whole cloves and dust with paprika. Top with a real pineapple top. Serve with crackers. Serves 25.

**Mrs. William Lee Wood, Jr. (Frances Elizabeth Bush)**
**Macon**

# HOT CRAB COCKTAIL DIP

3  8-ounce packages cream
  cheese
3 large cans KING crab
½ teaspoon garlic salt
½ cup mayonnaise

2 teaspoons prepared mustard
¼ cup sauterne
2 teaspoons confectioners' sugar
1 teaspoon onion juice
½ teaspoon seasoned salt

Melt cream cheese in top of double boiler. Add remaining ingredients; mix well. Place in chafing dish; serve warm with crackers or chips. (May be frozen and reheated.)

**Mrs. George Arthur Horkan, Jr. (Virginia Davis)**
**Moultrie**

# SHRIMP SPREAD

¼ cup milk
1 cup mayonnaise
1 tablespoon Worcestershire
  sauce
3 drops Tabasco sauce
1 small onion, chopped

1 5-ounce can shrimp, drained
½ pound medium or sharp
  cheese, grated (when using
  medium cheese, you get more
  shrimp flavor)

Mix all ingredients except shrimp thoroughly. Add shrimp and process for just a second. Don't completely destroy shrimp. (May use blender or food processor for easiness.) Chill before serving. This is better after being chilled 2 to 3 days. Will keep up to 2 weeks in refrigerator. Makes 2 cups.

**Mrs. Roland Wetherbee (Diane Waller)**
**Albany**

# PINK SHRIMP MOUSSE

1 envelope Knox gelatin
½ cup cold water
1 8-ounce package cream
  cheese
1 8-ounce bottle Thousand
  Island Dressing
1 tablespoon fresh lemon juice

½ teaspoon prepared horseradish
½ teaspoon salt
2 cups cooked shrimp, finely
  chopped
¼ cup bell pepper, finely chopped
½ cup celery, finely chopped

Soften gelatin in cold water; then heat slowly until dissolved. Soften cream cheese with spatula and gradually add dressing, blending smooth. Add gelatin, lemon juice, horseradish, and salt. Fold in shrimp, bell pepper, and celery. Pour in 1-quart fish mold which has been previously rinsed with cold water and place in refrigerator to congeal. After unmolding place slice of olive for eye and serve with crackers.

**Mrs. John A. Shields, Jr. (Christine Thiesen)**
**Waycross**

# MARINATED SHRIMP

4 pounds cooked and peeled
  shrimp

1 large onion, thinly sliced

MARINADE
¾ cup vegetable or corn oil
⅓ cup tarragon vinegar
½ package Italian Good
  Seasons salad dressing mix

½ package garlic Good Seasons
  salad dressing mix
1 tablespoon water

Combine shrimp and onion in bowl. In cruet, mix vinegar, seasonings and water. Shake thoroughly. Add oil and shake. Pour over shrimp and onion and stir. Let marinate in refrigerator for at least 8 hours, stirring at intervals. Will keep in refrigerator for a week or more.

**Mrs. Alexander Lawrence Cann (Mary Gatewood)**
**Savannah**

# FAVORITE CANAPÉ

2 3-ounce packages cream
  cheese
7 ounces crabmeat (fresh,
  frozen, canned)
½ teaspoon mayonnaise

½ teaspoon Worcestershire sauce
¼ teaspoon seasoned salt
paprika
rounds of toast

Mix all ingredients (except paprika) thoroughly and place mixture in a covered bowl in refrigerator for 1 hour or more. Make rounds of toast and cover well with crabmeat mixture. Sprinkle top with paprika. Place under broiler. Toast until golden brown. Serve very hot. Makes 36 canapes.

**Mrs. Charles H. Werner (Elizabeth Cox)**
**Atlanta**

# BACON PECAN DATES

pitted dates
pecan halves
thin sliced bacon

Italian, or oil and vinegar
  dressing

Place pecan half in the center of each date. Wrap dates with thin bacon slices. Lap bacon and secure with a toothpick. Place dates in a bowl, pour dressing over dates and marinate overnight. When ready to bake dates, put them in a roaster pan on a rack. Bake at 350° to 375°. Watch closely. When bacon is brown remove from pan and drain on paper towel.

**Mrs. Malcolm Hardin Bogle (Marion Ann Reid)**
**Valdosta**

# CRAB AND BROCCOLI DIP

1 package chopped frozen
  broccoli
1 can mushroom soup
1 tube Kraft garlic cheese
1 small jar chopped
  mushrooms
1 can crab claw meat

¼ cup chopped onions
½ cup chopped celery
dash of Tabasco
dash of Worcestershire sauce
salt
pepper
⅛ cup white wine

Cook broccoli according to directions. Melt cheese with soup in a double boiler. Sauté onion and celery in butter until onions are clear. Combine crabmeat, cooked broccoli, cheese, soup mixture, wine, sautéed onions and celery, mushrooms, Tabasco, Worcestershire sauce, salt, and pepper in a baking dish. Heat at 325 degrees for 30 minutes. Use as a dip with cocktails. This is also good served over rice as a main course.

**Mrs. Agnes Conoly Brown (Agnes Conoly)**
**Valdosta**

## CHAFING DISH CRAB DIP

1  1-pound can fresh backfin
   lump crabmeat
2  8-ounce packages cream
   cheese
½ cup butter
½ cup half and half

1 to 2 tablespoons grated onion
1 teaspoon Worcestershire sauce
1 tablespoon lemon juice
⅛ teaspoon Tabasco sauce
½ teaspoon salt

Melt cream cheese, butter, half and half in top of double boiler. Combine until smooth. Add seasonings. Fold in crabmeat and transfer to chafing dish. Serve with Ritz crackers or plain rounds of melba toast.

**Mrs. Walter Rylander (Alice Harrison Walker)**
**Americus**

## SANTA ROSA CRAB SALAD DELIGHT

1 small carton low-fat cottage
   cheese
8 ounces crabmeat, fresh or
   canned
¼ teaspoon salt
½ green pepper, finely
   chopped
1 medium onion, finely
   chopped

1 tablespoon gelatin soaked in 2
   tablespoons of water
⅛ teaspoon white pepper
1 small jar finely chopped
   pimentos
4 stalks celery, finely chopped
1 cup Hellman's mayonnaise
grated peel and juice of 2 lemons

Mix all ingredients together except mayonnaise, lemon peel and juice. Add peel and juice to mayonnaise. Add enough of the mixture to the crab mixture so that it all binds when stirred about. Mold and refrigerate. Do not freeze. When serving use the remaining mayonnaise mixture over the top of the salad or as side accompaniment. Garnish with paprika. Serve on mildly flavored cocktail crackers.

**Mrs. William McKinley Luckie (Patricia Johnson)**
**Thomasville**

# SMOKED OYSTER ROLL

2 8-ounce packages cream
cheese
2 cans smoked oysters
2 teaspoons Worcestershire
sauce

2 to 3 tablespoons mayonnaise
⅛ teaspoon salt (or to taste)
1 large garlic bud, pressed
½ small onion, pressed
parsley flakes

Cream mayonnaise into cheese. Add Worcestershire sauce, pressed garlic
and onion. Combine well. Chop oysters fine and add. Chill 24 hours. Can be
rolled into a log, ball or put in a bowl. May be rolled in parsley flakes.
**Mrs. John Tyler Mauldin (Anne Scott Harman)**
**Atlanta**

# SHRIMP DIP

4 tablespoons milk
1 cup mayonnaise
1 tablespoon Worcestershire
sauce
dash garlic salt
1 onion, chopped

½ pound shrimp, cooked and
shelled
½ pound sharp Cheddar cheese,
cubed
3 drops Tabasco sauce

Put all ingredients in blender and blend. Serve with melba toast, plain or
rye. This makes two cups dip.
**Mrs. Michael Justice Taylor (Mary Bothwell Burdell)**
**Augusta**

# SHRIMP DIP

1 4½-ounce can shrimp
3 tablespoons mayonnaise
1½ tablespoons parsley flakes
(fresh may be used)

½ teaspoon grated onion OR ½
teaspoon onion juice
salt and pepper to taste

Quick and easy to fix for unexpected folks who drop by for a drink.
**Mrs. Ray Lowell Peacock, Jr. (Margaret Anne McGowan)**
**Augusta**

## GAZPACHO SHRIMP DIP

1 cup catsup
1 onion, chopped
1½ small cucumbers, peeled,
    seeded and chopped
2 tablespoons oil
1 large tomato, peeled, seeded
    and chopped

2 cloves garlic, chopped
1½ green peppers, chopped
2 tablespoons wine vinegar
2 to 3 drops Tabasco
salt and pepper to taste

Combine catsup, garlic, onions, 1 green pepper, 1 cucumber, vinegar, Tabasco, oil, salt and pepper in blender and pureé thoroughly. Refrigerate for several hours for taste to develop. Garnish with remaining pepper, tomato and cucumber. Makes 2 cups.

**Mrs. J. Madden Hatcher (Sue Mac Fox)**
**Columbus**

## INDIVIDUAL SHRIMP QUICHE

¾ cup cooked shrimp,
    chopped
¼ cup green onions, finely
    sliced
2 eggs
¼ teaspoon salt

pastry for two crusts
1 cup Swiss cheese, grated
½ cup mayonnaise
⅓ cup milk
¼ cup dried dill weed (optional)

On a floured surface roll out half of the pastry (either frozen or made by recipe) into a 12-inch circle. Cut six 4-inch circles. Repeat with remaining pastry. Fit into twelve 2½-inch muffin pan cups. Fill each with some of the onions, shrimp and cheese. Beat together milk, eggs, salt and dill. Pour over shrimp mixture. Bake in a 400 degree preheated oven for about 20 minutes or until browned. Makes 12 servings.

**Mrs. George Erwin (Mary Talley)**
**Athens**

# PÂTÉ

1 pound liverwurst
1 cup real mayonnaise
1 teaspoon unflavored gelatin
2 teaspoons lemon juice
Worcestershire sauce to taste

¼ cup bourbon
½ cup cold chicken or beef broth
⅛ teaspoon pepper
⅛ teaspoon garlic powder

Grease a 3½-cup mold. Mix liverwurst (room temperature) and bourbon until smooth. Stir in mayonnaise. Sprinkle gelatin over broth in small saucepan. Heat over low heat until gelatin is dissolved. Stir into liverwurst. Add lemon juice, Worcestershire sauce, pepper, and garlic powder. Blend well. Turn mixture into mold, cover, and chill overnight.

**Mrs. Edmond Archer Turner (Dorothy Holmes)**
**Quitman**

# PÂTÉ

2 pounds of calf's liver
½ pound of chicken liver
¼ pound of pork liver
2 eggs, beaten
¼ cup heavy cream
2 tablespoons fresh lemon
   juice

1 clove garlic, crushed
pinch of powdered bay leaf
dash of salt and freshly ground
   pepper
½ pound sliced bacon
4 tablespoons brandy

Preheat oven to 325 degrees. Mince the livers, or put through grinder twice, using finest blade. Add all other ingredients to the livers except bacon and brandy. Mash into a paste with a fork. Warm the brandy in a saucepan, light, and pour slowly over the liver mixture. Mix well. Line a pâté mold or a bread-loaf pan with strips of bacon. Pack in the liver and cover with the remaining bacon strips. Cover the mold with aluminum foil and set into a large shallow roasting pan that contains one or two inches of water. Let stand in the oven for approximately 2 hours. Remove from oven, discard the foil, and "weight" the pâté with any heavy object that will cover the entire loaf. Chill overnight. Unmold and serve with a favorite garnish. Makes a 9-inch loaf.

**Mrs. Dykes Nelson (Martha Marshall Dykes)**
**Americus**

# EMERGENCY PÂTÉ

½ cup real butter
2 sticks Oscar Mayer Liver
   Sausage (Braunschweiger)
1 small can chopped ripe olives

½ cup finely chopped onions
⅓ cup brandy
¼ cup chives or parsley

Cream butter with sausage. Add onion, brandy, olives (to simulate truffles). Pack in 4-cup mold lined with cheese cloth. Chill. Unmold and cover with chives or parsley.

**Mrs. David Samuel Wainer (Emma Heyward Burnet)**
**Valdosta**

# CHICKEN LIVER PÂTÉ

1 pound chicken livers
½ cup butter (no substitute)
1 medium onion, chopped
   finely
1 bud garlic, minced
3 tablespoons brandy or sweet
   sherry

1 teaspoon salt
¼ teaspoon freshly ground
   pepper
½ teaspoon mixed herbs

Melt ½ cup butter. Add onion and garlic. Sauté. Add livers, salt, pepper and herbs. Cook for about 10 minutes. The livers should be bright pink on inside. Remove from stove. Pour all into blender with brandy. Blend until smooth. Cool. Cream remaining ½ cup of butter. Add to liver mixture. Mix until thoroughly blended. Place in serving container. This pâté is smooth enough to pipe onto toast squares from a decorator's bag. Otherwise, serve with melba toast or regular toast. Serves 6.

**Grace Latimer Durham**
**Edinburgh, Scotland**

# CHIPPED BEEF APPETIZER

| | |
|---|---|
| 2 jars chipped beef | 1 large jar pimento |
| 2 cans cheese soup | 1 package sliced almonds |
| 1 large can sliced mushrooms | ½ cup milk |

Empty 2 cans cheese soup in double boiler. Add ½ cup milk. Shred chipped beef and fold in. Add remainder of ingredients. Serve hot on Melba toast. If desired a small amount of sherry may be added. Serves 20.

**Mrs. Cornelius Elliott Heath (Sarah Clark DeSaussure)**
**Atlanta**

# SWEET AND SOUR MEATBALLS

| | |
|---|---|
| 1½ pounds ground beef | 1 tablespoon soy sauce |
| ¾ cup rolled oats | 1 teaspoon Accent |
| 1 can water chestnuts, drained and chopped | ½ teaspoon onion |
| | ½ teaspoon garlic salt |
| ½ cup milk | ¼ teaspoon salt |
| 1 egg, slightly beaten | dash of Tabasco |

Form mixture into very small meatballs. Brown and drain.

SAUCE

| | |
|---|---|
| 1 8½-ounce can crushed pineapple | ½ cup red wine vinegar or lemon juice |
| 1 cup brown sugar | 2 tablespoons soy sauce |
| 2 tablespoons cornstarch | ⅓ cup chopped green pepper |
| 1 cup beef bouillon | |

Mix pineapple juice, sugar and cornstarch. Gradually stir in liquids. Cook, stirring until thick. Add pineapple, green pepper. Simmer with meatballs for 35 minutes.

**Mrs. William Hanger (Sudie Clark)**
**Atlanta**

## COCKTAIL TAMALES

1 14½-ounce can hot tamales ("Gebhardt" and "Old El Paso" are good brands)

1 pound thin sliced bacon, minus a few slices

Pour off and discard tomato sauce, carefully unwrap tamales and discard wrappings. With sharp knife cut each tamale crosswise into 4 pieces. Wrap each piece in ½ slice of bacon, folding to cover all of tamale if possible. Secure with toothpicks. (It is easier to cut the whole pound of bacon at once, when cold, then warm slightly to facilitate wrapping.) Place tamales in baking pan in pre-heated 375 degree oven, cook for about 30 minutes, turning once or twice, until bacon is nicely browned. Drain on paper towels. Serve hot. This recipe makes about 24. (If desired, tamales may be wrapped, then frozen and kept for later cooking, or may be frozen after cooking, then thawed and reheated 20-30 minutes in 350 degree oven.)

**Mrs. Albert Sidney Britt Jr. (Annie McIntosh)**
**Savannah**

## ANTIPASTO

½ cup catsup
½ cup oil
1  12-ounce can tomato sauce
1 whole bay leaf
1 teaspoon salt
½ teaspoon each black pepper & Tabasco
2 or 3 cloves crushed garlic
1 teaspoon Accent
1 teaspoon chili powder

2 2-ounce cans anchovy filets with oil
½ cup diced celery
½ cup diced carrots
1 6-ounce can solid pack tuna
1 5-ounce jar pickled onions (drained)
1 cup cauliflower florettes
1 cup sliced sweet pickles
1 6-ounce can button mushrooms

In a 3-quart saucepan, combine the first 10 ingredients (listed in column one) in the order given. Bring to a boil. Cook 2 or 3 minutes, stirring well. Remove from heat. In separate pan, blanch celery and onions in small amount of water until barely tender. Drain thoroughly and then add to previous mixture and carrots, tuna, cauliflower, pickles and mushrooms. Return to heat and boil gently for 5 minutes, stirring gently. Remove from heat and cool. Pack in covered jars. Store in refrigerator where it will keep indefinitely. Do not freeze. To serve, place in pretty bowl and surround with a variety of crackers. Will serve 18 to 20 as an hors d'oeuvre.

**Mrs. Flewellyn Plant Murphy (Valeria McCullough)**
**Macon**

## LEFTOVER LAMB CURRY BALLS

¼ pound cream cheese,
  softened
2 tablespoons mayonnaise
1 cup chopped cooked lamb
1 tablespoon chopped chutney

1 tablespoon curry powder
½ teaspoon salt
1 cup blanched slivered almonds
½ cup grated coconut

Mash cream cheese. Add mayonnaise, lamb, curry, chutney, salt, and almonds. Mix well and roll into balls approximately 1 inch in diameter. Roll in coconut. Chill. May be refrigerated 2 days in advance or frozen. Makes 3½ dozen balls.

**Mrs. Charles J. Heinemann, Jr. (Eloise Champion)**
**Albany**

# BOLOGNA WEDGES
*(Makes 16 appetizers)*

12 thin slices bologna
1 3-ounce package cream
  cheese (softened)
2 tablespoons milk

1 teaspoon grated onion
1 teaspoon horseradish
¼ teaspoon hot-pepper sauce

Early on serving day or day before: In small bowl with fork, *mix well* cream cheese, milk, onion, horseradish and pepper sauce. Spread half of cream cheese mixture on five slices of bologna. Stack these slices and top with unspread, plain slice of bologna. Repeat process and make amother stack of 5 *spread* slices of bologna. Top with unspread, plain slice. Wrap in waxed paper until serving time.

*Before serving:*
With a sharp knife cut each stack of bologna slices into 8 equal wedges. Garnish each wedge with small piece of parsley—keep cold.
Note: 12 slices ham, chicken or turkey may be used instead of bologna.

**Mrs. Forman Dismukes (Florence Barber)**
**Brunswick**

# MARINATED RIPE OLIVES

1 can pitted ripe olives,
  drained

1 small bottle Worcestershire
  sauce

Place well-drained olives in a glass jar with the Worcestershire sauce and marinate in the refrigerator three days, shaking up occasionally. Pour off sauce and serve the chilled olives with drinks. The mixture is death on silver so serve in glass or pottery. Men particularly seem to like these.
**Mrs. William Leonard Erwin (Harriett Gilbert)**
**Athens**

# CREAM CHEESE STUFFED MUSHROOMS

small amount lemon juice,
  diluted with water
1 pound fresh mushroom caps
1  8-ounce package cream
  cheese, softened

1 small onion, grated
1 egg
salt and pepper

Wipe mushrooms with cloth dipped in lemon juice. Mix together cheese, egg, onion, salt and pepper. Fill caps with mixture. Place on baking sheet and broil until bubbly. Serves 6 to 8.
**Mrs. John Davidson Capers (Margaret Sherman)**
**Augusta**

# PICKLED MUSHROOMS

3 pounds mushrooms
1 quart water
2 medium onions, thinly sliced
½ cup distilled white vinegar

1½ teaspoons salt
½ bay leaf
¼ teaspoon whole black pepper
1  teaspoon olive oil

Cook whole or quartered mushrooms in water for fifteen minutes. Drain, reserving liquid. Arrange mushrooms and onions in layers in a crock or in jars. Simmer together vinegar, mushroom liquid, salt, bay leaf, and pepper for ten minutes. Strain over mushrooms. Float olive oil over the top and chill for at least 24 hours before serving.
**Mrs. Robert Reynolds (Elizabeth Hollingsworth)**
**Albany**

# SPINACH DIP

2 cups sour cream
1 cup mayonnaise
1 package Knorr's leek or
   onion soup
1 package frozen, chopped
   spinach (thawed or cooked
   and drained)

½ cup chopped green onions
½ cup chopped parsley
1 teaspoon dill weed
1 teaspoon salad seasoning
pinch of garlic powder

Mix all ingredients. Refrigerate several hours. Serve with chips or crackers. Serves 20 generously.

**Mrs. Fielding Lewis Walker, IV (Sarah Wise Turpin)**
**West Dundee, Illinois**

# BUFFET HOT DOGS IN BOURBON

¾ cup of bourbon
2 pounds hot dogs
1½ cups catsup
   (14-ounce bottle)

1 cup brown sugar
1 teaspoon grated onion
½ teaspoon oregano
¼ teaspoon rosemary

Combine all ingredients in ovenproof dish. Bake for 1 hour uncovered in a 350 degree oven. Serve in a chafing dish with toothpicks for a hearty cocktail buffet.

**Mrs. William C. Thomas (Nancy Harrold)**
**Richmond, Virginia**

## HOT BACON-CHEESE ROLL-UPS

| | |
|---|---|
| thin sliced white bread | 1 jar Old English cheese spread |
| bacon slices, cut in half | |

Trim crusts from thinly sliced white bread. Cut each slice in half. Spread lightly with Old English cheese spread. Roll up; wrap with a half slice of bacon; and secure with a wooden toothpick. Preheat oven to 400 degrees. Bake on a rack until bacon is crisp. These may be cooked halfway, cooled, and frozen until needed. When ready to use, put frozen roll-ups on cookie sheet and bake.

**Mrs. Henry Turner Brice, Jr. (Myra Jane Holman)**
**Valdosta**

## MRS. BRUMBY'S COCONUT CURLS

| | |
|---|---|
| 1 fresh coconut | salt |

Pierce eyes and drain coconut. Set in a very hot oven, 450 degrees or more, for about 10 minutes, the larger the coconut the longer it must stay. Remove and crack. If it does not come out easily, it may be returned broken to the oven until the meat no longer adheres to the shell. With a vegetable peeler which is very sharp, shave off the brown rind. Holding the piece of white meat in the hand so that the edge of the break is convenient, shave off long strips of the coconut meat. Spread strips out on a cookie sheet and set in an oven of 200 degrees or lower and slowly toast, stirring them occasionally. When one edge has reached a pretty brown, remove from the oven and sprinkle with salt while hot. Store in an airtight container until needed to serve with drinks.

**Mrs. Harben Daniel (Caroline Noble Jones)**
**Savannah**

## SUGARED NUTS

1½ cups granulated sugar      ½ teaspoon cinnamon
½ cup sherry                  2 or 3 cups pecan halves

Combine sugar with sherry and boil until it will form a soft ball in cool water. Add cinnamon and nuts, stirring until cloudy. Turn mixture onto a well-buttered cookie sheet, separating nuts. (Walnuts may be used instead of pecans.) These keep well in covered jars.

**Mrs. Hurt Starbuck (Elizabeth Hurt)**
**Columbus**

## ALMONDS GLAZED AND SALTED

2 pounds almonds, blanched    coarse salt (Kosher salt does well
1 egg white                       for this)

Coat the dried blanched almonds with the unbeaten egg white, being sure that they are only sticky and not wet. Immediately roll them in coarse salt and put them on a lightly buttered baking sheet, and bake in 300 degree oven until just brown enough to please you.

**Mrs. W. H. Zimmerman (Frances Barrett)**
**Columbus**

# Soups

Mary F. Panaclaigue

## MAE'S VEGETABLE SOUP

1 large soup bone
4 pounds lean stew meat
3 16-ounce cans tomatoes
1 15-ounce can tomato sauce
1 can Campbell's tomato soup
5 large carrots, chopped
3 cups onion, chopped

1 pound frozen shoe peg corn
1 pound frozen cut okra
1 cup macaroni or spaghetti
3 cups Irish potatoes, chopped
2 cups celery, chopped
1 can tiny English peas
salt and pepper to taste

Boil soup bone and stew meat until tender. Cook in a two gallon size container to hold all ingredients. Then add chopped vegetables, tomato sauce, tomatoes, Campbell's soup, macaroni, etc. Season to taste. Cook slowly for an hour and a half. This soup may be put in small containers and frozen. Serves about 20 people.

**Mrs. J. Derry Burns (Hazel Holmes)**
**Macon**

## VIRGINIA ILLGES' GAZPACHO

5 tomatoes, peeled and seeded
2 unpeeled cucumbers
1 whole bell pepper, cored and
   seeded
1 10-ounce can beef consommé
3 tablespoons olive oil
Tabasco or red pepper to taste
¼ lemon

1 small onion
½ cup parsley
1 small clove garlic
1 16-ounce can Italian tomatoes
4 tablespoons tarragon vinegar
1 teaspoon cumin powder
2 teaspoons salt

Blend tomatoes, cucumbers, pepper, onion, parsley, garlic, canned tomatoes, and consommé until thoroughly blended. After blending, add 3 tablespoons olive oil, 4 tablespoons tarragon vinegar, ¼ lemon, 1 teaspoon cumin powder, 2 teaspoons salt and a good dash of Tabasco or red pepper. Mix well. Put in refrigerator overnight and rectify seasoning if necessary.

**Mrs. L. Neill Bickerstaff (Sara Bussey)**
**Columbus**

# TOMATO BISQUE

1 16-ounce can of select
  tomatoes
2 cups strictly fresh milk
6 saltine crackers, crushed
1 heaping tablespoon sugar

¼ teaspoon soda
¼ teaspoon salt
¼ stick margarine or butter
dash of nutmeg

Pour tomatoes into boiler, preferably thick boiler. Mash tomatoes. Add ¼ teaspoon soda (don't forget). Stew for five minutes or until some of the liquid has cooked out. Remove from heat. Into this pour 2 cups of cold milk—bring just to a boil or scald. Add 6 crushed crackers, 1 heaping tablespoon sugar and the margarine. Add ¼ teaspoon salt last. Heat before serving (never boil—may curdle). Into each cup or bowl put dab of corn oil and dash or more of nutmeg. Fills 3 measuring cups.

**Mrs. Robert Flowers (Nettie Winn)**
**Thomasville**

# JELLIED BEET SOUP

6 large beets
2 cans consommé
4 tablespoons sherry
2 tablespoons plain gelatin,
  soaked in ½ cup cool water

1 tablespoon lemon juice
1 pint heavy cream
3 small jars caviar
salt and pepper

Grate beets. Cook slowly for 45 minutes in 2 cans of consommé and 2½ cups water. Add salt and pepper. Strain through cheese cloth but do not squeeze. Add 4 tablespoons sherry, 1 tablespoon lemon juice. Stir in gelatin which has been soaked. Pour into cups you are going to serve it in and chill at least 6 hours. Just before serving, top each serving with whipped cream and one tablespoon caviar.

**Mrs. Henry Garlington (Jeanne Morrell)**
**Savannah**

# OKRA SOUP

1 3 to 4 pound chuck roast or
   brisket
4 large onions, chopped
1 clove garlic, minced
4 16 ounce cans tomatoes

2 packages frozen cut okra
2 teaspoons salt
½ teaspoon black pepper
1 teaspoon Kitchen Bouquet
hot rice, cooked

Simmer roast in 5 quarts water with one half of the onions, the garlic, salt, pepper and Kitchen Bouquet for two hours or until tender. Add remaining onion, tomatoes and okra. Simmer one hour longer. Adjust seasonings. Serve in a bowl with a spoonful of hot rice. The longer this soup simmers the better. For a larger quantity, add more tomatoes and okra. Makes 5 to 6 quarts.

**Mrs. James G. Hardee III (Mary Cunningham)**
**Savannah**

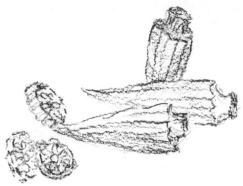

# COLD CURRIED SQUASH SOUP

9 summer squash
1 can chicken broth
½ teaspoon salt
dash pepper
½ onion

2 tablespoons, more or less to
   taste, of curry powder
juice of one lemon
½ pint of light cream or milk
chopped chives

Slice the squash and onions, cook in the chicken broth until tender. It takes 5 minutes in a pressure cooker and retains the moisture. Put this mixture in a blender. Add the lemon juice, salt, pepper and curry. Blend well. Add the cream or milk to the desired thickness—adjust curry to your taste. Chill. Sprinkle with chives before serving. May be made the day before. Makes 5 cups.

**Miss Isabelle Harrison**
**Savannah**

## SUMMER SOUP

2 cups cooked squash or broccoli or a pound can of asparagus, beets, carrots or other vegetable

1 cup of sour cream (buttermilk for less calories)
1 13¾-ounce can of chicken broth or homemade

Blenderize 3 ingredients together. Serve cold. Vary with curry or other herbs mixed in, or chives on top. Since sour cream can be kept in freezer, you can keep all ingredients on hand for emergencies.

**Mrs. Joseph Harrison (Louise Lynah)**
**Savannah**

## COLD AVOCADO SOUP

1 medium size ripe avocado
1 can consommé
1 medium onion, peeled and grated
1 cup sour cream
1 tablespoon lemon juice

½ cup milk to thicken
½ teaspoon dill weed or 1 teaspoon fresh dill, chopped
1 teaspoon Beau Monde seasoning

.Peel and cut up avocado in large pieces. Put all ingredients in blender and blend until smooth. Chill thoroughly and serve in bouillon cups.

**Mrs. Richard Stone (Mary Marshall)**
**Savannah**

## VICHYSQUASH

1 medium onion, sliced
⅓ stick butter
6 medium summer squash, sliced
½ cup chicken broth

salt
freshly ground pepper
1 cup milk or light cream
chopped chives

Sauté onion in butter in a large pan. When it is wilted but not brown, add the squash and broth. Cover and cook briskly about 25 minutes. Cool. Puree the squash with the cooking liquid in a blender or put through a food mill. Season the soup with salt and pepper. When it is cold, add the milk or cream. Serve it sprinkled with chives.

**Mrs. Alexander Barrett (Julia Hill)**
**Augusta**

## BLENDER VICHYSSOISE

1 14-ounce can of clear chicken
  broth soup, chilled
1 teaspoon salt
1 cup sour cream
1½ cups cold diced cooked
  potatoes

½ teaspoon pepper
½ small onion, sliced
chopped chives

In blender combine onion, broth, salt, pepper, and potatoes. Cover, blend at high speed for 8 seconds. Add sour cream, cover, and blend 10 seconds. Refrigerate until well chilled. Garnish with chives.

**Mrs. Claude Scarbrough Jr. (Ida Pease)**
**Columbus**

## EMERALD VICHYSSOISE

1 cup chopped scallions
2 tablespoons butter
1 10-ounce package frozen
  spinach
2 cans potato soup

2 tablespoons lemon juice
2 cups light cream
1½ cups chicken broth
½ teaspoon salt
½ teaspoon pepper

Sauté scallions in butter. Add frozen spinach and chicken broth. Cook, covered for 10 minutes. Add potato soup, undiluted, and lemon juice. Cook 10 minutes. Cool. Put through blender. Add cream and thin with more broth if necessary. Salt and pepper to taste. Serves 8.

**Mrs. John Phillips Pickett (Eulalie Converse Harris)**
**Cedartown**

# ICED CUCUMBER SOUP

2 cups unpeeled chopped
  cucumbers
1 teaspoon salt
2 cups clear chicken broth (can
  use bouillon cubes)
1 cup peeled, finely chopped
  cucumbers
1 medium onion, chopped

dash cayenne pepper
2 tablespoons cornstarch
1 cup light cream
  (not half-and-half)
3 drops green food coloring
chopped mint or chives as
  garnish

Cook together until very tender the unpeeled cucumbers, onion, salt, pepper and broth. Blend cornstarch with small quantity of cold water and add to boiling mixture, stirring constantly. Boil 2 minutes. Sieve and chill. When ready to serve, add finely chopped cucumbers, food coloring and cream. Garnish and serve. Serves 3 to 4.

**Miss Emily R. Jerger**
**Thomasville**

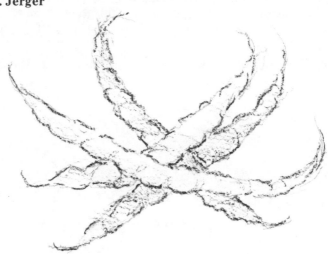

# EASY COLD SQUASH SOUP

12 yellow squash
1 onion
salt and pepper to taste
juice of 1 lemon

1½ cups chicken stock
6 tablespoons sour cream
6 tablespoons heavy cream

Boil squash with onion, salt and pepper. Cook and drain well. Add remaining ingredients; blend and chill. Delicious! Serves 6 generously.

**Mrs. Albert Lehman (Eugenia Seldon)**
**Augusta**

# SPLIT PEA SOUP

1 pound split green peas, rinsed
2 quarts of water
2 cups carrots, chopped small
2 cups celery and tops, chopped small
2 cups onion, chopped small
½ cup chopped parsley

1 meaty smoked ham bone *or* a little over a pound of ham hocks with some bone on them. Trim fat
1 tablespoon oregano leaves
1 tablespoon salt
½ teaspoon ground black pepper
1 bay leaf
several twists freshly ground black pepper

In 6 to 8 quart Dutch oven or heavy pot combine all ingredients. Heat to boiling, stirring frequently. Reduce heat, and simmer covered one hour and 30 minutes, until peas have cooked down to a thick soup. Stir occasionally to prevent sticking. Remove ham bone or hocks and cut meat coarsely. Return meat to soup, discard bone and fat. Reheat gently, covered, before serving. Freezes well. Always stir often when heating. Thin with a little cream if desired.

**Mrs. Warrington Maxwell Oliver, Jr. (Mary Young Roberts)**
**Valdosta**

# SOUP FOR SATURDAY LUNCH

2 cups diced Irish potatoes, cooked
½ cup chopped celery, cooked
¼ cup margarine
2 cups milk
2 cups cream style corn

½ cup chopped carrots, cooked
¼ cup chopped onions, cooked
¼ cup flour
10 ounces sharp Cheddar cheese, shredded
parsley or chives

Make a cream sauce of ¼ cup margarine, ¼ cup flour and 2 cups milk. Stir in 10 ounces sharp Cheddar cheese, shredded. Add to this sauce the vegetables and their broth, and 2 cups cream style corn. Heat, but do not boil. Garnish with parsley or chives.

**Mrs. J. Madden Hatcher (Sue Mac Fox)**
**Columbus**

# CRÈME DU BARRY (CAULIFLOWER SOUP)

2 cups cauliflower
1 tablespoon dehydrated onion
  flakes
3 packets instant chicken
  broth
¼ cup evaporated skimmed
  milk

parsley, chopped for garnish
2 tablespoons celery, chopped
½ teaspoon rosemary
4 cups water
salt and white pepper to taste

Put cauliflower, celery, onion flakes (or a tablespoon of chopped fresh onion), rosemary, and chicken broth in a pan. Add water and simmer slowly until celery and cauliflower are tender. Put half in a blender and blend until smooth. Blend second half. Add milk. Season with salt and pepper. It may not need salt if the broth is very salty. Either heat and serve hot with parsley for a garnish or chill and serve cold. If in cooking the vegetables the liquid has reduced too low, add water sufficient to make four servings.

**Mrs. Robert Murray Soule (Katherine Parks)**
**Athens**

# CORN SOUP

2 cups of corn, cut off cob
  (about 6 ears)
2 tablespoons finely chopped
  onion
2 tablespoons butter

2 cups milk
2 teaspoons salt
white pepper
2 tablespoons flour
2 cups half-and-half cream

Put corn, butter, onion, salt and pepper, one cup milk in skillet. Heat slowly, then simmer for 15 minutes. Put through blender. Stir the flour into the other cup of milk, put in large saucepan and add the corn mixture from the blender. Cook, stirring constantly, until quite thick. Add the half-and-half and heat. Makes 5 or 6 cups. Garnish, if desired, with chopped parsley or crumbled crisp bacon. (Canned corn may be used if fresh is not available, but it is not as good.)

**Mrs. Joseph T. Higgins (Virginia Jemison)**
**Thomasville**

# MULLIGATAWNY SOUP

1 small chicken
1 stalk celery
1 small onion
parsley
pepper
2 ounces rice
1 eggplant, peeled

1 quart chicken stock
2 ounces butter
2 ounces flour
1 tablespoon curry powder
1 quart half and half cream
½ pound apples, unpeeled
cinnamon wafers or toast

Cook chicken with onion, celery, and chopped parsley until done. Save one quart of stock and add rice and 1 cup chopped eggplant. Cook until done. Make a roux of butter and flour and curry powder. Add half and half cream and cook until it thickens. Add stock mixture to roux slowly. Add boned and cut up chicken and season with salt and pepper. Add ½ pound diced apples and boil at least 2 minutes. Serve with cinnamon wafers or crisp toast.

**Mrs. Malcolm N. Fleming (Cora Wynn)**
**Atlanta**

# BROCCOLI SOUP

broccoli
6 cups chicken broth

4 tablespoons flour
4 tablespoons margarine

Chop a nice bunch of broccoli and cook in six cups well seasoned chicken broth until tender. Blend liquid and broccoli together in blender or reserve liquid and chop cooked vegetable finely with knife, then add to liquid. Make a roux with four tablespoons flour and four tablespoons margarine cooked over low heat. Slowly add the blended broccoli and chicken stock. Soup may be served hot or cold.

**Miss Ellen Callaway Merry**
**Augusta**

# BROCCOLI BISQUE

1½ pounds fresh broccoli (or 2
   10-ounce packages frozen
   broccoli)
2 cans (13¾ ounces) chicken
   broth
1 medium onion, quartered
2 tablespoons margarine
1 teaspoon salt

1 to 2 teaspoons curry
   (or to taste)
dash pepper
2 tablespoons lime juice
8 slices lemon
½ cup sour cream
1 tablespoon chopped chives

Trim broccoli, and cut in chunks; put in boiler with broth, onion, margarine, salt, curry and pepper. Bring to boiling; reduce heat and simmer, covered, 8 to 12 minutes, until broccoli is tender. Pour mixture, half at a time, into electric blender, and blend thoroughly. Stir in lime juice. Cover and chill at least 4 hours. Serve topped with lemon slice, spoonful of sour cream, and chopped chives. Serves 6 to 8.

**Mrs. Joseph P. Zollo (Margaret Glenn)**
**Columbus**

# ONION SOUP

soup bone
3 tablespoons butter
1 soup bunch*
6 rounds hard French bread

6 medium onions
1 salt spoon mace
salt and white pepper
6 slices Swiss cheese

If the bones of a rib roast of beef which has been cooked rare are saved, they will serve very well indeed for onion soup, if there are no rare beef bones, a soup bone will do. Put the bones into a large kettle with reserved water from canned artichoke hearts, asparagus, or hearts of palm, the water from fresh green peas or zucchini, and add other water to cover the bones well. Without the vegetable water add a "*soup bunch" of stalk of celery, small onion, several sprigs of parsley, cover with water and salt very lightly. Cook until all the savor and strength are extracted from the soup bones. In a new kettle, under medium heat, melt the butter and add the onions which have been cut in thin lengthwise slices. Sauté until limp. Strain the beef stock into the onion kettle and cook over low heat until reduced to about six cups. While cooking, add the mace (the secret seasoning of good onion soup) and white pepper and salt to taste, remembering that it will be saltier as it reduces. Before serving check for seasoning. Pour into six ovenproof bowls. Top with a slice of crusty bread covered with Swiss cheese. Set in the oven under the broiler until the cheese is melted. Serve with grated Parmesan cheese, if desired.

**Mrs. Sewell Marion Brumby (Mary Hart)**
**Athens**

# MEXICAN BEAN SOUP

¼ cup salad oil
4 cloves minced garlic
1 cup chopped onion
½ cup chopped green pepper
1 pound hamburger meat
  (browned)
2 cans beef broth

4 cups water
1 16-ounce can tomatoes
2-4 tablespoons chili powder
2 cans Mexican chili beans (Van
  Camp's)
1 heaping teaspoon salt
½ teaspoon pepper

Sauté first four ingredients until tender. Mix together with remaining ingredients and simmer 1 hour. If crock pot used, simmer 4 hours.
**Mrs. James Bowen (Frances Rylander)**
**Americus**

# CANADIAN CHEESE SOUP

¼ cup butter
½ cup onion, diced
½ cup carrot, diced
½ cup celery, diced
¼ cup flour
1½ tablespoons cornstarch
2 tablespoons parsley, chopped

1 quart chicken stock
1 quart milk
⅛ teaspoon soda
8 ounces processed Cheddar
  cheese, grated
¼ teaspoon salt
¼ teaspoon pepper

Melt butter in 3-quart soup pot. Add onions, carrots, and celery. Sauté over low heat. Add flour and cornstarch. Cook until bubbly, add milk to make smooth sauce. Add stock, add soda and cheese, grated. Season with salt and pepper. Add parsley a few minutes before serving.
**Mrs. Charles Wood Pittman (Margaret Black)**
**Brunswick**

# CHINESE CHICKEN AND CORN SOUP

4 ounces chicken breast,
  minced
2 egg whites
2 quarts chicken stock
1 teaspoon salt
2 tablespoons chopped ham

2 tablespoons chopped green
  onions
1 tablespoon sesame oil
4 tablespoons cornstarch stirred
  into ½ cup water
1 can sweet corn, 12 ounce size

Put minced chicken in a bowl and add one egg white at a time, mixing with your hand until thoroughly combined. Bring chicken stock to a boil, add corn and salt and cornstarch and water. Stir well until thickened. Reduce heat to low, add chicken and stir until blended. Pour into serving bowl and sprinkle with chopped ham and green onions and sesame oil. Serves at least 6 people.

**Mrs. Thomas Clay (Anita Lippitt)**
**Savannah**

# SENEGALESE SOUP

4 cups chicken stock
4 egg yolks
2 cups cream
1 cup cooked, minced chicken

grated rind of 1 lemon
1 teaspoon curry powder
¼ teaspoon cayenne
¼ teaspoon salt

In the top of a double boiler, heat chicken stock to scalding point. In separate bowl, and with wire whisk, beat egg yolks, curry, cayenne, salt and cream. Stir in ½ cup hot stock. Add this mixture to remaining stock and cook until thickened, stirring constantly. Remove and cool. Chill in refrigerator, and add minced chicken and grated lemon rind at last minute. This recipe can be used as a base for other soups . Instead of chicken, just add spinach, broccoli, artichokes or avocados.

**Mrs. John Lawrence Brown (Plant Ellis)**
**Fort Valley**

# CHICKEN CHOWDER

5 slices bacon
1 can (about 4 ounces) sliced
  mushrooms
½ cup chopped onion
⅛ teaspoon thyme leaves
1 10¾-ounce can cream of
  celery soup

½ cup chopped canned tomatoes
1 can chicken vegetable soup
1 soup can water
2 cups diced cooked chicken
1 can (8 ounces) whole kernel corn
  (undrained)

In saucepan cook bacon until crisp. Remove and crumble. Pour off all but 2 tablespoons drippings. Brown mushrooms and cook onion with thyme in drippings until tender. Add bacon and remaining ingredients. Heat, stirring occasionally. Makes about 5½ cups. Recipe may be doubled easily.

**Mrs. T. Schley Gatewood (Anna Laura Griffin)**
**Americus**

# CHRISTINE'S SHRIMP STEW

2 pounds picked shrimp
¼ cup celery, chopped
½ onion, chopped
½ cup flour (or less)
1 tablespoon dry mustard
½ teaspoon salt

¼ cup bell pepper
1½ pints milk
1 pint cream (or milk)
1 tablespoon butter
pepper, Worcestershire sauce, and
  sherry added to taste

Sauté celery, onion and bell pepper in butter until limp. Put milk, cream, celery, onion and bell pepper to cook in top of double boiler. Mix flour and mustard to a paste with a little of the hot milk. Add to mixture. Add shrimp. Keep heat high and stir until mixture begins to thicken, then turn heat low and let cook for approximately an hour. Season with butter, pepper, salt, Worcestershire sauce and sherry. This may also be used for crab stew or substitute 1 quart of oysters cut in pieces.

Recipe of Christine Anderson, cook for Mrs. Anton P. Wright.

**Mrs. Augustine T. Smythe Wright (Mary Morris)**
**Bluffton, S. C.**

## RUDOLPH'S OYSTER BISQUE

1 pint milk
1 pint oysters
½ onion, chopped
1 tablespoon butter
1 tablespoon flour

salt
pepper
1 tablespoon sherry
paprika

Bring first three ingredients to the boil but do not boil. Strain through colander, save milk, put oysters through meat grinder or blender. Combine oysters in double boiler with salt, pepper and paste made from butter and flour. Stir until mixture thickens. Before serving add sherry and sprinkle with paprika.

(Rudolph Capers, a man of many capacities, was in devoted service to Miss Ophelia Dent of Hofwyl Plantation near Darien, Georgia.)
**Mrs. Walter Hartridge Strong (Julia Dancy Eve)**
**Savannah**

## THE HARDEE GIRLS' OYSTER STEW

¼ cup butter or margarine
1 12-ounce container of fresh
  standard oysters
2 tablespoons minced onion
2½ cups whole milk
½ cup coarsely crushed oyster
  crackers

1½ teaspoons Worcestershire
¾ teaspoon salt
⅛ teaspoon black pepper
⅛ teaspoon Tabasco sauce
1½ teaspoons freshly squeezed
  lemon juice

Melt the butter in a saucepan. Sauté the minced onion in the butter until tender and clear, but not brown. Use a medium setting to avoid too quick cooking. Add the oysters and simmer gently until the edges curl. Add the milk and increase beat slightly. Heat almost to boiling, but do not allow to boil. Add oyster crackers, Worcestershire sauce, salt, pepper and Tabasco. Finally add lemon juice. Pour into hot tureen or individual bowls and serve immediately.
**Mrs. Lowry W. Hunt (Caroline H. Candler)**
**Madison**

# SHRIMP BISQUE

1 10-ounce can cream of shrimp
  soup
1 10-ounce can cream of celery
  soup
1 4½-ounce can sliced
  mushrooms with broth
1 small onion, chopped (¼-⅓
  cup chopped onion)
1 pound raw, peeled and
  deveined shrimp

2 tablespoons sherry
2 tablespoons butter
2 cups milk
2 tablespoons chopped pimento
1 tablespoon Worcestershire sauce
1 8-ounce can minced clams and
  juice

Sauté chopped onion and sliced mushrooms in butter. Add soups and milk
which have been blended together until smooth. Heat. Add pimento, Worcestershire sauce, minced clams and juice, mushroom broth and sherry.
Stir over heat. Add raw shrimp. Stir. Simmer gently until shrimp turn
pink. Never allow to boil. Serves 6.

**Mrs. Lloyd Guyton Bowers (Effie Campbell Siegling)**
**Columbus**

# SHRIMP STEW

1 pint of milk, boiling hot
1 cup cream
grated rind of 1 lemon
sherry wine to flavor
juice of 1 lemon

2 egg yolks
1 tablespoon flour
1 pint cooked shrimp, broken in
  pieces (not cut)

Put hot milk into cream. Add juice and grated rind of lemon, yolks of 2
eggs. Mix in 1 tablespoon flour, shrimp and flavor with sherry.

**Mrs. Raymond M. Demere (Josephine Mobley)**
**Savannah**

# OYSTER SOUP

1 tablespoon flour
1 tablespoon butter
1 quart milk
½ cup celery, finely chopped
1 small green pepper, finely
   chopped

½ onion, finely chopped
1 teaspoon Worcestershire sauce
1 quart oysters, put through
   grinder or processor

Sauté vegetables in butter and stir in salt and flour. Pour in heated milk and cook, stirring constantly until slightly thick. Add Worcestershire sauce and oysters. Keep warm in top of double boiler, but do not allow to boil as soup will curdle.

**Mrs. Malcolm Maclean, Jr. (Frances Grimball)**
**Savannah**

# OYSTER BISQUE

1 quart oysters (selects)
1 quart half and half
1 pint milk
½ stick butter
1 teaspoon Worcestershire
   sauce

chopped parsley
celery stalks, chopped
1 onion, chopped
salt and pepper to taste

Cook oysters in butter until they begin to curl slightly. Then put in blender and chop. Mix with oysters all other ingredients in double boiler and cook for 30 or 40 minutes. Strain and serve.

**Mrs. Joseph E. Birnie (Octavia Norfleet Riley)**
**Atlanta**

# GRUYÈRE SOUP

½ cup butter
½ cup flour
1 quart half and half
4 cups chicken stock
1 heaping tablespoon Dijon
    mustard

2½ cups grated Gruyère cheese
2-3 dashes Tabasco
chopped parsley for garnish

Melt butter in a 2-quart saucepan. Add flour and cook the roux, stirring constantly, over low heat for several minutes. Stir in cream and cook until slightly thickened. Blend mustard into chicken stock and add to cream sauce mixture. Just before serving, stir in cheese and Tabasco. Heat gently, but do not allow to boil. This soup is delicious hot or chilled. Serves 8.

**Mrs. William B. Hardegree (Eleanor Glenn)**
**Columbus**

# FISH SOUP

¾ cup cooking oil
1 cup flour
1 28-ounce can stewed
    tomatoes
1 12-ounce can tomato paste
3 onions, diced
1 cup chopped bell peppers
8 cups diced, cooked fish
1 cup chopped celery

2½ quarts water (use more or less,
    depending on how thick you like
    soup)
season to taste with salt, pepper, a
    little sugar, garlic salt, lemon
    pepper, lemon juice, parsley
    flakes, marjoram, tarragon
    leaves

Make brown roux of oil and flour, add onions, celery and bell pepper and cook until soft. Add stewed tomatoes and tomato paste. Cook slowly for 5 minutes. Add water and seasonings and simmer one hour. Add fish. When heated, serve over rice in soup plates.

This is a good recipe to make in a large quantity and then freeze.

**Mrs. Archibald Lovett Morris (Elizabeth Putnam Carswell)**
**Savannah**

# Seafood

Mary F. Panaulaique

# CRAB IMPERIAL

½ cup butter or margarine
1 teaspoon grated onion
½ cup flour
2 cups milk
½ cup cream
3 egg yolks
2 tablespoons chopped chives
2 tablespoons chopped parsley
2 tablespoons chopped
    mushrooms (broiled in
    butter)

salt and pepper to taste
½ teaspoon paprika
1 teaspoon Worcestershire sauce
3 tablespoons sherry
1 teaspoon prepared mustard
1 pound crabmeat
2 eggs, hard-boiled, chopped
buttered bread crumbs
grated Swiss cheese

Melt butter, add grated onion and flour. Mix and gradually add milk and cream. Stir until thick and smooth. Mix in egg yolks and chives, parsley and mushrooms. Stir until thick and smooth. Season with salt and pepper, paprika, Worcestershire sauce, sherry and mustard. Heat but do not boil and add crabmeat and eggs. Fill 6 crab shells or small ramekins. Sprinkle with bread crumbs and cheese. Bake until bubbling and light brown. Serve at once. These freeze well (before being baked). Serves 6.

**Mrs. Thomas Clay (Anita Lippitt)**
**Savannah**

# CRAB DISH

2 cups milk
8 tablespoons butter
4 tablespoons flour
1½ teaspoons salt
2 teaspoons prepared
    mustard

onion to taste, grated
1 cup mayonnaise
4 eggs, hard cooked, sliced
4 teaspoons lemon juice
1 pound lump crabmeat
1 cup cracker crumbs

Make white sauce of milk, butter and flour. Add salt, mustard, onion, mayonnaise, eggs, lemon juice and crabmeat to white sauce. Put in 2-quart baking dish or individual shells. Top with cracker crumbs and dot with butter. Bake until heated through and brown on top in 350 degree oven. Serves 4 to 6.

**Mrs. Howard Dasher (Mary McCulley)**
**Valdosta**

# DEVILED CRAB IMPERIAL

1 tablespoon butter
1 cup cream
2 tablespoons flour
1 teaspoon salt
½ pound mushrooms
2 tablespoons green pepper,
    minced

1 tablespoon dry mustard
dash of cayenne
3 tablespoons pimento, minced
1 tablespoon parsley, minced
2 tablespoons Worcestershire
    sauce
1 pound crabmeat

Make a white sauce of first 4 ingredients. Mix crabmeat with seasonings. Add white sauce. Fill well-buttered shells or casserole with mixture. Sprinkle with bread crumbs and dot with butter. Place under broiler until browned.

**Mrs. George Claussen Jr. (Virginia Houston)**
**Augusta**

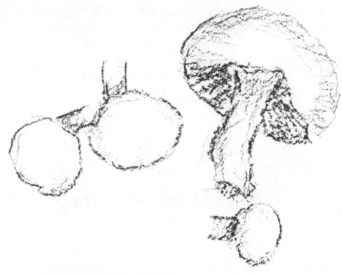

# IMPERIAL CRAB

1 pound backfin lump crab
    (fresh)
enough mayonnaise to make
    consistency of salad

½ teaspoon dry mustard
salt to taste

Pick crabmeat. Mix all ingredients. Pack loosely in crab shells or ramekins. Ice over the top of each with additional mayonnaise. Bake in hot oven, approximately 425 degrees, until top is browned and crab is bubbly hot. Serves 4-6.

**Mrs. F. Daly Smith (Berthenia Crocker)**
**Macon**

# CRAB MARY

2 cans white shoulder lump
  crabmeat (6½-ounce)*
1 one-pound carton sour cream
2 tablespoons butter
1 teaspoon Worcestershire
  sauce

freshly ground white pepper, to
  taste
1 medium onion, sliced
2 tablespoons flour
½ teaspoon salt

*1 one-pound can may be substituted

In heavy saucepan or deep skillet (cast aluminum), melt butter. Add onion and cook over medium heat for a few minutes until onion is translucent but not brown. Discard onion but retain seasoned butter. To this add cream which has been well blended with flour, *no lumps*. Cook over low heat until flour is done and sauce is thickened. Taste will tell you when flour is done. Add salt, Worcestershire and crabmeat which is free of all fiber. When hot through (do not let boil), add pepper and adjust salt to your taste. Serve in freshly made hot toast cups and garnish with small parsley bouquets. Serves 4.

**Mrs. Brumby McGehee (Mary Brumby)**
**Atlanta**

# RACHEL'S DEVILED CRAB
*(Rachel has been Mrs. Frank M. Chisholm's*
*cook for 52 years.)*

3 tablespoons butter
2 tablespoons flour
2 cups half and half cream
salt to taste
red pepper to taste

3 cups crabmeat
2 tablespoons mayonnaise
¼ cup minced bell pepper
10 Ritz crackers

Make cream sauce out of first 5 ingredients, by melting butter in double boiler, add flour and stir until smooth. Mix in cream, stir constantly until thick. Add salt and pepper to taste. Mix in mayonnaise and bell pepper with the crabmeat and stir into the cream sauce. Stuff mixture into crab shells or baking shells. Sprinkle tops with crushed Ritz crackers and pat in firmly. Bake in 350 degree oven for 25 minutes. Makes 8 servings.

**Mrs. Frank A. Chisholm (Katherine Crutcher)**
**Savannah**

# CRAB MORNAY

½ cup butter
½ cup chopped green onions
½ cup chopped parsley
2 tablespoons flour
1 pint half and half cream
1 cup grated Swiss cheese

1 tablespoon sherry
¼ teaspoon red pepper
1 pound white crabmeat, picked
salt to taste
½ teaspoon Worcestershire sauce

Melt butter in pan and sauté onions. Add parsley right before onions are soft. Pour off two tablespoons butter from this into top of double boiler. Add crabmeat, pepper, sherry, and a little salt to onion-parsley mixture. Set aside.

Blend flour, then half and half, then cheese in double boiler. Add crabmeat mixture to double boiler after cheese melts. Add Worcestershire sauce, stir and pour into chafing dish. Serve with toast or pastry shells, poached egg and toast for brunch or light supper. 6 to 8 large portions.

**Barbara Bunn Vereen**
**Moultrie**

# CRABMEAT MORNAY

4 tablespoons margarine
4 tablespoons flour
1 cup milk
1 heaping tablespoon grated Parmesan cheese
1 pound lump crabmeat
½ cup white wine

1 heaping tablespoon grated Swiss cheese
1 tablespoon sweet butter
½ cup sliced mushrooms
1 teaspoon finely chopped onion
bread crumbs

Melt margarine, add flour, then milk to make white sauce. To white sauce add white wine. Over hot fire, cook until ⅓ original volume. Add Parmesan cheese, Swiss cheese and sweet butter. This is about one cup Mornay sauce. Sauté mushrooms (canned may be used) and onion in two tablespoons margarine. Combine this to sauce. Add crabmeat. Fill greased crab shells (scallop shells). Sprinkle with bread crumbs and Swiss cheese equally and lightly. Brown in oven at 400 degrees. Feeds six or fills six shells.

**Mrs. Ray Lowell Peacock, Jr. (Margaret Anne McGowan)**
**Augusta**

## CRAB AND SHRIMP CASSEROLE

1 pound crabmeat
1 pound medium shrimp
½ cup green pepper, chopped
⅓ cup fresh parsley, chopped
2 cups cooked rice

1½ cups mayonnaise
2 packages small frozen green peas
    thawed but not cooked
salt and pepper

Toss lightly. Place in greased casserole. Refrigerate overnight covered. Bake 1 hour at 350 degrees covered. Serves 6 to 8.

**Mrs. Raymond Dunlap Hill (Ruth Berrien Waller)**
**Augusta**

## CRAB S-T-R-E-T-C-H

1 6½-ounce can crabmeat
1 cup uncooked shell macaroni
½ cup Parmesan cheese,
    grated
2 eggs hard-boiled, chopped
1 can mushroom soup
1 cup milk

1 tablespoon chopped onions
1 tablespoon chopped parsley
1 tablespoon lemon juice
½ teaspoon horseradish
½ teaspoon prepared mustard
dash Tabasco sauce
1 teaspoon Worcestershire sauce

Grease one-quart pyrex baking dish. Combine all ingredients except cheese and put in baking dish. Top with cheese. Cover and refrigerate overnight. Bake the next day at 350° uncovered for one hour. Serves 5.

**Mrs. C. P. Whiting (Louise Osborne)**
**Albany**

## CRAB CASSEROLE

1 pound crabmeat
2 cups milk
2 tablespoons finely chopped
    onion
1 tablespoon dry mustard
1 tablespoon lemon juice

¼ tablespoon horseradish
1 tablespoon paprika
¼ teaspoon salt
½ cup flour
¼ cup butter

Sauté onion in butter. Add mustard, horseradish, paprika, and salt, and blend in flour. Put in double boiler (optional) and add milk. Cook and stir until thickened. Add crabmeat and lemon juice. Serve over rice.

**Mrs. John Cantey Oliver (Edith Burwell Lowry)**
**Valdosta**

# CRABMEAT CASSEROLE

1 pound fresh crabmeat,
  picked over for shell pieces
8 tablespoons butter
4 tablespoons flour
2 cups milk
4 teaspoons lemon juice
2 teaspoons dry mustard
2 teaspoons salt

3 eggs, hard-boiled, chopped
1 cup mayonnaise
onion to taste
1 teaspoon Worcestershire sauce
½ teaspoon seasoning salt
dash Tabasco
1 cup drained sliced mushrooms

Make a cream sauce with butter, flour and milk. Add remaining ingredients. Place in long flat baking dish. Top with bread crumbs (or finely crumbled cheese crackers). Sprinkle with Parmesan cheese and dot with butter and dash of paprika. Bake at 350° until bubbly and lightly brown. Serves 6-8.

**Frances Stewart Chandler**
**Albany**

## LUNCHEON CRAB CASSEROLE

2 tablespoons butter
2 tablespoons flour
1½ cups coffee cream
½ cup white wine
1 pound crabmeat

dash of mace
grated rind of ½ lemon
salt and pepper
Parmesan cheese

Make cream sauce with first four ingredients. Add crabmeat and seasonings. Pour into 4 small or 1 large greased casserole. Sprinkle with Parmesan cheese. Bake at 350 degrees until bubbly.

**Mrs. William Haley Atkinson (Nell Glover)**
**Savannah**

## CRABMEAT CASSEROLE

one pound crabmeat
3 eggs
1 cup milk
2 tablespoons flour

2 teaspoons butter
¼ cup wine
salt and pepper to taste
1 cup grated cheese

Make cream sauce of milk, flour, and butter. Season highly. Add beaten yolks and cheese. Shred crabmeat, cover with wine. Let stand for twenty minutes; combine with sauce; fold in beaten whites. Bake in buttered casserole in medium oven (375 degrees) for forty-five minutes.

**Mrs. Ladson Vereen (Mary Ladson)**
**Moultrie**

## CRABMEAT AU GRATIN

3 cups fresh crabmeat
1 4-ounce can sliced
  mushrooms
6 tablespoons butter
3 tablespoons all-purpose
  flour
1 cup whole milk
1 cup "half and half" or light
  cream
1 teaspoon salt

1 teaspoon onion salt
⅛ teaspoon paprika
7-8 grinds black pepper
½ teaspoon Worcestershire
  sauce
¼ teaspoon Tabasco sauce
dash of nutmeg
3 tablespoons pale dry sherry
bread crumbs
grated Parmesan cheese

Drain mushrooms, then sauté in 1 tablespoon of butter. Set aside. Make cream sauce as follows: Melt over low heat 5 tablespoons butter, stir in flour. In separate saucepan, mix together milk and cream and bring just to boiling point. Stir thoroughly into butter-flour mixture. Add all seasonings, one at a time, stirring constantly, over low heat, till smooth and thickened. Remove from heat and add sherry. Lightly stir mushrooms into crabmeat, which has been previously picked over for shell and cartilage. Try not to break up lumps of crabmeat. Add cream sauce, mixing lightly. Spoon into well-buttered 1½-quart casserole, or 6 or 7 au gratin dishes, or about 14 small crab shells. (I prefer Pyrex shells, but natural ones, well-scrubbed, may be used.) Sprinkle with bread crumbs, grated Parmesan cheese, and a dash of paprika. Bake in 350 degree oven 20 to 30 minutes (till lightly browned). Serves 6-8.

(If desired, you may omit mushrooms, bread crumbs, and Parmesan cheese, and serve a *Basic Creamed Crab*, hot from a chafing dish, with toast points, or for a cocktail party, with tiny patty shells.)

**Mrs. Albert Sidney Britt, Jr. (Annie McIntosh)**
**Savannah**

## DEVILED CRAB

1 pound fresh lump crabmeat
2 lemons, juiced
2 eggs, beaten
1 tablespoon cream

1 handful bread crumbs
1 tablespoon Durkee's dressing
½ tablespoon mustard
salt and pepper

Mix all ingredients. Put into six greased clam baking shells. Sprinkle with cracker meal. Dot with butter. Bake 25 minutes in a 350° oven. Garnish with paprika, lemon slice and parsley.

**Mrs. John Phillips, Jr. (Aynn Kirtley)**
**Albany**

# CRABMEAT IN AVOCADO MORNAY SAUCE

3 avocados
6 green onions—diced
1½ pounds crabmeat
½ cup butter

¾ cup sherry
2 cups mornay sauce
2 ounces grated Parmesan cheese

Halve avocados—scoop out meat and dice. Lightly sauté diced avocado, green onions and crabmeat in butter. Add ¾ cup sherry; stir well. Add mornay sauce. Pile mixture into seafood shells. Sprinkle with Parmesan cheese. Heat in 400° oven for 5 minutes. Serves 6.

MORNAY SAUCE

¼ cup butter
½ cup flour
1 cup chicken stock
1 cup cream
dash of salt and pepper

dash of nutmeg
2 tablespoons shredded Swiss
   cheese
¼ cup grated Parmesan cheese

Melt butter, stir in flour. Cook 2 or 3 minutes. Stir in chicken stock and cream. Cook, stirring constantly until smooth. Add salt, pepper, nutmeg and cheeses. Stir until smooth.

**Mrs. Eugene McNeel (Louise Inman)**
**Brunswick**

# DEVILED CRAB

Mix together:
2 boiled egg whites, chopped
½ cup celery, chopped
½ cup green pepper,
   chopped

½ pound (or more) crabmeat
½ cup toasted bread crumbs
salt, red and black pepper to
   taste

Mix together and add to first mixture:

2 boiled egg yolks, mashed
2 tablespoons Worcestershire
   sauce
½ cup melted butter

1 tablespoon prepared mustard
2 teaspoons vinegar
½ cup boiling water

Pour in buttered casserole and bake in 350 degree oven for about ½ hour. Sprinkle with bread crumbs and dot with butter before baking. Serves 6.

**Mrs. James A. Anderson, Jr. (Mary Neel)**
**Thomasville**

# LUMP CRABMEAT

1 pound lump crabmeat
¼ cup real butter
1 tablespoon flour
1 cup half and half
1 tablespoon ketchup
1 tablespoon prepared
    mustard

1 tablespoon chili sauce
Worcestershire sauce
onion juice
juice of one lemon
4 Ritz crackers, crushed coarsely
Ritz crackers, crushed very fine

Make cream sauce with butter, flour and half and half. Add to this all seasonings. Fold in crabmeat and the four, crushed Ritz crackers. Sprinkle finely crushed crackers on top, dot with butter. Bake 15 minutes in preheated 350 degree oven. Do not over cook. Can be cooked in casserole or ramekins.

**Mrs. Warrington Maxwell Oliver, Jr. (Mary Young Roberts)**
**Valdosta**

# BAKED FLOUNDER AU GRATIN

4 fillets of flounder
1 teaspoon salt
½ cup corn meal

½ cup Parmesan cheese
2 tablespoons butter or margarine

Place flounder fillets skin side down on flat, greased baking dish. Season with ½ teaspoon salt. Sprinkle with corn meal seasoned with ½ teaspoon salt. Sprinkle with Parmesan cheese and dot butter. Bake in 350 degree oven for 15 minutes. Turn on broiler until top is golden brown. Serves 4.

**Mre. William Porter Price (Ann Flowers)**
**Charlotte, N.C.**

# CRAB CASSEROLE

1 pound crabmeat
1 small onion, chopped fine
1 cup mayonnaise
1 cup soft bread crumbs
1 teaspoon Worcestershire
    sauce
1 cup toasted bread crumbs,
    buttered

1 teaspoon lemon juice
½ cup celery, chopped
½ cup bell pepper, chopped
½ teaspoon salt
⅛ teaspoon pepper
¼ cup butter

Pick shell out of crabmeat. Sauté onions, bell pepper and celery in butter until slightly browned—not too long. Mix all ingredients together except the buttered crumbs. Put mixture into a greased casserole and top with buttered bread crumbs. Bake in a 375° oven 30-40 minutes.

**Mrs. James P. Champion, Jr. (Jane Luthy)**
**Albany**

# CRABMEAT CASSEROLE

4 tablespoons butter
4 tablespoons flour
½ pint cream
dash Worcestershire
small can sliced mushrooms,
  drained

1 pound crabmeat (lump or claw)
4 tablespoons sherry
¾ cup sharp grated cheese
salt and pepper to taste

Make a cream sauce with the butter, flour and cream. Add salt, pepper, Worcestershire and sherry. Remove from fire and add crabmeat which has been picked over to remove shell, and mushrooms. Pour mixture into a buttered casserole or individual ramekins. (This much can be done ahead.) Sprinkle with grated cheese and cook in 400 degree oven until cheese melts. (Do not overcook.) Serves 4.

**Mrs. Lloyd H. Megahee (Frances Philips)**
**Thomasville**

# CRABMEAT IN PATTY SHELLS

1 can crabmeat, white
1 teaspoon onion, grated
1 package pie crust mix
1 lemon, juice and peel

1 cup mayonnaise
3 tablespoons celery,
  chopped fine

Combine crab, mayonnaise, onion, lemon juice and peel, and celery, chopped very fine. Let stand in refrigerator for at least one hour. Fill shells with crab just before serving. Make the patty shells by rolling out the pie crust mix, which has been prepared according to directions. Roll very thin and cut in rounds and place in doll muffin pans to bake. Prick center of each with a fork and bake by package directions. Makes 12.

**Mrs. Albert Dobbs Sams, Sr. (Anita Burke)**
**Athens**

# FRESH BROILED TROUT

fresh trout
2 tablespoons Mazola or other
  good oil
2 tablespoons Worcestershire
  sauce

2 tablespoons fresh lemon juice
½ teaspoon dry mustard
salt to taste
pepper as desired

Combine all ingredients, except trout, into a sauce. Beat together until well-mixed. Roll each fish in the sauce until well-covered. Pour any leftover sauce over fish in broiling pan. Broil slowly until done, but not overcooked.

**Mrs. Sam Merritt (Janet Scarborough)**
**Americus**

## SENSATIONAL STUFFED BASS

3 to 6 pound bass or similar fish, cleaned with head intact if possible.

THE MARINADE

1 cup white wine or bottled
   lemon juice
½ cup soy sauce

¼ cup Worcestershire sauce
¼ cup salad oil

THE STUFFING

1½ cups herb-flavored stuffing
   mix
⅔ cup warm water
½ cup butter
½ unpeeled red apple, diced
¼ cup diced onion

¼ cup diced celery
1 teaspoon curry powder
2 tablespoons raisins
½ teaspoon salt

Mix marinade ingredients and marinate fish for at least two hours, turning every half hour. Remove and rub fish inside and out with salt.

Mix stuffing with warm water and butter, after butter has melted. Add remaining ingredients. Place fish in oiled pan, pat mixture into cavity. Some may overflow. No need to skewer. Dot generously with butter; sprinkle well with paprika and cover loosely with aluminum foil, bake at 300° until tender from 40 minutes to 1½ hours, depending on size of fish. Do not dry fish out by overcooking. Remove fish to hot platter. Replace fish's eye with parsley sprig or raisin. Sprinkle fish with additional paprika. Serve with lemon wedges and/or melted butter to which lemon juice has been added.

**Mrs. John Joel Rucker (Alma Pancost)**
**Moultrie**

## BROILED SPANISH MACKEREL

1 mackerel filet
parsley for garnish
lemon wedges for garnish

¼ cup butter
capers for garnish
salt and pepper to taste

Squeeze lemon juice on fish, add salt and pepper. Melt ¼ cup butter and pour over filet. Place pan under broiler and broil for 10 minutes, or until fish is flaky and browns on top. Garnish with capers, parsley and lemon wedges. Serves 1.

**Mrs. Jack C. Hughston (Sarah Hardaway)**
**Columbus**

# BAKED SHAD WITH ROE

3½ to 4 pound boned shad with
  roe
1 tablespoon finely chopped
  parsley
1 tablespoon grated onion
4 tablespoons butter

½ cup soft bread crumbs
salt
pepper
¼ cup dry white wine (optional)
¼ cup flour
lemon and parsley for garnish

Scald one pair shad roes in boiling salted water for two minutes. Drain, split the roes and scrape out the eggs. Add to them one tablespoon butter, finely chopped parsley, grated onion and soft bread crumbs, with salt and pepper to taste. Blend thoroughly. Use this mixture to stuff fish.

Tie the fish, or secure with toothpicks, and place in generously oiled shallow baking pan. Sprinkle with flour, seasoned with salt and pepper. Dot well with butter and bake in a hot oven (450 degrees) for 25 to 35 minutes or until the fish is tender when tested with a toothpick, basting frequently with butter. A little dry white wine may be added to the pan before baking and used for basting. Remove fish to platter, garnish with lemon and parsley.

**Mrs. John Wright Carswell (Elizabeth Putnam)**
**Savannah**

# LOBSTER DELIGHT

3 large packages cream
  cheese
2 cans lobster (or crabmeat)
½ teaspoon garlic salt
1 cup mayonnaise
2 teaspoons prepared
  mustard

¼ cup white sauterne
2 tablespoons confectioners'
  sugar
2 teaspoons onion juice
½ to 1 teaspoon seasoned salt

(Crabmeat may be substituted for lobster.) Combine all ingredients in chafing dish and heat. Serve hot as a cocktail dip or on toasted half of English muffin for light meal, or cooled and stuffed in tomato. Prepare day of party or make ahead and freeze, using Hellman's mayonnaise. No cooking needed. Just heat and serve. Serves 6.

**Mrs. Jack L. Stephenson (Winifred Harriss)**
**Atlanta**

# SCALLOPS ISABELLA

1 quart bay or sea scallops,
    quartered
1 cup green pepper, minced
1½ ounces capers
2 teaspoons monosodium
    glutamate
2 teaspoons Spanish paprika

1 cup onion, minced
1 teaspoon salt
½ teaspoon garlic, crushed
1 cup good cream sherry
½ cup good olive oil

Place scallops in an ovenproof dish. Combine green pepper, onion, capers, salt, garlic, monosodium glutamate, sherry, olive oil, and paprika. Pour over scallops. Broil under highest heat, stirring occasionally, until scallops are lightly browned. Marinade will reduce during cooking. Serve with toast points or in timbales.

**Mrs. Wesley Turnell Hanson, Jr. (Marie McHatton)**
**Rochester, New York**

# COQUILLES SAINT JACQUES

1½ pounds fresh or frozen
    scallops
¾ cup dry white wine
1 tablespoon lemon juice
½ teaspoon salt
1 cup sliced fresh mushrooms
2 tablespoons thinly sliced
    shallots or green onions

1 clove garlic, minced
¼ cup butter or margarine
⅓ cup all-purpose flour
⅛ teaspoon ground nutmeg
dash white pepper
1 cup soft bread crumbs
2 tablespoons butter or margarine,
    melted

Thaw scallops, if frozen. Halve any large scallops. In a saucepan combine the scallops, wine, lemon juice, and the ½ teaspoon salt. Bring to boil. Reduce heat; cover and simmer for 2-4 minutes until scallops are opaque in appearance. Drain, reserving 1 cup of the wine mixture, adding water if necessary to make 1 cup liquid. Cook mushrooms, shallots and garlic in the ¼ cup butter or margarine until tender, stirring occasionally. Blend in the flour, nutmeg, white pepper and ¼ teaspoon salt. Add milk and the reserved 1 cup of wine mixture, all at once. Cook and stir until thickened and bubbly. Add scallops and heat through. Spoon the mixture into 6 buttered shells (makes 8 if shells are small). Shallow individual casseroles or 6-ounce custard cups will do for baking. Toss bread crumbs with the 2 tablespoons of melted butter and sprinkle over the scallop mixture. Bake in 400 degree oven about 10 minutes or until brown.

**Mrs. Lovick P. Corn (Elizabeth Turner)**
**Columbus**

# SCALLOPS

| | |
|---|---|
| 1 pint scallops | 3 finely diced shallots |
| 8 fresh mushrooms | 2 tablespoons flour |
| 2 tablespoons chopped | 3 tablespoons cream |
|    parsley | buttered bread crumbs |
| ½ pint dry white wine | ½ teaspoon salt |
| 2 tablespoons butter | ¼ teaspoon pepper |

Place salt in saucepan with white wine. Boil scallops in wine for five minutes. Remove scallops and save wine. Wash and slice mushrooms and sauté in butter. Add shallots, parsley, ¼ teaspoon salt, and pepper to mushrooms. Cook slightly, stir in flour. Slowly stir in 1 cup of the wine mixture in which scallops were cooked. Add cream and scallops. Place scallop mixture in buttered, ovenproof shell ramekins. Top with crumbs. Broil until brown and heated-through. Serves 4.

**Mrs. John Vander Horst (Helen Lawrence)**
**Marietta**

# SCALLOPED OYSTERS

| | |
|---|---|
| 1½ pint stewing oysters | 2 eggs |
| ½ cup butter | 1 tablespoon Worcestershire sauce |
| 1½ packs saltine crackers from | 1 teaspoon Tabasco |
|    box | salt and pepper |
| 2 cups milk (scant) | |

In well-greased 2-quart casserole, crumble layer of saltine crackers. Dot butter on top with a fork, lift each oyster from carton and layer on top of saltines. Salt and pepper oysters. Crumble another layer of saltines. Dot with butter. Again put oysters, salt and pepper on top. The top of casserole will have crumbled crackers and butter.

In 1 2-cup dish, beat eggs, add Tabasco, Worcestershire sauce and milk. Pour mixture over casserole. Bake in preheated 375 degree oven for 15 to 20 minutes until bubbly. Serves 6.

**Mrs. James T. Flynn (Julia Powell)**
**Moultrie**

## OYSTERS WITH PARSLEY RICE

¼ cup butter
4 shallots
1 onion
6 stalks celery
6 slices lemon, finely chopped
1 bay leaf, crumbled
1 clove garlic (optional)
1 tablespoon Worcestershire
   sauce
3 tablespoons butter

3 tablespoons flour
1 6-ounce can mushrooms, with
   their juice
½ pint whipping cream
1 teaspoon gumbo filé
1 quart oysters
1 quart soft bread crumbs, as
   desired
½ teaspoon salt, hot pepper sauce

Sauté shallots, onions and celery in ¼ cup butter until they are soft. Make a roux of 3 tablespoons of flour and 3 tablespoons of butter. Cook this until it is brown and add mushrooms with their juice. To this add Worcestershire sauce, gumbo filé, hot pepper sauce and ½ teaspoon salt. Heat oysters only until they curl around the edges. Add bread crumbs.

### PARSLEY RICE
1 cup Uncle Ben's Converted
   Rice
2 cups water
1 onion, sliced

3 chicken bouillon cubes
1 teaspoon salt
1 cup fresh parsley, chopped

Boil all ingredients in covered saucepan for 20 minutes, except parsley which should be added last. Serves 8.

**Mrs. Lawrence Vaughan Howard (Purcell Chamberlain)**
**Atlanta**

## SCALLOPED OYSTERS

1 quart oysters
½ cup cracker crumbs
2 tablespoons butter

¼ teaspoon pepper
1 teaspoon salt

Place ½ quart oysters in baking dish after draining oysters and reserving liquor. Sprinkle salt, pepper and some butter broken into bits over them, then sprinkle with half the crumbs. Make another layer of oysters, salt and pepper, rest of crumbs and butter. Pour oyster liquor over all and bake in hot oven for one-half hour.

**Mrs. Richard Platt (Mary Stuart Gordon)**
**Savannah**
**Recipe of Harriet Montague Wellford**
        **Sabine Hall Plantation, Warsaw, Va.**

# OYSTERS WITH ANCHOVY SAUCE

3 tablespoons flour
3 tablespoons butter
½ cup grated Cheddar
  cheese
½ cup white wine, dry
½ cup milk

⅓ cup buttered bread crumbs
1½ teaspoons anchovy paste
1 tablespoon grated lemon rind
salt to taste
1 pint oysters (1½ pints is even
  better), well-drained

Make sauce by blending butter, flour, anchovy paste, adding heated milk, stirring until thick and smooth. Add wine. Stir until smooth. Blend in grated lemon rind and grated sharp cheese. Stir until cheese is melted and the sauce is smooth. Add salt to taste. Drain oysters, then lay them out on paper towels and pat with another paper towel to remove excess liquid. Place oysters in buttered casserole. Pour sauce over oysters. Cover with buttered bread crumbs. Bake in the casserole in a 400 degree oven for 7 minutes. Serves 4.

**Mrs. Lloyd Guyton Bowers (Effie Campbell Siegling)**
**Columbus**

# OYSTER ARTICHOKE RAMEKINS

1 14-ounce can artichoke
  hearts, chopped
2 dozen oysters with their
  liquid
4 tablespoons butter
2 tablespoons flour
3 green onions
¼ teaspoon thyme
1½ teaspoons Worcestershire
  sauce

1 tablespoon pimento, chopped
⅛ teaspoon cayenne
1 to 2 tablespoons dry sherry
  (optional)
salt and pepper to taste
½ cup bread crumbs mixed with 2
  tablespoons Parmesan cheese

Cook oysters with liquid in 2 tablespoons butter until edges curl. Make a dark roux with 2 tablespoons butter and flour. Add onions and cook 2 minutes. Add chopped artichokes, Worcestershire sauce, pimentos, thyme, cayenne, salt and pepper, and sherry. Add oyster liquid and blend to make a sauce. Add oysters. Place mixture in ramekins and sprinkle with bread crumbs and dot with butter. Cook 10 minutes in hot (450 degree) oven or until brown.

**Mrs. John Ely Simpson (Marjorie McKinnon)**
**Savannah**

# OYSTERS IN CASSEROLE

1 quart standard oysters          ½ cup butter
saltines (about ¾ pound)          milk

Drain oysters. Grease 2-quart casserole with butter. Cover bottom with crushed (by hand) crackers. Place layer of oysters, salt and pepper and several dots of butter. Then cover with crackers. Repeat layers until oysters are used. Top with crackers. Just before cooking, add milk to top so that just a small amount remains in bottom of casserole after it soaks up the milk. Bake 30 minutes in oven at 325 degrees.

**Mrs. Edgar C. Holmes (Mary Frances Broach)**
**Atlanta**

# OYSTER PIE

1 pint oysters                    3 well-beaten eggs
12 saltine crackers               2 tablespoons butter
⅔ cup evaporated milk             ½ teaspoon salt
⅔ cup water                       dash of pepper

Put layer of oysters in one quart casserole. Sprinkle with salt and pepper. Crush 6 saltines on top. Dot with butter. Then a second layer of oysters and crackers. Combine beaten eggs, milk and water. Pour over oysters. Milk mixture should be on top. Bake at 400° until brown—about ½ hour. Serves 3.

**Mrs. Henry Green (Mary Frances Yates)**
**Brunswick**

# JUNIOR LEAGUE MINCED OYSTERS

1 quart oysters                   2 tablespoons parsley, chopped
2 eggs, well-beaten               ½ cup cream
2 heaping tablespoons butter      1 cup fine bread crumbs. Reserve ½
4 tablespoons onion, chopped         of these for topping
4 tablespoons celery, chopped     salt and pepper to taste

Drain oysters and put through meat grinder. Mix well with other ingredients and heat in a double boiler for 15 minutes. Place in a greased casserole and top with the reserved bread crumbs. Dot with butter and bake in 350 degree oven until brown.

**Mrs. Abraham Illges (Virginia Howard)**
**Columbus**

# UNION LEAGUE OYSTERS

| | |
|---|---|
| 1 quart select oysters | ½ cup Parmesan cheese, grated |
| 2 tablespoons butter | ½ teaspoon salt |
| 1 tablespoon Worcestershire sauce | ¼ teaspoon pepper |
| | 6 slices toast, cut into triangles |

Melt butter and add Worcestershire sauce. Arrange oysters in 1 layer in a large baking dish. Sprinkle with salt and pepper. Pour butter and Worcestershire sauce mixture over and let sit for ½ hour. Sprinkle with Parmesan cheese and broil until the edges begin to curl, about 5 minutes. Serve hot on toast triangles, spooning juice over oysters. Serves 6.

Good as a first course.

**Mrs. Francis Willson Daily (Alice Hunt)**
**Savannah**

# SHRIMP

| | |
|---|---|
| boiled shrimp | sherry wine |
| water chestnuts | slivered almonds |
| Campbell's Cheddar Cheese Soup | |

In double boiler put the soup, water chestnuts and wine (not too much to make it too thin) and boiled shrimp. Be sure it is thoroughly heated. Serve over rice or in timbales with asparagus. Sprinkle almonds over shrimp before serving.

**Miss Elizabeth Anderson Brown**
**Atlanta**

# SHRIMP CURRY

| | |
|---|---|
| 2 onions, chopped | ¾ teaspoon salt |
| 3 tablespoons Wesson oil | ½ cup raisins |
| 3 tablespoons flour | ½ lemon, juice and grated peel |
| 1 teaspoon curry powder | dash pepper |
| 1 cup water | 2 cloves |
| 1 pound raw shrimp, cleaned | |

Cook the onions in 3 tablespoons Wesson oil for 5 minutes. Mix in flour, curry powder, salt, pepper, water, raisins, cloves. Stir until thick. Add lemon juice and peel and raw cleaned shrimp. Cover, cook slowly 15-20 minutes. Serve with rice and assorted accompaniments for curry. Serves 4.

**Mrs. Edmond Archer Turner (Dorothy Holmes)**
**Quitman**

## SHRIMP CREOLE

2 pounds raw shrimp, peeled
2 tablespoons
  butter/margarine
1 tablespoon flour
6 medium tomatoes or 10
  ounces
½ teaspoon salt
1 cup water

1 clove garlic, minced
⅛ teaspoon black pepper
1 cup chopped onions
½ cup chopped green pepper
⅓ teaspoon sage
⅓ teaspoon clove
⅓ teaspoon bay leaf

Melt butter in skillet. Add flour and cook slowly until light brown. Add onion and green pepper. Sauté gently about 5 minutes. Add shrimp. Let color slightly and then add tomatoes, water, sage, clove, bay leaf, garlic, salt and pepper. Simmer covered for about ½ hour, stirring often. Serve over steamed rice. Freezes nicely. 4 to 6 servings.

**Mrs. William Newell Kennon (Emma West Green)**
**Atlanta**

## SHRIMP CREOLE

1½ pounds green shrimp
1 tablespoon Worcestershire
  sauce
2 tablespoons melted butter
1 cup chopped onions
1 cup chopped green pepper
½ clove garlic, chopped

1 cup chopped celery
⅛ teaspoon paprika
2 cans cream of tomato soup
⅜ teaspoon salt
2 pinches pepper
2 pinches curry powder

Peel shrimp, wash and remove sand vein. Melt butter and stir into it the onion, green pepper, celery and garlic. Let this simmer until pepper is tender, then add tomato soup, salt, pepper, paprika, and curry powder. Boil for five minutes. Add shrimp (green) and boil ten minutes longer. Serves 8.

**Mrs. Sam Noble Roberts (Mary Stanton)**
**Atlanta**

# PAPA'S SHRIMP DINNER

6 pounds medium fresh shrimp
   (allow 1 pound per person)
3 onions, quartered
2 or 3 cloves garlic, peeled

4 lemons, squeezed and then
   quartered (reserve juice for
   sauce)
salt and pepper to taste

Pour about 6 inches of water in a large pot (enough to cover the shrimp) and add onions, garlic, lemons, salt and pepper. Steep at least an hour or until ready to cook shrimp. Bring mixture to full boil and add the shrimp. When water comes back to a boil, cook 5 to 10 minutes more. *Do not overcook.* Test after 5 minutes. Shrimp are done when pink and beginning to come away from shell. Drain. Remove onion, garlic, lemon and serve at once. These are peeled at the table, so provide bibs and stacks of paper napkins and a large bowl for the shrimp hulls.

## LEMON BUTTER SAUCE

1 pound butter
fresh horseradish (optional)

juice of 2 lemons (more lemon
   juice may be served in pitcher)

Heat butter and lemon juice thoroughly, stirring with a wooden spoon. Serve sauce in individual ramekins.

## PAPA'S SPECIAL SALAD

2 heads iceberg lettuce,
   shredded
2 saltine crackers
1 bottle small cocktail onions

1 package (8 ounces) sliced Swiss
   cheese, cut in match sticks
French dressing

Toss lettuce, cheese and onions with French dressing. Crumble crackers over top and lightly toss again.

## PECAN ICE CREAM BALLS
   WITH AMARETTO

½ gallon vanilla ice cream
Amaretto

2 cups crushed pecans

Soften ice cream and form into balls (1 per person). Refreeze. Roll balls in crushed pecans and return to freezer. A few minutes before serving, remove from freezer and serve. Serve with small pitcher of Amaretto.

**Mrs. J. W. Feighner (Margaret Richards)**
**Columbus**

## CURRIED SHRIMP IN RICE MOLD

1½ pounds raw fresh shrimp
3 chicken bouillon cubes
½ teaspoon salt
3 tablespoons flour
5 cups cooked rice

3 cups milk
1 tablespoon curry powder
¼ teaspoon white pepper
3 tablespoons butter
3 eggs, hard-boiled

Dissolve bouillon cubes in ¼ cup hot water. Moisten curry powder with the bouillon water. Add the salt and pepper. Melt the butter in a saucepan and stir in the flour. Stir in the milk with the curry mixture. Cook over low heat, stirring constantly until the mixture reaches the proper thickness for cream sauce. Pack the hot cooked rice into a greased ring mold and place the mold in a pan of water, which prevents sticking. Bake in a 350 degree oven for about fifteen minutes. Add the raw, peeled and deveined shrimp to the hot cream sauce and cook until the shrimp turn pink and are done. Unmold the rice ring on a heated platter. Pour the curried shrimp into the center of the ring. Decorate the edge of the platter with a parsley ring and serve very hot.

**Mrs. Leon Milton Leathers (Sarah Pharr Erwin)**
**Athens**

## SHRIMP DE JONGHE

2 cloves garlic, finely minced
½ teaspoon each finely
  chopped parsley, scallion,
  shallot, chives, chervil,
  tarragon and thyme
¼ pound butter at room
  temperature
1 cup fresh bread crumbs

1 pound uncooked shrimp, shelled
  and deveined
¼ cup dry sherry
Tabasco sauce to taste
⅛ teaspoon grated nutmeg
1 teaspoon grated mace
salt and freshly ground pepper to
  taste

Preheat oven to 400 degrees F. Combine the garlic, parsley, scallion, shallot, chives, chervil, tarragon, thyme and butter in a mixing bowl. Blend well. Add the bread crumbs, wine, Tabasco, nutmeg and mace. Add salt and pepper to taste. Drop the shrimp into boiling water and cook three minutes. Drain. Add one tablespoon or so of the butter mixture to each of four scallop shells. Arrange equal amounts of shrimp on top. Top with equal portions of the butter mixture and smooth it over. Bake 10 to 15 minutes or bake 10 minutes and run the dish under the broiler to brown. Serves 4.

**Mrs. W. Graham Ponder (Adelaide Wallace)**
**Madison**

# SHRIMP CASSEROLE

2 to 3 pounds shrimp, cooked,
  peeled, and cleaned
1 cup cooked rice
1 cup sharp cheese, grated
1 can mushroom soup

½ cup chopped green pepper
½ cup chopped green onion
½ cup chopped celery
½ cup butter
8 lemons, sliced very thin

Mix first 4 ingredients together. Sauté green peppers, green onions, and celery in the butter. Add to shrimp mixture. Put in long flat casserole and completely cover top with sliced lemon. Cook covered for about 20 minutes at 375 degrees. May be frozen ahead. Serves 6.

**Mrs. Moragne A. Whitney (Margaret Sinkler)**
**Bluffton, S.C.**

# HOT SHRIMP SALAD CASSEROLE

1 pound deveined cooked small
  shrimp
2 cups sliced celery
½ cup sliced canned water
  chestnuts
2 hard-boiled eggs, chopped

2 tablespoons grated onion
¾ cup mayonnaise
2 tablespoons lemon juice
½ teaspoon salt
½ cup shredded American cheese
1 cup crushed potato chips

Combine shrimp, celery, chestnuts, eggs and onion. Blend mayonnaise, lemon juice and salt. Stir in shrimp mixture. Place in greased 8-inch round glass baking dish. Top with cheese and potato chips. Bake at 400 degrees for 20 minutes. Serves 4 to 6.

**Mrs. Robert Rutledge King, Jr. (Marianna Barrett Bush)**
**Augusta**

# SHRIMP AND CHEESE CASSEROLE

6 slices white bread
1 pound cooked shrimp
½ pound Old English cheese
¼ cup margarine, melted

½ teaspoon dry mustard
3 whole eggs, beaten
1 pint milk
salt to taste

Break bread in pieces about the size of a quarter. Break cheese into bite sized pieces. Arrange shrimp, bread and cheese in several layers in greased casserole. Pour melted butter over this mixture. Beat eggs. Add mustard and salt to eggs, then add the milk. Let stand a minimum of 3 hours, preferably overnight in refrigerator, covered. Bake 1 hour in 350 degree oven, covered. Serves 4.

**Mrs. Frederick F. Williams, Jr. (Suzanne Hill)**
**Savannah**

# SHRIMP VICTORIA

½ pound raw shrimp, peeled & deveined
1 small onion, finely chopped
2 tablespoons butter or margarine
1½ teaspoons all-purpose flour
⅛ teaspoon of salt

½ cup commercial sour cream
1 teaspoon sherry
¼ pound mushrooms
1 tablespoon lemon juice
dash of pepper
1½ cups hot cooked rice

Sauté shrimp and onion in butter 10 minutes or until tender. Add mushrooms and cook over low heat 5 minutes. Sprinkle with flour, salt and pepper. Stir in sour cream and cook gently 10 minutes. Do not allow to boil. Before serving add 1 tablespoon of sherry. Serve with rice. Serves 2.

**Mrs. Frank Atkinson Little (Sarah Renfroe)**
**Thomasville**

# SHRIMP CHATEAUBRIAND

½ pound boiled shrimp
1 8-ounce box mushrooms
¼ cup shallots
⅛ teaspoon cayenne pepper
⅛ teaspoon garlic salt
2 tablespoons sherry
⅛ teaspoon paprika

⅛ teaspoon oregano
1 tablespoon flour
3 tablespoons butter
1 tablespoon Parmesan cheese
¾ pint whipping cream
1 tablespoon parsley flakes

Sauté mushrooms in butter. Drain and add shrimp, shallots, cayenne pepper, salt and flour. Heat and stir. Pour in cream. Add garlic salt, cheese, paprika, oregano, and parsley flakes. Spill sherry on this and thicken. Serves 4.

**Mrs. William E. Hamilton (Foster Adair)**
**Atlanta**

# SHRIMP PIE

1 pint cooled cooked shrimp
2 cups bread crumbs
1 cup milk
2 tablespoons melted butter
1 teaspoon salt

½ teaspoon black pepper
1 teaspoon Worcestershire sauce
2 tablespoons sherry
⅛ teaspoon mace
¼ teaspoon nutmeg

Soak bread in milk. Add shrimp, butter, and seasonings. Place in a buttered 1-quart baking dish and bake in a moderate oven (375 degrees) for 30 minutes.

**Mrs. James Clyde Mixon (Elizabeth Edwards Gaillard)**
**Atlanta**

# SHRIMP FRITTERS

1 cup small or medium raw,
    peeled shrimp
1½ teaspoons salt
4 or 5 grinds fresh black
    pepper

1 egg
1 cup flour
½ teaspoon baking powder
⅔ cup milk
½ teaspoon salt

Salt and pepper shrimp. Set aside while preparing batter as follows: Sift together flour, baking powder, and ½ teaspoon salt. Separate egg, beat yolk, add milk and flour, stir. Blend into this mixture the egg white which has been beaten stiff.
Drain shrimp of any moisture. Stir into batter. Drop by spoonfuls into hot cooking oil (1 to 2 inches deep if frying pan is used, or according to directions if deep fat fryer). Fry 3 to 5 minutes, or until nicely browned. Drain on paper towel and keep piping hot. Serve with seafood cocktail sauce, as an appetizer or main dish. Serves 3 to 4.

**Mrs. Albert Sidney Britt, Jr. (Annie McIntosh)**
**Savannah**

# PINK SHRIMP

1 pound uncooked peeled
    shrimp
4 teaspoons butter
½ pound fresh mushrooms,
    sliced

1 cup sour cream
1 teaspoon soy sauce
paprika
salt and pepper
½ cup grated sharp cheese

Melt butter. Stir in mushrooms and sauté 5 minutes. Add shrimp and sauté 3 minutes. Put sour cream (at room temperature) in saucepan. Add salt, pepper, soy sauce and enough paprika to turn pink. Heat but do not boil. Stir in shrimp and mushrooms and cook until mixture thickens. Spoon into 4 shells, sprinkle with grated cheese and put under broiler until cheese bubbles. Serves 4.

**Mrs. Henry F. Garlington (Jeanne Morrell)**
**Savannah**

# SHRIMP PILAU

2 cups cooked rice
2 cups cooked and picked small
  shrimp
4 strips bacon
4 tablespoons fresh bacon
  grease

1 cup chopped onion
1 cup chopped bell pepper
salt, pepper and curry powder to
  taste

Sauté the onion and bell pepper in the bacon grease until opaque. Do *not* brown. Add shrimp and sauté briefly. Turn in cooked rice and continue turning in until all bacon grease and flavorings are absorbed. Add salt, pepper and curry powder to taste. Add crisp bacon, crumbled, and chopped parsley if desired.

If you omit the shrimp, this makes a delicious curried rice dish to use with sour cream chicken or lamb.

**Mrs. M. Heyward Mingledorff (Marjory Heyward)**
**Savannah**

# SHRIMP CURRY

½ cup chopped onion
¼ cup butter (melted)
¼ cup plain flour
1 teaspoon salt
dash of pepper
1¾ cups chicken broth

1½ teaspoons curry powder
½ cup apple sauce
1½ pounds cooked and cleaned
  shrimp
2 cups cooked, fluffy dry rice
condiments of your choice

Cook shrimp first. Put two whole bay leaves in water and let come to a boil. Put in cleaned shrimp—cook 5 minutes—*no more*. Remove from water—cover with ice—set aside.

Cook finely chopped onion in butter until tender and a golden brown. *Careful, don't burn*. Blend in flour, salt and pepper, add chicken broth—slowly. Cook until thick, stirring constantly. Have heat low. *Careful, don't scorch*. Add curry powder, apple sauce and shrimp. Heat and *heat only* because shrimp will become tough if over-cooked.

If you are not planning to serve right away, make curry sauce and set aside. Add apple sauce and shrimp to heated sauce when ready to serve. Serve on hot rice with your choice of condiments. Serves 6.

**Mrs. Forman Dismukes (Florence Barber)**
**Brunswick**

# NEW JERSEY SEAFOOD CASSEROLE
*(Served in the Governor's Mansion in Trenton, New Jersey)*

¼ cup butter
¼ cup flour
1½ cups milk
⅛ teaspoon dry mustard
½ teaspoon salt
¼ teaspoon dried dill
⅛ teaspoon pepper
3 tablespoons butter
1 lemon, juice only
⅛ teaspoon thyme

2 cups Cheddar cheese, grated
½ pound mushrooms, sliced (or 8 ounce can sliced)
1 pound shrimp, boiled
1 pound crabmeat (not claw)
1 quart oysters, poached until edges curl
½ cup additional grated Cheddar cheese

Melt butter in top of large double boiler. Add flour and when well-blended, stir in milk. Add dry seasonings and 2 cups grated cheese. Keep warm over boiling water. Sauté sliced mushrooms in 3 tablespoons butter. Boil shrimp 7-9 minutes and drain. Poach oysters and drain. Add shrimp, crabmeat, oysters and mushrooms to cheese sauce. (At this point recipe may be held over simmering hot water until needed.) Before serving, stir in juice of lemon, pour into 3 quart casserole, sprinkle ½ cup cheese on top and bake in 450 degree oven until top is golden brown, about 10 minutes. Serves 8 generously.

**Mrs. Francis Willson Daily (Alice Lincoln Hunt)**
**Savannah**

# CRAB AND SHRIMP CASSEROLE

3 tablespoons butter
2 tablespoons flour
1 cup milk
½ pound crabmeat, flaked
½ pound cooked shrimp
salt to taste
dash of white pepper
¼ cup chopped bell pepper

1 2½-ounce can sliced mushrooms
1 10¾-ounce can mushroom soup
½ cup slivered almonds
1½ cups grated cheese
½ cup sherry
¾ cup bread crumbs

Melt butter in saucepan. Add chopped peppers, cook until tender. Sauté mushrooms in butter. Push aside. Add flour and cook until mixture bubbles. Add milk slowly, stirring constantly until it thickens. Remove from fire, add undiluted mushroom soup, sherry, crabmeat, cooked shrimp, 1¼ cups grated cheese, slivered almonds, salt and white pepper. Pour into 2-quart buttered casserole. Top with bread crumbs and ¼ cup cheese. Bake uncovered 30 minutes in oven at 350 degrees. Serves 8.

**Mrs. Harold I. Tuthill (Hazelle Beard)**
**Savannah**

# SEAFOOD SAN SIMEON

4 tablespoons butter or
  margarine
4 tablespoons flour
2 cups milk
½ teaspoon salt
1½ teaspoons curry powder
1 cup packed grated cheese
  (medium sharp or sharp
  American)

1 cup sour cream
1 pound raw shrimp, peeled
1 pound uncooked fish fillets or
  scallops
1 4-ounce can sliced mushrooms
  (optional)
½ cup almond slivers, toasted
accompanying dish of cooked rice

Melt butter in saucepan. Stir in flour until it is a thick paste. Gradually add milk, stirring constantly until it is smooth and thickened. Add salt, curry and cheese, stirring until melted. Cool. Fold in sour cream. Spread a thin layer of sauce in a greased two quart pyrex baking dish, add uncooked seafood and mushrooms and cover with balance of sauce. Sprinkle with almond slivers. Bake at 300 degrees for 20 minutes or until fish is just done. Serve with rice. Serves 6 to 8.

**Mrs. S. William Clark (Susan Lott)**
**Waycross**

# SEAFOOD CASSEROLE

2 tablespoons butter
2 tablespoons flour
3 cups milk
2 tablespoons mayonnaise
¼ teaspoon Worcestershire
  sauce
dash Tabasco sauce
dash paprika

1 pound crabmeat
2 pounds shrimp
¼ teaspoon seasoning salt
¼ teaspoon onion powder
2 tablespoons sherry wine
½ teaspoon lemon juice
salt and pepper to taste

Make a cream sauce by melting butter, add flour and blend. Add milk slowly and stir until thickened. Add seasoning salt, onion powder, sherry wine; salt and pepper to taste. Cool. Add two tablespoons mayonnaise, ½ teaspoon lemon juice, Worcestershire sauce and paprika. Go through 1 pound crabmeat for shell and add 2 pounds cooked and cleaned shrimp. Add Tabasco sauce and put seafood mixture in a buttered baking dish. Cover with crumbs. Bake in 350 degrees for thirty minutes.

**Mrs. Ralph B. Willis, Jr. (Lillian Neely)**
**Augusta**

## ARTICHOKE, SHRIMP, CRAB CASSEROLE

1 can artichoke hearts
1 pound crabmeat
1½ pounds cooked shrimp
1 pint coffee cream
2 tablespoons butter
3 teaspoons flour
1 tablespoon Worcestershire
   sauce

½ teaspoon paprika
1 tablespoon lemon juice
2 tablespoons ketchup
1 tablespoon sherry
1 teaspoon salt—dash of pepper
1 cup grated sharp cheese
bread crumbs

Slice artichokes. Put in layer of artichoke, shrimp and crabmeat. Make sauce of cream, butter, flour. Add Worcestershire, paprika, lemon juice, ketchup, sherry, salt and pepper. Add to casserole, then add cheese mixed with bread crumbs. Bake for 30 minutes at 350 degrees.

**Mrs. Isaac M. Aiken (Alice Harrison)**
**Brunswick**

## CRAB-SHRIMP CASSEROLE

2 medium bell peppers,
   chopped
2 medium onions, chopped
4 long stalks celery, chopped
2 cups crabmeat
2 cups buttered bread crumbs,
   crumbled fine

1½ (21 ounces) bags of frozen,
   cooked shrimp
½ teaspoon black pepper
½ teaspoon salt
2 teaspoons Worcestershire sauce
2 cups mayonnaise

Drop shrimp into rapidly boiling water and let boil one minute; drain; cool. Chop into rather large pieces. Mix onions, celery, crabmeat, bell pepper, salt, Worcestershire sauce, shrimp, and mayonnaise together and pour into generously buttered casserole (preferably oblong); sprinkle with the buttered crumbs; bake in 350 degree oven for one hour, uncovered. Serve hot. Serves 10.

**Mrs. John Goss Stone (Anna Thomas)**
**Atlanta**

# SALMON MOUSSE WITH CUCUMBER SAUCE

2 pounds red salmon, broken in
  bits
4 egg yolks
4 tablespoons vinegar
1 cup water
1 teaspoon salt

2 teaspoons dry mustard
2 cups milk
2 tablespoons butter
2 tablespoons gelatin
2 teaspoons sugar

Combine dry mustard, sugar, salt, butter and egg yolks. Stir in milk gradually and over low heat, cover mixture to make a very thick custard, stirring constantly. Soak gelatin in one half of the cup of water and dissolve in the other half cup which has been brought to a boil. Add vinegar and then turn into the custard mixture. Add salmon and pour into a lightly greased ring mold. Set in refrigerator to congeal. Serve with the following cucumber sauce or caviar sauce.

## CUCUMBER SAUCE

½ pint sour cream
salt and pepper to taste

2 cucumbers, chopped
few drops green food coloring

Combine sour cream and cucumber and check for salt and pepper. Add a drop or two of green coloring if desired.

## CAVIAR SAUCE

2 cups fresh mayonnaise
small jar caviar

2 eggs, hard boiled
juice of 1 lemon

Put mayonnaise in center of ring of mousse. Arrange over the mayonnaise the hard-boiled eggs, with the whites and yolks put through a sieve separately and topped with the caviar. Squeeze the lemon over the eggs and caviar.

**Mrs. Howell Cobb Erwin (Lucy G. Yancey)**
**Athens**

# SALMON MOUSSE de BEAUZON

2 cups cold flaked salmon
2 tablespoons grated onion
2 tablespoons Worcestershire
    sauce
2 tablespoons capers
1 cup mayonnaise
salt and Tabasco to taste

1½ tablespoons gelatin
½ cup cold water
⅓ cup lemon juice
1 dozen cooked, split shrimp for
    garnish
watercress or lettuce

Soften gelatin in the water. Heat gently, stirring until gelatin dissolves. Add lemon juice and set aside. Combine salmon with onion, capers, Worcestershire sauce, mayonnaise, Tabasco, and salt. Fold in the gelatin and water and pour into a three cup mold, which has been rinsed in cold water. Chill until set. Unmold on watercress or lettuce and garnish with split shrimp. Serve Sauce Verte separately.

SAUCE VERTE (for SALMON
    MOUSSE de BEAUZON)

1 cup mayonnaise
1 cup sour cream
1 teaspoon dry mustard
2 cucumbers, peeled and
    chopped

1 drop green food coloring
2 tablespoons chopped chives or
    parsley

Mix mayonnaise and sour cream together. Remove 2 tablespoons of this mixture and mix with dry mustard. Return to mayonnaise mixture. Add cucumber, green coloring, and chives or parsley. Serve separately with Salmon Mousse de Beauzon.

**Mrs. Bell Young**
**Valdosta**

# SALMON CROQUETTES

1 pound can salmon
½ can cream mushroom soup
1 tablespoon grated onion
¼ cup chopped celery
1 tablespoon chopped parsley

½ cup Pepperidge Farm dressing
1 egg
2 tablespoons water
cracker meal

Drain salmon, discard any bone and skin, flake with fork and mix with next five ingredients. Form into 12 croquettes. Roll in cracker meal, then in egg beaten with water, again in cracker meal. Place in refrigerator to dry at least 1 hour. Fry in deep, hot oil until golden.

**Mrs. Shelby Myrick Jr. (Alice Barrow)**
**Savannah**

# SALMON MOUSSE

2 envelopes unflavored gelatin
2 slices onion
4 tablespoons lemon juice
1 cup boiling water
2 tall cans red salmon, drained

2 teaspoons dill weed
½ cup mayonnaise
½ teaspoon paprika
½ pint heavy cream, whipped
salt to taste

Put gelatin, onion, lemon juice and water in blender at high speed for 40 seconds. Add salmon, mayonnaise, paprika, dill, salt and blend until salmon is puréed. Fold in whipped cream. Pour in a greased mold. Chill until firm. Serve with lettuce and dill sauce.

DILL SAUCE

½ cup mayonnaise
½ cup sour cream

dill weed
dash curry powder

Mix and chill.

**Mrs. Charles Lanier (Elizabeth Sheffield)**
**Americus**

# SEAFOOD SUPREME

1 medium green pepper,
  chopped
1 cup chopped celery
6 or 8 stalks parsley, chopped
1 tablespoon Worcestershire
  sauce
1 cup mayonnaise

1 medium onion, chopped
1 pound of shrimp
1 6½-ounce can of crabmeat
1 6-ounce can of lobster
1 cup Pepperidge Farm Herb
  dressing
salt and black pepper to taste

Sauté green pepper, celery, onion and parsley until transparent (not brown). Add all ingredients except Pepperidge dressing. Put in greased casserole, sprinkle top with dressing (mash the dressing into crumbs). Bake 45 minutes at 350°.

**Mrs. Hollis Lanier (Virginia Owens)**
**Albany**

# SALMON TETRAZZINI

4 ounces spaghetti
1 16-ounce can salmon
about 2 cups milk
2 tablespoons butter or
  margarine
¼ cup all-purpose flour
¼ teaspoon salt

¼ cup sliced pitted ripe olives
2 tablespoons grated Romano
  cheese
2 tablespoons dry sherry
1 cup soft bread crumbs
1 tablespoon butter or margarine
1 3-ounce can sliced mushrooms

Cook spaghetti in boiling, salted water until just tender. Drain. Drain salmon, reserving liquid. Add milk to salmon liquid to measure 2¼ cups. Break salmon into chunks discarding skin and large bones. In large saucepan, melt the butter or margarine; blend in flour and salt. Add milk mixture all at once. Cook and stir until thickened and bubbly. Add mushrooms, olives, cheese, sherry, salmon and spaghetti. Turn into 1½-quart casserole. Combine bread crumbs and 1 tablespoon butter. Sprinkle on top. Bake at 350 degrees for 35 to 40 minutes. Serves 6.

**Mrs. Gordon C. Turner (Mary Moore)**
**Augusta**

# SALMON MOUSSE

1 large can salmon
chicken stock
2 packages gelatin
½ cup parsley, chopped
½ green pepper, chopped
½ medium onion, chopped
1 to 2 stalks celery, chopped

1 cup mayonnaise
3 tablespoons lemon juice
½ teaspoon Worcestershire sauce
½ teaspoon Tabasco sauce
½ teaspoon dill
1 to 2 teaspoons salt

Drain salmon into measuring cup and add enough liquid (chicken stock) to make 1 cup. Sprinkle gelatin into cold liquid. Let set 2 to 3 minutes and slowly heat until dissolved. Pour parsley, green pepper, onion, celery into bowl. Add 1 cup mayonnaise, salmon, lemon juice, Tabasco sauce, Worcestershire sauce, dill and salt. Combine. Pour into 6-cup mold, oiled. Place in freezer for 1 hour or refrigerate 2 to 3 hours. Sprinkle dill on top.

**Mrs. Alexander Barrett (Julia Hill)**
**Augusta**

## RED CLAM SAUCE FOR SPAGHETTI

3 8-ounce cans minced clams
3 tablespoons olive oil
3 cloves garlic, minced
4½ tablespoons fresh parsley,
    chopped
1½ teaspoons dried oregano
¼ teaspoon dried basil

½ teaspoon salt
¼ teaspoon pepper
1 28-ounce can tomatoes
1 15-ounce can tomato sauce
1 8-ounce bottle clam juice
juice of 1 lemon

Drain clams, reserving liquid. Cook garlic until it begins to brown in olive oil in medium saucepan. Add parsley, oregano, basil, salt, pepper, tomatoes, tomato sauce, reserved clam liquid, bottled clam juice and lemon juice. Simmer 30 minutes, stirring occasionally. Add clams and cook until clams are heated through. Serve over spaghetti. Serves 6 to 8.

**Mrs. Lowell Harry Hughen (Jan Paullin Whitfield)**
**Atlanta**

## SEAFOOD CASSEROLE

1 7½-ounce can Alaskan king
    crab
1 4½-ounce can shrimp
1 cup mayonnaise
1 cup Pepperidge Farm Herb
    Stuffing

¼ cup green pepper, chopped
1 tablespoon Worcestershire sauce
½ cup celery, chopped
¼ cup onion, chopped

Mix all ingredients and put into buttered quart and a half size baking dish. Do not pack down. Bake at 350° for 30 minutes.

**Mrs. Malcolm Hardin Bogle (Marion Ann Reid)**
**Valdosta**

# Meats

Mary F. Passailaigue

# EYE OF ROUND ROAST FOR PARTY

| | |
|---|---|
| 1 eye of round roast | 1 can mushroom soup |
| ⅓ cup soy sauce | ½ cup diced onions |
| ⅓ cup wine | ½ cup diced celery |
| ⅓ cup water | ½ cup diced bell peppers |

Marinate roast for 1 hour in mixture of soy sauce, wine, water, onions, bell peppers and celery. Turn several times. Bake roast and marinade inside "Brown-in-bag" placed in a pan at least 2 inches deep for 1 to 1½ hours at 275 degrees. Remove from bag. Thicken cooked marinade and meat juices with 1 can mushroom soup to make gravy. Serve with rice. Makes 8 to 10 servings.

**Mrs. Bonner Milwee Durham (Nina Kathleen Fuller)**
**Americus**

# ROUND STEAK SAUERBRATEN

| | |
|---|---|
| 1½ pounds round steak, ½ inch thick | 2 cups water |
| | ½ teaspoon salt |
| 1 tablespoon shortening | 2 tablespoons wine vinegar |
| 1 envelope French's Brown Gravy mix | 1 teaspoon Worcestershire sauce |
| | ¼ teaspoon ground ginger |
| 1 tablespoon instant minced onion | 1 bay leaf |
| | ¼ teaspoon pepper |
| 1 tablespoon brown sugar | hot buttered noodles |

Cut meat in one inch squares, brown in hot shortening. Remove meat from skillet, add gravy mix and water. Bring to boil, stirring constantly. Stir in onion, sugar, vinegar, Worcestershire sauce, ginger, bayleaf, salt and pepper. Add meat. Put in 1½ quart casserole, cover and bake at 350 degrees for 1½ hours. Remove bay leaf. If desired, thicken with cornstarch. Serve on noodles. Makes 5 or 6 servings.

**Mrs. Henry Freeman Inglesby (Leila James)**
**Savannah**

# BEST CHUCK ROAST

1 six to seven pound chuck
   roast
2 medium green peppers,
   chopped
4 medium onions, chopped
1 teaspoon salt
1 teaspoon black pepper
1 clove garlic
2 bottles catsup (20 ounces)
½ cup sugar

1 teaspoon chili powder
10 whole cloves
1 teaspoon dry mustard
1 teaspoon cinnamon
1 teaspoon allspice
2 bay leaves
2 tablespoons Worcestershire
   sauce
1 cup cider vinegar
1 teaspoon ginger

Pour all ingredients above over roast and cover pan. Bake at 225-250 degrees for 6 to 6½ hours. Slice or shred with two forks. Serve sliced or on seed buns. It may also be served on rice or noodles. Serves 12 to 15.

**Mrs. Paul Bouzigues (Lucy Hatcher)**
**Atlanta**

# APPLE POT ROAST

4 pounds chuck blade-bone pot
   roast
2 tablespoons vegetable
   shortening or oil
1½ teaspoons salt
¾ teaspoon ground ginger
5 whole cloves
1 bay leaf

¼ teaspoon black pepper
1 cup apple juice
½ cup dry red wine
4 medium Washington State
   apples, cored and quartered
   (nice with skin left on)
2 large onions, sliced

In Dutch oven (or roaster) brown roast on both sides in hot shortening. Add ginger, salt, pepper, cloves, bay leaf, apple juice and wine to meat. Bring to boiling, reduce heat, cover and simmer 2 hours. Add apple and onion slices to meat, cover. Return to simmer and cook ½ hour longer. Remove meat to heated platter and surround with apples and onions. Serves 6.

**Mrs. J. Robert Logan (Virginia Connerat)**
**Savannah**

# BEEF MEDALLIONS SAUTÉED WITH WILD RICE

4 small filets about 1½ inches
   thick
2 tablespoons butter
½ teaspoon Dijon mustard
2 tablespoons sliced shallots
⅓ cup Noilly Prat vermouth

salt
¼ teaspoon sage
¼ teaspoon basil
2 teaspoons capers
1 6-ounce package wild rice mix

Sprinkle filets lightly with salt. In medium-sized skillet over high heat, melt 1 tablespoon butter and stir in the sage, basil and mustard. Add filets and brown until done as preferred. Allow 3 minutes a side for rare filets. Place filets on bed of wild rice mix prepared by instructions on package. Keep warm. To the skillet add the remaining 1 tablespoon butter, vermouth and capers and boil rapidly until reduced about half; stir occasionally. Pour these juices over meat and sprinkle with shallots.

**Miss Frances Huguenin Ellis**
**Columbus**

# POT ROAST JARDINEVE

3-4 pound chuck or round roast
shortening for browning meat
1 can beef broth
1 teaspoon salt
¼ teaspoon pepper

¼ teaspoon rosemary
4 small carrots, halved lengthwise
2 medium turnips, cut in fourths
8 small onions, whole
parsley for garnish

Brown meat on all sides in large heavy pan in a small amount of shortening. Put meat in 3-quart deep baking dish. Add soup. Cover and bake 2½ hours in 325 degree oven. After baking for 2½ hours add salt, pepper, rosemary, carrots, turnips and onions. Cover and continue baking for 1 hour. Remove to heated platter and garnish with parsley. Serves 4 to 6.

**Mrs. J. Converse Bright (Lucia Duval Chase)**
**Valdosta**

# GOURMET STEW

3 pounds lean stew meat
1 can celery soup
1 can mushroom soup
1 package dried onion soup

⅓ cup red wine
1 4-ounce can mushrooms, drained
1 can water chestnuts, drained

Mix all ingredients. Cook in a covered vessel for 3 hours in a 325° oven. Serve over rice or Chinese noodles. Serves 6 to 8.

**Mrs. John Phillips, Jr. (Aynn Kirtley)**
**Albany**

# SAUTÉ TENDERLOIN OR SIRLOIN TIPS WITH MUSHROOMS IN SAUCE

3 pounds 4 ounce tenderloin or sirloin tips trimmed. (Fat free and about 1½ inches square)
10 ounces mushrooms

4 ounces shallots
1 ounce margarine
1¼ quarts brown sauce
1¼ ounces burgundy wine
2 ounces salad oil

Slice beef tips on bias. Wash mushrooms and slice, lifting from water. Sauté shallots and mushrooms in margarine and combine with hot brown sauce. Add burgundy wine. Simmer slowly while preparing beef tips. Heat cooking oil and cook beef quickly in large frying pan. Mix cooked beef with mushroom sauce. Have cooked rice to serve with.

BROWN SAUCE
(ESPAGNOLA)

½ pound onions, medium diced
¼ pound carrots, diced
5-ounces flour (all purpose)
4-ounces tomato puree

¼ pound celery, diced
5-ounces oleo
1¼ quarts beef bouillon
½ bay leaf

Sauté all vegetables in saucepan. Add flour and cook slowly 10 minutes. Add hot bouillon and tomato puree, stirring until slightly thickened and smooth. Add bay leaf, and salt and cook slowly for 1½ hours. Adjust flavor and consistency. Serve on rice.

**Mrs. John Sheffield, Sr. (Emily Cheves)**
**Americus**

# FLANK STEAK TERIYAKI

1 teaspoon ginger
1 clove garlic, minced
⅓ cup grated onion
2 tablespoons sugar

½ cup soy sauce
¼ cup water
1½ to 2 pounds flank steak

Combine first six ingredients. Pour over steak and let stand 3 to 4 hours turning often. Preheat grill, cook steak 4-5 minutes, brushing with marinade and turning often. Cut into thin slices on the diagonal. Will serve 5.

**Mrs. Aubrey Matthews (Sue Earnest)**
**Rome**

## RAGOUT OF BEEF WITH ENGLISH WALNUTS

3 pounds lean beef, cubed
18 small white onions
¾ cup red wine
1 teaspoon parsley, minced
1 clove garlic, crushed
1½ teaspoons salt
¾ cup walnuts
2 teaspoons orange rind,
    shredded

3 tablespoons fat
5 teaspoons flour
¼ teaspoon thyme
2 bay leaves
2½ cups stock
½ teaspoon pepper
3 cups celery, sliced

Brown beef in fat or lard. Remove from Dutch oven. Cook whole onions until golden in fat. Mix in two teaspoons flour. Add wine and stock (or water with two beef cubes, if this is used do not add salt as the beef cubes are very salty). Add parsley, garlic, salt, thyme, bay leaves and pepper. Return meat to Dutch oven and cover and cook at 350 degrees for one hour. Add celery and nuts and continue cooking for one hour or until the meat is tender. If the gravy is too thin, thicken with remainder of the flour by putting the flour in a small pan and adding some of the hot gravy while stirring vigorously. Return to Dutch oven. Sprinkle orange rind over the dish before serving. Serve with very hot noodles, or rice.

**Mrs. Howell Cobb Erwin (Lucy G. Yancey)**
**Athens**

## FILET JOSEPH

½ pound mushrooms, sliced
3 tablespoons butter
salt and pepper to taste
1 tablespoon brandy, warm
1 tablespoon sherry, warm
1 tablespoon Madeira, warm

¼ cup butter
1 teaspoon flour
1 tablespoon Dijon mustard
4 tenderloin filets, ¾ inch thick
butter

Sauté mushrooms in 3 tablespoons butter for about 5 minutes. Add salt and pepper and warm brandy, sherry and Madeira. Ignite the spirits; shake the pan until the flames die out. Stir in ¼ cup butter creamed with flour and mustard. Cook the sauce until slightly thickened. Pan broil 4 slices tenderloin of beef in butter. Spread sauce on filets. Serves 4.

**Mrs. John H. Cheatham, Jr. (Leila Gillian Barnes)**
**Griffin**

# SHISHKABOB IN A DISH

2 cups rice, cooked
2 pounds beef
5 medium tomatoes, quartered
1 package Adolph's tenderizer
   or marinade

3 medium onions, quartered
1 quart fresh mushrooms, sliced
1 large green pepper, cut in strips
2 tablespoons butter

Cut beef in large cubes, marinate in tenderizer or marinade five minutes on one side; turn and let soak on other side. Remove beef but reserve liquid. Heat large skillet very hot and braise beef. Set aside on paper towel. Sauté onions and pepper together with butter. In separate pan sauté mushrooms. Add them to onions and pepper, along with tomatoes. Cover and steam on low heat for five minutes. Add beef and reserved liquid. Mix and serve over two cups cooked rice. Serves 6-8.

**Mrs. William Glascock Bush (Marie Battey)**
**Augusta**

# NANCY'S PASTRAMI

1 fresh beef brisket, boned and
   trimmed
1 cup salt
1 box pickling spice

1 whole garlic, peeled, sliced
2 tablespoons saltpeter
water to cover

Choose a brisket with as little fat as possible. Mix pickling ingredients, except water. Using porcelain or glass container large enough to contain brisket, put ½ pickling mixture in bottom. Place meat in container; top with other ½ of spices. Cover with water and close container. Place in refrigerator for 10 days or 2 weeks, turning at end of 1 week. Keep covered. It looks bad. After pickling, remove from brine and run under water lightly to rinse. Boil in new water in porcelain pan until tender—a long time but not falling apart. Refrigerate until very cold. Slice very thin. Freezes well.

**Mrs. James Dickson Maddox (Rebecca Wall)**
**Rome**

# ROULADEN

2 pounds lean beef (flank,
round, or chuck)
½ teaspoon thyme, rosemary
or marjoram
salt and pepper
mild mustard
gherkins

cord or skewers
1 cup consommé
1 tablespoon flour
few sprigs parsley
bacon strips
finely chopped onion
¼ cup butter

Cut beef in ½ inch thick slices (or have butcher cut them); pound the strips as thin as possible. Sprinkle each with salt and pepper, spread each lightly with mustard. On each slice lay a thin strip of bacon, some onions, and thin slices of gherkins. Roll up the slices neatly and secure with cord or skewers. In a heavy skillet brown the beef rolls on all sides in butter. Pour in consommé, cover and simmer 1 hour or until very tender. Remove rolls from skillet, stir in flour mixed to a smooth paste with water. Season with thyme, rosemary, or marjoram and parsley, finely chopped. Simmer sauce for several minutes; return meat rolls and heat them through.

**Mrs. Joseph P. Zollo (Margaret Glenn)**
**Columbus**

# WELSH MEAT LOAF

⅓ cup shortening
½ cup onion, minced
½ cup green pepper, chopped
2 cups celery, chopped
2 tablespoons parsley, minced
2 cups soft bread crumbs
2 eggs, beaten
1 teaspoon salt

½ teaspoon pepper
1 cup milk
2 pounds ground beef
3 hard-boiled eggs (optional)
3 tablespoons fine dry bread
crumbs
½ teaspoon paprika

Save 2 tablespoons of shortening out and use the balance to sauté until light brown the onion, celery, green pepper, and parsley. Put ground beef in large bowl, add soft bread crumbs and mix; add vegetables and mix. Mix beaten eggs, salt, pepper, and milk and add to meat mixture. Mix well. Spread ½ of meat mixture in 10-inch by 6-inch greased loaf pan. Lay hard-boiled eggs lengthwise down the center. Place rest of the meat on top and shape slightly. Spread remaining 2 tablespoons of shortening over the top and sprinkle with dry bread crumbs, then a bit of salt, and paprika for a crusty brown top and moist inside. Bake in hot oven (400 degrees) for 1½ hours. Let cool in pan. Serve hot or cold in slices. (Can be cooked on top of stove in heavy frying pan.)

**Mrs. Frederick Eugene Fletcher (Sarah Jackson Sims)**
**Atlanta**

# BRUNSWICK STEW

1½ pounds round steak (cubed)
1½ pounds pork, fresh, lean
    (cubed or small strips)
½ cup white vinegar
2 -28 ounce cans tomatoes
2 cups Irish potatoes (diced
    and cooked)
2 cups cream corn

1-16 ounce can English peas, small
2 cups tomato catsup, Heinz
¾ cup onion, chopped
1 tablespoon salt
3 slices bread, whole wheat, ½ inch
    thick
Red Hot pepper sauce, optional

Cook meat with vinegar in pressure cooker 40 minutes or until shredded. Remove gristle, bone and fat. In a 4 quart Dutch oven pan, put tomatoes, potatoes, corn, peas, catsup, onion and salt. Add bread torn into small pieces for thickening. Add shredded meat with juices. Simmer together 45 minutes to 1 hour to blend flavors. Makes 4 quarts and freezes well.

Serve in cream soup bowls with English muffins buttered in slits on top, sprinkled with paprika and Parmesan cheese, then toasted until crusty.

**Mrs. Frank Willingham (Mary Watson)**
**Macon**

# CHILI

½ pound pinto beans
4 cups water
8 cups canned tomatoes
3 cups chopped green peppers
4 cups chopped onions
4 tablespoons salad oil
2 large cloves garlic, crushed
½ cup chopped parsley
½ cup butter or margarine

2½ pounds ground beef
1 pound ground pork
5 tablespoons chili powder
2 tablespoons salt
1 teaspoon black pepper
½ teaspoon crushed red pepper
1½ teaspoons cumin seed
1½ teaspoons Accent (optional)

Wash beans. Soak overnight in water. Simmer in same water until tender. Add tomatoes and simmer five minutes. Sauté green peppers in oil five minutes. Add onions. Cook until tender, stirring often. Add garlic and parsley. Melt butter and sauté meat for fifteen minutes, until all meat has changed color. Add meat to onion mixture. Stir in chili powder and cook for ten minutes. Add meat mixture, salt, black pepper, red pepper, cumin seed, and Accent to bean mixture. Simmer, covered for 1½ hours. Cook, uncovered, for 30 minutes. Serves 8 to 10.

**Mrs. Hubert Gregory Veal (Mary Martha Lanier)**
**St. Simons Island**

# CHILI CON CARNE

6 tablespoons butter
6 medium onions, sliced
3 pounds ground beef (good
　round)
3 20-ounce cans tomatoes
1 6-ounce can tomato paste

1 cup beer or ale
1 tablespoon salt
½ teaspoon Tabasco sauce
2 to 4 tablespoons chili powder
2 12-ounce cans whole kernel corn

A sound, all-around chili, made distinctive by the addition of corn.

Melt the butter in a large saucepan. Add the onions and cook until tender. Add the beef and cook until lightly browned. Add the tomatoes, tomato paste, beer, salt, Tabasco sauce and chili powder. Cover and simmer 45 minutes. Add the corn and simmer 15 minutes longer.

**Mrs. Charles Thomas Huggins (Sada Mason)**
**Augusta**

# BOEUF EN DAUBE

4 pounds stew beef
3 tablespoons flour
1 teaspoon salt
½ teaspoon black pepper
⅛ teaspoon nutmeg
½ cup onion, chopped

½ cup carrots, grated
¾ cup dry red wine
1 cup beef broth, canned
½ teaspoon thyme
1 bay leaf
3 tablespoons bacon drippings

Toss beef in mixture of flour, salt, pepper and nutmeg. Add onions, carrots and beef to bacon drippings in a large skillet. Cover over medium heat until well-browned. Add wine, beef broth, thyme and bay leaf. Cover and cook over low heat 1½ hours or until meat is tender. Serve over egg noodles.

**Mrs. Erle Allen Taylor (Anna Elizabeth Brannen)**
**Moultrie**

# SHEPHERD'S PIE

2 cups well-seasoned mashed
　potatoes
2 eggs, beaten
⅛ teaspoon salt
2 cups cooked lamb or veal,
　finely chopped

⅓ cup cream
2 tablespoons parsley
paprika
butter

Fold beaten eggs into potatoes. Place ½ mixture in buttered casserole. Combine meat, cream, and parsley. Cover potatoes with mixture. Top with remaining potatoes and dot with butter. Preheat oven to 350 degrees. Bake for 30 minutes. Serves 4.

**Mrs. J. Thomas Daniel, Jr. (Martha Alexandria Bell)**
**Thomasville**

# CORN BEEF CASSEROLE

| | |
|---|---|
| 1 can corn beef | 1 cup sharp Cheddar cheese, grated |
| ½ package medium noodles | 1 onion, chopped |
| 1 can cream of celery soup | 1 bell pepper, chopped |
| dash of cayenne pepper | |

Sear onion and bell pepper in salad oil. Heat soup, add cheese and onion and bell pepper. Cook noodles 9 minutes, drain, add soup mixture. Fold in corn beef torn up. Do not stir too much. Put in greased casserole (1½ quart). Heat in 350 degree oven until bubbly. Can be made ahead. Serves 6 amply.

**Mrs. Frances Martin Cable (Frances Nelson Martin)**
**Albany**

# LASAGNE CASSEROLE

| | |
|---|---|
| 1 tablespoon salad oil | ¼ rounded teaspoon pepper |
| 2 cloves garlic, crushed | ½ teaspoon oregano |
| 2 pounds ground beef, crumbled | ½ pound lasagne noodles |
| | 12 ounces mozzarella cheese or |
| 1 16-ounce can tomato sauce | Monterrey jack or mild Swiss |
| 1 16-ounce can tomatoes | 1 pound cottage cheese (or ricotta) |
| 1½ teaspoons salt | ¾ cup Parmesan, grated |

Sauté ground beef and garlic in oil, then add next 5 items and simmer 20 minutes. While simmering, cook noodles in boiling, salted water about 15 minutes; drain. Now fill 3-quart buttered casserole with alternate layers of noodles, cheese, tomato sauce, and Parmesan, ending with a layer of sauce and Parmesan. Bake uncovered at 375 degrees for 20 minutes.

**Mrs. William F. Toole (Bertha Barrett Lee)**
**Augusta**

# SPICED BEEF LOAF

| | |
|---|---|
| 2 pounds ground steak | 2 tablespoons ground cinnamon |
| ½ pound ground pork | 2 tablespoons brown sugar |
| 1½ cups cracker crumbs | 2 tablespoons dry mustard |
| 2 eggs | 2 tablespoons allspice |
| red pepper | 1 tablespoon Worcestershire sauce |
| 2 teaspoons salt | |

Form into loaf and bake in moderate oven (350 degrees) for about 45 minutes.

**Mrs. William A. Winburn III (Emily Coxe)**
**Savannah**

# SPICY BEEF BUNS

4 tablespoons
  margarine/butter
1 medium onion, chopped
¼ cup green pepper, diced
½ cup celery, chopped
1 pound ground chuck
8 wiener buns, split on side

½ cup catsup
1 teaspoon salt
¼ teaspoon pepper
1 tablespoon Worcestershire sauce
1 cup Cheddar cheese, shredded
1 tablespoon prepared mustard

In large skillet, melt 2 tablespoons butter/margarine. Sauté green pepper, celery, onion for 5 minutes. Add ground chuck and cook just until all redness is gone. Drain. Add other ingredients. Simmer 10 minutes, stirring occasionally. Hollow out inside of buns and spread with mixture of 2 tablespoons margarine and mustard. Refrigerate buns and meat for 2 hours. Fill each bun with meat, filling full. Wrap in foil and freeze. Preheat oven to 350 degrees and heat in foil for 30 to 40 minutes.

**Mrs. John Tyler Mauldin (Anne Scott Harman)**
Atlanta

# HAMBURGER QUICHE

1 pound ground beef
1 cup onion, chopped fine
1 cup mayonnaise
1 cup milk

1 cup grated cheese
4 eggs
2 tablespoons flour
2 unbaked pie shells

Brown ground beef with onion. Combine with remaining ingredients and pour into the pie shells. Bake for 40 minutes in a 350° oven. Each quiche serves 4-6.

**Mrs. R. E. Champion, Jr. (Mary Barrett)**
Albany

# CORDON BLEU

6 veal cutlets
6 slices Swiss cheese (do not
  buy sliced)
6 slices Canadian bacon
2 eggs
12 small slices of stale French
  bread

2 tablespoons sweet (unsalted)
  butter
4 tablespoons Mazola oil
1 cup flour

Have butcher slice cutlets ½ to ¾-inches thick. With a very sharp knife make a pocket in each cutlet. Slide a slice of cheese and a slice of Canadian bacon into each pocket. Heat butter and Mazola Oil in iron skillet. Cook when thoroughly heated on low. Set up an assembly line and dip cutlets in following:
1. Flour
2. Well-beaten eggs
3. Bread crumbs (made from French bread).
   Do the crumbs ahead of time.

Cook slowly until browned and done.

**Mrs. Thomas T. Hawkins (Harriet Waddell)**
**Thomasville**

# VEAL SCALLOPINI

2 pounds veal cutlet
1 cup marsala wine
2 tablespoons vermouth
2 tablespoons lemon juice
2 cups sliced mushrooms

1 garlic clove
2 tablespoons tomato paste
6 or 8 peppercorns
salt to taste

Have butcher cut veal cutlet very thin. Flour the cutlet and brown it in butter.

Add marsala wine (madeira or sherry may be used, marsala wine is better), vermouth, lemon juice, mushrooms. Add garlic clove, finely chopped (or cut garlic cloves in half and remove from dish just before serving), tomato paste, peppercorns and salt to taste.

Cover the pan and cook veal slowly 1½ hours. Serves 4 to 6.

**Mrs. Malcolm Maclean Jr. (Frances Grimball)**
**Savannah**

# LEG OF LAMB WITH SAUCE

small leg of lamb
fresh cracked or coarse grind
  pepper
½ cup water
¼ cup vinegar

1 tablespoon Worcestershire sauce
2 tablespoons catsup
1 teaspoon coarse salt
½ teaspoon cracked pepper

Sear lamb on range until brown. Place in roasting pan, sprinkle liberally with pepper and cover. Cook for 1 hour in 300 degree oven. Mix next six ingredients in small saucepan and heat, pouring heated sauce over lamb after it has cooked 1 hour. Turn oven down to 230 degrees, recover lamb and cook until meat thermometer measures 180 degrees. Cool pan drippings, remove layer of fat, and thicken with cornstarch or arrowroot for gravy.

**Mrs. Henry Brown (Patti Smith)**
**Rome**

# LAMB STEW

½ leg lamb (cut in ¾ inch
  cubes) not cooked
1 medium onion (coarsely
  chopped)
½ large green pepper (coarsely
  chopped)

1 pound carrots
3 heaping tablespoons butter or
  margarine
6 ounces gin
salt and pepper to taste

Sauté coarsely chopped onion and pepper in 1 tablespoon butter until tender, but not too brown. Salt and pepper lamb and lightly brown in balance of butter. Add sautéed onion and pepper and cook over medium heat until nearly done. In another pan boil carrots until almost done. Drain and put in with lamb. Pour in 1 jigger of gin per person. Gives delicious flavor. Cook 10 minutes more. Serves six.

**Mrs. Leonard John Mederer (Hyta Plowden)**
**Valdosta**

# LAMB CHOPS

4 loin lamb chops (2 to 2½"
  thick)
1 crushed garlic bud

¼ teaspoon dry ginger
1 tablespoon curry powder
¾ cup soy sauce

Marinate chops 3 or 4 hours or overnight. Brush with same marinade as they broil.

**Mrs. F. P. Wetherbee (Patty Eppes)**
**Albany**

# PASTITSIO
*(Lamb with Macaroni)*

3 tablespoons butter
1 pound lamb, ground
2 small onions, chopped
3 garlic cloves, minced
2 16-ounce cans tomatoes
½ teaspoon oregano
½ teaspoon nutmeg
⅛ teaspoon cinnamon

3 eggs, beaten
Parmesan cheese
1 pound macaroni, cooked in
    salted water and drained
1 large eggplant
olive oil
custard sauce

Heat 3 tablespoons butter in large pan until it foams. Add the lamb, onions and garlic and sauté until lamb is brown. Add tomatoes and juice of tomatoes, oregano, nutmeg and cinnamon. Simmer, uncovered, until liquid has evaporated. Remove from heat and cool. Add the eggs and Parmesan to taste (½ cup or more). Carefully mix in macaroni and pour into an open, greased baking dish. Peel and slice eggplant into ¼ inch slices. Arrange on a baking sheet, sprinkle with olive oil and broil until both sides are golden. Layer the eggplant on top of lamb and pasta. Pour custard over eggplant, sprinkle with more Parmesan, dot with butter. Bake in preheated 325 degree oven until custard sets, about 35-40 minutes. Let stand 10 minutes before serving. Serves 8.

CUSTARD SAUCE

3 tablespoons butter
3 tablespoons flour
3½ cups warm milk
½ teaspoon salt

pepper to taste
4 eggs, lightly beaten
1½ cups ricotta

Melt butter in heavy sauce pan and add flour. Stir over low heat 2 minutes. Add milk, salt and pepper. Stir until mixture thickens, about 5 minutes. Remove from heat and stirring constantly, add eggs and ricotta. Mix well.
**Mrs. Heyward B. Clarke (Ann Williams)**
**Waycross**

# MARTHA BALL'S LAMB CARDINAL

6 to 8 slices cold cooked lamb
¼ cup currant jelly
¼ cup tarragon vinegar

½ cup tomato catsup
scant teaspoon prepared
    horseradish

Heat together all sauce ingredients, add to lamb and cook for about 10 to 15 minutes on medium heat.
**Mrs. Lloyd Hiram Megahee (Frances Philips)**
**Thomasville**

# STUFFED SHOULDER OF LAMB

1 boned shoulder of lamb
1 pound sausage
1 onion, chopped
1 tablespoon parsley,
  chopped
½ teaspoon pepper
1 onion, sliced
pinch thyme

1 clove garlic
2 tablespoons flour (more or less)
1 egg
1 cup bread crumbs
1 teaspoon salt
1 carrot, sliced
1 bay leaf
1 cup beef bouillon

Make stuffing from sausage, onion, parsley, egg, bread crumbs, salt and pepper. Spread mixture on lamb. Roll up and tie with string. Put lamb in roasting pan and add onion, carrot, thyme, bay leaf, garlic, and bouillon. Cook for 2 hours. Remove roast and add flour to pan juices and more bouillon as needed to make gravy.

**Mrs. William Shivers Morris, III (Mary Sue Ellis)**
**Augusta**

# HAM MOUSSE

2½ cups cooked, ground ham
  (country ham preferred)
2 cups milk
6 eggs

8 tablespoons flour
8 tablespoons butter
2 teaspoons lemon juice
1 teaspoon salt

Make a cream sauce of the butter, flour and milk. Add lemon juice and salt. Add ground ham and beaten egg yolks. When cool, add stiffly beaten egg whites and pour into 2 well buttered loaf pans or one large casserole dish if you do not wish to unmold. Bake for 20 to 25 minutes at 400 degrees. Carefully loosen around sides of pans and invert on serving dish. Especially good served with Supreme Sauce spooned over loaves and garnished with broiled peach halves which have been filled with chutney. Serves 10 to 12.

SUPREME SAUCE

2 tablespoons butter
3 tablespoons flour
1 cup chicken stock, heated
¼ teaspoon salt
⅓ cup cream

dash of pepper
1 egg yolk
6 fresh mushroom caps, sliced and
  sautéed in butter

Melt butter, add flour, salt and pepper. Stir until well blended. Add stock slowly, stirring constantly. Bring to boiling point. Boil 2 minutes. Add cream and just before serving add beaten egg yolk and sautéed mushroom caps.

**Mrs. John A. Shields, Jr. (Christine Thiesen)**
**Waycross**

# HAM AND MUSHROOMS IN PATTY SHELLS

1 pound fresh mushrooms,
  sliced
3 tablespoons flour
¼ teaspoon white pepper
2½ cups milk
2 cups cooked ham, cut in
  julienne strips

8 patty shells, prepared by
  directions
8 tablespoons butter
½ teaspoon salt
½ teaspoon prepared mustard
½ cup sharp cheese, shredded
2 teaspoons lemon juice

Wash and slice mushrooms. Under medium heat, drop 3 tablespoons butter in saucepan and add the mushrooms and lemon juice. Sauté gently until heated through. If mushrooms are cooked too long they give off a great deal of liquor and shrivel down and lose texture. Set aside. Melt remaining 5 tablespoons butter in a saucepan. Blend in flour, salt, pepper and mustard. Gradually add milk stirring constantly to prevent lumping. Cook over medium heat, or over hot water until cream sauce consistency. Add ham and stir in cheese until melted. Add mushrooms and as much mushroom juice as sauce will take without too much dilution. Serve in warm patty shells.

**Mrs. Thomas Walter Rogers (Mary Emma Gee)**
**Athens**

# STUFFED HAM

17 pound processed ham
2 cups celery, diced
2 cups onion, chopped
2 cups fat, cut from ham after
  boiling
4 tablespoons brown sugar

2 loaves stale bread, crumbed
2 cups parsley, chopped
8 tablespoons whole mustard seed
8 tablespoons celery seed
1 cup vinegar

Simmer ham in deep water for three hours. Allow to cool in water. Remove bone and stuff cavity and cover top with stuffing. To make the stuffing, knead the celery, parsley, bread crumbs, ham fat, mustard and celery seed and brown sugar with the hands until well mixed. After stuffing the ham, bake in a 300 degree oven for two hours with one cup of water and one cup vinegar in the pan.

**Mrs. Hubert B. Owens (Anna Torian)**
**Athens**

## HAM POTATO CASSEROLE

2 or 3 cups chopped, cooked
  ham
2 medium potatoes, sliced and
  cooked

1½ cups grated Cheddar cheese
6 tablespoons margarine
6 tablespoons all-purpose flour
2½ cups milk

Make a thin white sauce using the margarine, flour, and milk. In a slightly greased 2-quart casserole alternate layers of potatoes, ham, cheese, in that order. Pour white sauce over the mixture. Cover and bake for 30 minutes at 350 degrees. Makes 6 generous servings.

**Mrs. John K. Thomas (Martha Paine)**
**Fitzgerald**

## COMPANY PORK CHOPS

8 or 10 pork chops
2 cups rice, uncooked
2 cans condensed onion soup
½ cup sherry
1 8-ounce can mushrooms
  (stems and pieces)

1 large onion, chopped
1 green pepper, chopped
2 stalks celery, chopped
salt and pepper to taste

Mix rice, onion soup, mushrooms, sherry, onion, green pepper, celery, salt and pepper in three-quart baking dish. Season chops and place over rice mixture. Bake covered in 325° oven for one and half hours. Uncover and bake at 350° for another half hour. Serves 8 to 10.

**Mrs. Lewis Johnson Hubbard (Alice Brinson)**
**Moultrie**

## BAKED PORK CHOPS

10 pork chops
10 onion slices
10 lemon slices
⅔ cup brown sugar

1/12 teaspoon salt
⅜ teaspoon pepper
3 teaspoons lemon juice
⅔ cup chili sauce

Brown pork chops in skillet. Arrange in large baking dish. Cover each chop with onion and lemon slice. Blend remaining ingredients. Pour over chops. Bake uncovered at 325 degrees about 1½ hours.

**Mrs. Vance Watt (Mercer Pendleton)**
**Thomasville**

# PORK CHOPS

6 pork chops, 1-inch thick
salt, pepper, garlic salt
3 cups cooked brown rice
½ cup chopped (coarsely)
    cashews
½ cup chopped celery

¼ cup chopped onion
3 tablespoons soy sauce
¼ teaspoon ground ginger
1 can cream of mushroom soup
½ cup sour cream
¼ cup milk

Brown pork chops, salt, pepper, and garlic salt in small amount of butter. Combine next six ingredients and spread in a 9x13 inch baking dish. Place chops on top. Cover. Bake for 1 hour in 350 degrees preheated oven. Combine mushroom soup, sour cream, and milk and heat. Do not boil. Serve soup mixture with casserole.

**Mrs. William B. McMath (Henryetta Glover)**
**Americus**

# PORK CHOP DELIGHT

2 pork chops 1½ inches thick
2 cans of sauerkraut
1 apple

Worcestershire sauce
garlic salt

Sear chops in heavy iron skillet with Worcestershire sauce and garlic salt. In covered deep dish place one can of sauerkraut, then chops. Slice apple on that; then add other can of sauerkraut. Cover and cook for 1½ hours at 375°. It should almost fall off bone.

**Miss Sally E. Wetherbee**
**Albany**

# PORK AND PRUNES

1½ pounds prunes
½ bottle dry white wine
8 slices fillet or pork (or loin
    chops)
2 tablespoons butter

2 tablespoons seasoned flour
1 tablespoon red currant or
    gooseberry jam or jelly
1½ cups cream
salt and pepper to taste

Soak prunes for six hours or overnight in the wine. Turn the pork slices in the seasoned flour and fry in butter on both sides until golden. Cook gently with lid on pan until meat is done. Meanwhile simmer the prunes for half an hour in the wine in which they soaked. Drain prunes, retaining juice, and arrange on a serving dish with pork. Add prune liquor to the meat juices, reduce, add the jam and blend with the cream. Pour over the pork and prunes and serve very hot with boiled parsley potatoes. Serves 8.

**Grace Latimer Durham**
**Edinburgh, Scotland**

## CHINESE BARBECUE SPARERIBS

2 pounds lean spareribs (pork)

Marinate for 6 hours in following mixture:

3 slices fresh ginger
2 green onions, chopped
5 tablespoons soy sauce (light)
2 tablespoons wine (rice wine
   or sherry)

2 tablespoons sugar
1 tablespoon Horsin sauce (readily
   available at Oriental food store)
½ teaspoon red food coloring

Roast ribs in 350 degree oven for about 1 hour until brown. Cut into slices and serve.

Mrs. Thomas Clay (Anita Lippitt)
Savannah

## NOODLES JOHNSETTE

2 tablespoons Crisco
2½ cups chopped onions
1 chopped green pepper
1 pound lean ground pork
1 10½-ounce can tomato soup
½ soup can water

½ pound sliced fresh mushrooms
   (optional)
2 teaspoons salt
2 cups cooked noodles
½ cup shredded sharp Cheddar
   cheese

Sauté onions and green pepper in Crisco until soft but not brown. Add pork and stir until all meat is seared. Add soup, water, mushrooms, salt, and noodles. Mix well and put in greased casserole dish. Sprinkle with cheese, cover, and bake at 350 degrees for one hour. Serves 6. This recipe may be made the day before and reheated.

Mrs. Robert T. Sessions (Jean Warren)
Marietta

## SAUSAGE PILAU

2 cups rice
1½ pounds ground hot
   sausage

1 cup diced celery
1 cup diced onion
⅓ cup butter

Steam rice. Sauté sausage, celery and onions, pour off fat. Combine all ingredients and either steam or bake in casserole with cover until hot. Serves 6.

Mrs. Beverly Leigh (Elizabeth LeHardy)
Savannah

# CANNELLONI DI CAPRI

½ pound sausage meat, cooked
and drained
1 box frozen spinach, cooked
and chopped fine
1 cup finely chopped cooked
chicken
¼ cup grated Parmesan
cheese

⅛ teaspoon thyme
⅛ teaspoon pepper
butter
1 cup milk
2 eggs, slightly beaten
½ cup sifted flour
1 teaspoon baking powder
½ teaspoon salt
cheese sauce (recipe below)

Mix first 6 ingredients to make stuffing. To make crêpe batter: heat 2 table-spoons butter and the milk until butter is melted; cool slightly and add next 4 ingredients; mix until smooth. Drop by spoonfuls into hot skillet to form about 18 thin 3-inch crêpes. Fry until brown on both sides. Cool and spread each pancake with some of the stuffing, roll up and put in shallow baking dish in one layer. Cover with cheese sauce. Half an hour before serving heat in oven at 350 degrees until bubbling and run under broiler to brown.

CHEESE SAUCE

3 tablespoons butter
3 tablespoons flour
1½ cups light cream

½ cup Parmesan cheese or ¼ cup
Parmesan and ¼ cup provolone
salt and white pepper

Melt butter and blend in flour. Gradually add 1½ cups light cream and cook, stirring until thick. Stir in cheese. Season with salt and pepper. Serves 6. Can be frozen.
**Mrs. Thomas Clay (Anita Lippitt)**
**Savannah**

# SAUSAGE CASSEROLE

1 pound whole hog ground
sausage
1 cup diced green pepper
1 cup diced celery

1 cup white rice
1 cup diced onion
2 cans chicken broth (or 2 cups
chicken stock)

Brown sausage in 10-inch skillet. Add green pepper, celery, and onion. Continue browning until all are sautéed. Turn into casserole. Add broth and uncooked rice and bake in 350 degree oven for 1 hour.
**Mrs. William W. Alexander (Elise Clarke)**
**Thomasville**

## SPAGHETTI SAUCE

3 pounds ground chuck
½ bell pepper, chopped
1 medium onion, chopped
¾ cup celery, chopped
2 tablespoons bacon drippings

1 tablespoon Worcestershire sauce
salt, pepper, garlic powder to taste
3 small cans tomato sauce
1 can mushrooms (stems and
    pieces—any size can)

Sauté celery, bell pepper, and onions in bacon drippings. Add ground meat and stir until browned. Add all other ingredients. Simmer for at least one hour. Ladle off and discard fat that cooks to the top. Keep lid on pot. Serves 8.

**Mrs. Robert Engram Fokes, Jr. (Romanz Cook)
Moultrie**

## HOT CARAMEL APPLES

3 pounds tart, crisp apples
1 cup light brown sugar
juice one lemon

½ cup butter
¼ teaspoon cinnamon
2 ounces good brandy

Peel, core, and cut the apples in sixes. Drop the butter in a hot skillet and sauté the apples for five minutes, moving them about constantly. Add other ingredients and turn into a baking dish. Bake at 325 degrees for one hour, uncovered. Serve hot. When apples are being prepared in quantity for a large party, the lemon juice squeezed over the apples will prevent them from discoloring.

These apples make a good side dish to serve with pork. Bananas are equally delicious prepared in this manner. Six large bananas are the right quantity for the above other ingredients.

**Mrs. John Michael Gregory (Helen Louise Theuss)
Athens**

# Poultry and Game

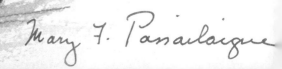

## COUNTRY CAPTAIN MIRA HART

Since the origins of Georgia's state dish still seem obscure and it was origi-nated by a Colonial Dame, this might be the time to set the record straight. About sixty-five years ago my mother ordered a cookbook by Alexandro Fillipini, the chef of Delmonico's for many years. Of all the marvelous dishes of Filippini's this is the only one mother changed radically. At that time you could not even obtain curry powder locally and it is, as far as I know, the first party dish of this kind to be served in Georgia. Hence its great popularity. Army friends took it all over the world and when mother's butler-chef went to the White House with Mr. Roosevelt as chef there, it received even wider recognition. Only recently, in an English cookbook which did not give a recipe, I discovered the origins of the odd name. This book said that a "country captain" was a corruption of "country capon" and was a simple curry with few ingredients and sambals.

| | |
|---|---|
| 12 chicken breasts | fluffy white rice |
| 2 onions, sliced fine | 2 large spoonfuls lard |
| 2 one-pound tins tomatoes | 2 green peppers, sliced |
| 2 beans garlic, crushed | 1 teaspoon parsley, chopped |
| 2 teaspoons curry powder | ½ teaspoon white pepper, crushed |
| ¼ pound almonds, slivered and toasted | 2 saltspoons thyme |
| | 3 generous spoonfuls currants |
| salt | little wine to soak currants |

Coat chicken with flour and a little salt. Heat lard in skillet and fry chicken gently until brown. Remove the chicken from skillet and put into a large casserole and keep warm. Gently wilt the onion and green pepper in the skillet along with the garlic. Add the tomatoes, white pepper, thyme and curry and mix well. Check for salt, pepper, and acidity. Some tinned to-matoes are more acid than others and want a little sugar. Pour the tomato sauce over the chicken in the casserole. Deglaze pan and add. Cover tightly and cook until the chicken is very tender. Curries are much better if made a day ahead. The seasonings blend into the meat much better. The rice can be cooked a day ahead, sealed in foil and re-heated with the Country Captain. Blanch, sliver and toast the almonds. When the dish is to be served, re-heat gently. Put the currants in a little wine and warm to plump. Place the chicken breasts on a warmed platter. Make a ring of rice around them. Add the currants to the tomato sauce and pour over rice and chicken. Scatter almonds over top of rice.

**Mrs. Sewell Marion Brumby (Mary Hart)**
**Athens**

# LAYERED CHICKEN CASSEROLE

1 hen
bread, very thinly sliced
4 hard boiled-eggs, chopped
2 cans water chestnuts,
    sliced
1 can cream of mushroom soup

1½ cups sweet milk
1 can pimentos, chopped
1 can sliced mushrooms
sharp cheese, sliced
1 can cream of celery soup

Boil hen until tender in salty water. Remove bones and cut in small pieces. In the bottom of a 3 quart oblong Pyrex dish, place thin slices of bread. Cover bread with diced chicken, at least one inch thick. Sprinkle chicken with hard cooked eggs. Pour 1½ cups of sweet milk over this. Place water chestnuts evenly over dish. Next, spread a layer of pimentos and mushrooms evenly over top. Cover entire mixture with sliced sharp cheese. Spread mushroom soup and celery soup over top. Cover with plastic wrap and *place in refrigerator overnight.* Before using, take out of refrigerator and allow to reach room temperature. Bake 1 hour at 350 degrees. Sprinkle top with bread crumbs or toast.

**Mrs. Joyce Ferdinand Mixson, Jr. (Elizabeth Stitt)**
**Valdosta**

# PARTY CHICKEN-SPAGHETTI FOR EIGHTEEN PEOPLE

4 or 5 pound hen
2 onions, chopped
1 small can pimentos
1 large can mushrooms
1 teaspoon salt, added slowly
    to taste
2 cups chicken broth

2 green peppers, chopped
2 cups canned tomatoes
1 large box fine spaghetti
¼ teaspoon pepper
½ pound New York cheese, grated
1 teaspoon poultry seasoning
butter to dot top casserole

Cook hen in lightly salted water with poultry seasoning. Cool. Remove skin and bones. Cut meat in bite sized pieces, not too fine. Simmer in broth very briefly the green peppers and onions. Add tomatoes, mushrooms and pimentos. Cook and drain spaghetti. Butter large flat casserole. Arrange layers as follows: First, spaghetti; second, chicken; third, sauce; fourth, cheese. Repeat for a second time, ending with cheese. Bake in preheated 350 degree oven for 1 hour.

**Mrs. Sam Merritt (Janet Scarborough)**
**Americus**

## CAMOOSE CREEK CHICKEN

10 chicken breasts, skin removed
5 tablespoons butter or margarine
8 ounces fresh mushrooms, sliced
1 can water chestnuts, sliced
soy sauce
1½ 10¾-ounce cans cream of chicken soup
1½ cups dry white wine

Lightly brown chicken breasts in bubbly butter. Place in baking dish. Brown mushrooms in remaining butter. Drain water chestnuts and sprinkle generously with soy sauce. Place mushrooms and water chestnuts over chicken breasts. Mix together soup and wine and pour over chicken, mushrooms and water chestnuts. Bake 1¼ hours in 350 degree oven. Serves 8 to 10.

**Mrs. Claggett Gilbert, Jr. (Barbara Guild)**
**Savannah**

## PHILLIPINE CHICKEN

1 fryer
1½ teaspoons white corn syrup
1½ cups soy sauce
¼ cup vinegar

Cut up fryer. Salt to taste with a sprinkle of garlic salt. Lay chicken flat in casserole. Mix corn syrup, soy sauce, and vinegar. Pour over chicken. Cover and bake at 350 degrees for 1 hour. Serves 4.

**Mrs. John Tyler (Alice Roane Cross)**
**Thomasville**

## LEMON CHICKEN WITH WINE

1 fryer, quartered
1 lemon, sliced
½ cup lemon juice
½ cup white wine
3 tablespoons cooking oil
2 tablespoons butter

Salt and pepper chicken lightly. Brown in oil, preferably in iron skillet which can go in oven. If not, lift to casserole dish. Pour lemon juice and wine over chicken. Place sliced lemon and sliced butter on top. Cover well and place in oven. Cook at 350 degrees for 1 hour. Serves 4.

**Mrs. Thomas Hal Clarke (Mary Louise Hastings)**
**Atlanta**

## LEMONED CHICKEN BAKE

2 broiling chickens, quartered
2 lemons
⅔ cup flour
1 tablespoon salt
1 teaspoon paprika

½ cup cooking oil
¼ cup brown sugar
2 cups chicken broth or bouillon
1 teaspoon Angostura bitters

Wash chickens and dry well. Squeeze juice of 1 lemon over pieces of chicken. Combine flour, salt and pepper in paper bag. Put chicken in bag and shake until coated. Brown chicken in oil; arrange in baking dish. Thinly slice remaining lemon and arrange over chicken. Dissolve sugar in broth; add bitters and put over chicken. Cover and bake in 375 degree oven or simmer over low heat until tender (about 1 hour).

**Mrs. Thomas Benton Eaton, Jr. (Margaret Nesbitt Teague)**
**Augusta**

## CHICKEN AND AVOCADO WITH CURRIED RICE

1½ pounds boned chicken
  breasts
salt and ground pepper
2 tablespoons butter or
  margarine
1 tablespoon chopped green
  onion
¼ pound sliced mushrooms
2 tablespoons Cognac

1½ cups whipping cream
1 avocado
2½ tablespoons butter or
  margarine
2 tablespoons chopped onion
½ teaspoon garlic powder
1 cup uncooked rice
1 tablespoon curry powder
1½ cups chicken broth

Cut each chicken breast into several strips, salt and pepper to taste. Heat butter in heavy skillet. (Wok may be used.) Add chicken strips and cook over high heat until chicken loses raw look. Stir continuously with wooden spoon. Remove chicken and set aside. Add chopped green onions to same skillet along with mushrooms and cook slightly, adding Cognac by sprinkling. Add whipping cream and cook over high heat for several minutes. Salt and pepper to taste. Peel and slice avocado into strips and add to the cream mixture and cook gently to blend. Add previously cooked chicken strips and cook gently.

In a large saucepan melt 1 tablespoon of butter and cook chopped onion to lose color while adding garlic powder. Stir continuously. Add rice and stir to coat all grains then sprinkle in curry powder and blend. Add chicken broth, stir in to mix well and transfer to a casserole with a cover. Bake in 400 degree oven for approximately 15 to 20 minutes. Serve on curried rice. Serves 6.

**Mrs. James S. Peters, Jr. (Carolina Burt)**
**Atlanta**

## CHICKEN NOODLE CASSEROLE FOR COMPANY

1 hen
2 tablespoons Wesson Oil
1 bell pepper, diced
2 onions, diced
1 pound fresh mushrooms,
  sliced
2 cups chicken stock, strained
salt to taste
Worcestershire sauce
10¾ ounce can mushroom soup

2 stalks celery leaves
1 onion cut in quarters to cook
  with hen
1 cup dry sherry *(or)*
  1 cup sauterne
1 8-ounce carton sour cream
1 package thin noodles (no
  substitute)
Parmesan cheese

Cook hen until tender in water (to cover) with celery, salt and onion. Remove. Debone meat and cut into small pieces. Reserve strained stock. In skillet add Wesson Oil (be sure to use oil, it keeps noodles separate). When oil is very warm, add bell pepper, onions, and sliced mushrooms. Stir until coated with oil. Keep stirring until a bit tender. Add chicken stock. Let simmer until all is tender. Add wine and simmer another minute. Into a deep bowl, pour sour cream and mushroom soup. Mix well. Add cooked mushrooms, onions and peppers. Add 2 cups diced chicken. Stir well. Cook noodles in chicken stock until done. Mix with ingredients in bowl. Add 3 dashes Worcestershire sauce. Stir. If too thick, add a small amount of chicken stock. Place all in pyrex pan. Shake Parmesan cheese over all and bake at 350° until bubbly. *May be prepared the day before* baking. Serves 8 to 10.

**Mrs. Bonner Milwee Durham (Nina Kathleen Fuller)**
**Americus**

## CHICKEN BREAST WITH ARTICHOKE HEARTS

8 to 10 chicken breasts, boned
2 teaspoons salt
2 teaspoons pepper
1 clove garlic, chopped fine
2 tablespoons flour

1 small scallion
2 14-ounce cans artichoke hearts
  (drain—save juice)
2 lemons
1 cup whipping cream

Brown chicken in margarine—add garlic and chopped scallions and brown. Add juice of 2 lemons to juice from 2 artichoke cans and add to chicken. Add 1 cup heavy cream mixed with 2 tablespoons of flour. Put in skillet and simmer until chicken is tender. Slice artichoke hearts and simmer with chicken. This can be made ahead, put in casserole and warmed in oven. Serve over rice. Serves 8 to 10.

**Mrs. William Cobb Ball (Martha Brantley)**
**Thomasville**

# CHICKEN AND ARTICHOKE CASSEROLE

20 pieces of chicken, all
   breasts *or* breasts and second
   joints—10 cups of chicken
4 large cans artichoke hearts
4 4-ounce cans sliced button
   mushrooms
4-5 ribs celery
1 medium onion, chopped, *or*
   equivalent frozen chopped
5-10 peppercorns
3-4 tablespoons pale, dry
   sherry

Parmesan cheese (grated)
2-3 cups cream sauce
2 small cartons sour cream
1 can cream of mushroom
   soup—10¾-ounce can
1 can cream of celery soup—10¾-ounce
   can
1 teaspoon salt
1 teaspoon black pepper
1-2 dashes Worcestershire sauce
1-2 dashes Tabasco sauce
paprika

Place chicken in pot with water to cover. Add celery with ribs broken into 2 or 3 pieces each, onion, and peppercorns. Boil at medium heat until tender (about 30 minutes). Remove chicken to a large platter, pull off skin while warm, remove chicken from bones, cut into thin slices with sharp knife. Drain artichoke hearts and slice each crosswise into 2 or 3 pieces. Drain mushrooms and sauté 5-10 minutes in 2-3 tablespoons butter, adding a little salt and pepper while cooking. Make sauce by mixing together cream sauce, cream of mushroom soup, cream of celery soup, sour cream, salt, pepper, Worcestershire sauce, Tabasco sauce, sherry. Butter casseroles. Arrange alternately slices of chicken and artichoke, then spread sautéed mushrooms evenly on top. Pour sauce over all, pressing mushrooms down into sauce. Sprinkle lightly with grated Parmesan cheese and paprika. Bake in preheated 350 degree oven about 35-40 minutes till hot through, bubbly, and slightly browned on top. *Serves 15-20.* Do not overcook.

*Note:* For a festive buffet supper I served this with thin sliced ham, tomato aspic with shrimp and avocado, ripe olives, rolls, Gin Ice cream and butterscotch brownies, demi-tasse and liqueurs.

**Mrs. Albert Sidney Britt, Jr. (Annie McIntosh)**
**Savannah**

# LUNCHEON CASSEROLE

2 cans artichoke hearts (6 to 8
  in each can)
1 small carton fresh
  mushrooms
1 pound shrimp cooked (or) 1
  pound chicken breasts,
  cooked and diced

6 tablespoons margarine or butter
8 ounce carton sour cream
1 teaspoon Worcestershire sauce
1 tablespoon dried parsley
salt and pepper to taste
Parmesan cheese

Empty drained artichoke hearts into baking dish. In skillet, sauté mushrooms in butter about 10 minutes, drain and add to baking dish along with shrimp (or chicken), mix together lightly.

Pour sour cream into skillet with butter and blend well. Stir in Worcestershire sauce, salt, pepper and parsley. Pour over ingredients in baking dish. Sprinkle Parmesan cheese on top and bake in 350 degree oven for 20-30 minutes or until bubbly. (This recipe may be used for a chafing dish, served in toast cups, but artichoke, mushrooms and shrimp or chicken should be cut into small pieces.)

**Mrs. Archibald Lovett Morris (Elizabeth Putnam Carswell)**
**Savannah**

# HOT LUNCHEON DISH

2 avocados
2 cups cooked chicken,
  chopped

4 tablespoons Cheddar cheese
4 tablespoons toast crumbs

SAUCE

2 tablespoons butter
2 tablespoons flour

1 cup milk

Half avocados, remove seed, leave on skin. Melt butter, add flour, then slowly stir in milk until sauce bubbles and thickens. Add chicken. Spoon all into avocado cavities. Sprinkle cheese over top. Lightly dust with toast crumbs. Place in pan of warm water (about ½-inch deep). Put in 400 degree oven and heat for 4 to 5 minutes. Serves 4.

**Mrs. Henry Miles Cutler (Hazel Beamer)**
**Thomasville**

# CHICKEN CASSEROLE

6 chicken breasts
4 chicken thighs
2 packages frozen broccoli,
chopped and cooked in
salted water
2 cans cream of chicken soup

½ package seasoned Pepperidge
Farm dressing
¾ cup mayonnaise
1½ teaspoons lemon juice
2 teaspoons curry powder
¼ pound butter

Sprinkle chicken with salt and pepper and cook in water until done. Remove from bones and cut in bite size pieces. Save the chicken stock. Grease a 3 quart casserole and place chicken in bottom. Cover with broccoli. Mix chicken soup with one cup of saved chicken stock, mayonnaise, lemon juice, and curry powder. Pour over broccoli and sprinkle dressing over all. Melt butter and drizzle over the top. Bake at 350 degrees for 25 minutes. Serves 10 people.

**Mrs. Lawrence Austin (Dede Elizabeth Harrison)**
**Savannah**

# PRESSED CHICKEN

1 hen (cooked and cut into
small pieces)
1 cup celery, minced
1 cup almonds, minced
4 hard-boiled eggs, minced

salt to taste
2 cups cooked peas (cold)
2 cups hot skimmed chicken broth
1 package gelatin (4 envelopes)
1 cup cold water

Dissolve gelatin in cold water. Add chicken stock, then all other ingredients. Mold in refrigerator until firm. Serves 6-8.

**Mrs. Porter Wilkins Carswell (Elizabeth McMaster)**
**Augusta**

# JAPANESE CHICKEN CASSEROLE

2 2½ pound chickens, cut for
frying
4 tablespoons butter
½ cup water
2 tablespoons red wine vinegar

1 teaspoon powdered ginger
¼ cup soy sauce
¼ cup brown sugar
1 1-pound can crushed pineapple

Wash and dry chicken and dust with ginger. Melt butter in skillet and dredge chicken in flour and brown in the butter. Remove chicken to casserole. Mix soy sauce, water, wine vinegar, and brown sugar. Pour over chicken. Drain pineapple and add to chicken. Cover and cook in 350 degree oven until tender, about fifty minutes. Chicken should always be cooked until it is ready to leave the bone. Serve with hot rice.

**Mrs. Leon Milton Leathers (Sarah Pharr Erwin)**
**Athens**

# POULET DE NORMANDIE

2 cups cornbread stuffing
  for fowl
1 cup chicken broth (or water)
½ cup onions, chopped
¼ cup green onions or chives,
  minced
¾ teaspoon salt
1½ cups milk

1 cup Cheddar cheese, grated
½ cup margarine, melted
3 cups chicken boiled and diced
½ cup celery, sliced in crescents
½ cup mayonnaise
2 eggs
1 10¾ ounce can mushroom soup,
  undiluted

Mix melted margarine, chicken broth and stuffing together well. Spread half over the bottom of a 12x8 inch casserole which has been buttered. Mix together the chicken, onions, green onions or chives, celery salt and mayonnaise. Spread over the dressing in the casserole. Top with remaining dressing mixture. Refrigerate for at least four hours, overnight preferably. One hour before baking spread one can of soup over the top and sprinkle with grated cheese. Bake forty-five minutes to one hour, uncovered at 325 degrees. This dish freezes well. Make entirely up to the final baking and thaw before cooking for one hour. Men seem to like this particularly. Serves eight or ten.

Mrs. Joseph Britton Neighbors (Mary Cobb Erwin)
Athens

# FRENCH HERBED CHICKEN CASSEROLE

1 3-pound broiler, fryer
  cut-up
1 tablespoon shortening
1 8-ounce can small white
  onions
½ cup chopped carrots

½ cup chopped celery
1 clove garlic crushed
1 2-ounce can sliced mushrooms
1 cup sauterne or white wine
1 bay leaf

Brown chicken in shortening. Place in 2 quart casserole. Drain fat and add all other ingredients except celery and bay leaf. Sauté these and pour over chicken. Tuck in celery and bay leaf. Cover and bake 1¼ hours at 350 degrees. Serves 4.

Mrs. John Carroll (Martha Burney)
Covington

# CHICKEN SAUTERNE

1 fryer, cut up, or 8 to 10
chicken pieces
8 very small fresh onions or 1
can tiny onions
½ cup chicken stock or
bouillon
4 medium ripe tomatoes,
peeled and diced, or 1 pound
can tomatoes, drained
½ to 1 cup Sauterne wine
1 package slivered almonds,
roasted

⅓ cup flour
1 clove garlic, minced
2 tablespoons salad oil
2 teaspoons salt
2 teaspoons freshly ground black
pepper
½ pound fresh mushrooms, sliced
1 cup sliced pimentoes
1 cup pitted ripe olives cut in thirds

Brown chicken with garlic in hot oil in Dutch oven. Add onions, salt, pepper, chicken stock and tomatoes. Cover tightly. Bake in oven at 350 degrees for 1 hour. Add mushrooms, pimentoes, olives and almonds. Cook 15 minutes longer. Remove chicken from Dutch oven. Blend flour and Sauterne until smooth. Stir into cooked sauce. Cook, stirring constantly, on low heat atop stove until thickened. Return chicken to Dutch oven. Keep hot until ready to serve. Serve hot with rice.

**Mrs. Bonner Milwee Durham (Nina Kathleen Fuller)**
**Americus**

# CHICKEN BORDEAUX

6 pieces chicken breasts, boned
and skinned
¾ cup flour
1 teaspoon salt
1 cup sliced mushrooms,
cooked in butter
freshly ground black pepper to
taste

½ cup salad oil
1 cup canned tomatoes
1½ cups dry white Bordeaux
wine
1 clove garlic, very finely chopped
and cooked briefly in butter

Dredge chicken with ½ cup flour seasoned with salt and pepper. In a heavy skillet, heat the oil, add the chicken and brown on all sides. Cover the pan and cook slowly 25 minutes. Pour the oil from the skillet and add the tomatoes with their juice. Bring to a boil. Combine the remaining flour with a little water and sitr into the simmering tomatoes. Cook, stirring, until mixture thickens. Add the wine, mushrooms and garlic and cook until the chicken is tender, about 20 minutes longer. Serve hot. Serves 6.

**Mrs. S. A. Tyler (Sara Arechavala)**
**Columbus**

## PARTY CHICKEN CASSEROLE

3 cups chicken, cooked and
   diced
4 hard cooked eggs, chopped
2 cups cooked rice
1 small onion, chopped
1 cup mayonnaise
1 (3 ounce) package slivered
   almonds

1½ cups celery, chopped
2 (10¾ ounce) cans mushroom
   soup
1 teaspoon salt
2 tablespoons lemon juice
1 cup bread crumbs
2 tablespoons margarine, melted

Combine all ingredients except bread crumbs and margarine, mixing well.
Pour into 3 quart oblong casserole. Combine melted margarine and bread
crumbs and sprinkle over top. Bake at 350 degrees for 35 to 40 minutes or
until bubbly. Serves 12 to 15.

Mrs. George W. Cross (Eleanor Irene Calley)
Covington, Louisiana

## CHICKEN BAKED IN BUTTERMILK

3 pounds chicken breasts
1 egg, well beaten
¼ cup sesame seed
1 teaspoon Worcestershire
   sauce

1 cup buttermilk
1 cup cornflakes
2 tablespoons butter

Mix the buttermilk into the beaten egg and put the chicken breasts in the
mixture. Soak the chicken thus for at least one hour in a container with a
tight top. Mix the cornflakes with the sesame seed and roll the chicken
breasts in the mixture. Melt the two tablespoons butter (or more) with the
Worcestershire sauce and pour over the chicken breasts which have been
transferred to a shallow baking dish. Bake one hour and fifteen minutes in a
350 degree oven.

Mrs. Leon Milton Leathers (Sarah Pharr Erwin)
Athens

# MAGGIE'S SOUR CREAM CHICKEN

1 fryer, cut in pieces *or*
8 fryer pieces—thighs and/or
  breasts
1 cup sour cream

1 tablespoon lemon juice
1 tablespoon Worcestershire sauce
1 clove garlic, crushed
1 teaspoon celery salt

Spread chicken on tin foil on shallow pan. Sprinkle lightly with salt and pepper. Let stand at room temperature. Mix sour cream, lemon juice, Worcestershire sauce, garlic, and celery salt. Adjust seasoning to your taste and let stand for at least two hours. Coat all pieces of chicken with the sour cream mixture and return to the shallow pan. Bake in preheated oven at 300 degrees for one hour. Delicious with curried rice, tossed salad and spiced peaches or chutney.

**Mrs. M. Heyward Mingledorff (Marjory Heyward)**
**Savannah**

# CHICKEN HASH

1 quart cooked chicken or
  turkey, diced
1 cup half and half
6 tablespoons butter
4 tablespoons flour
2 cups milk
3 egg yolks, lightly beaten

½ teaspoon salt
white pepper to taste
1 teaspoon grated onion
½ cup grated Swiss cheese
1 cup mushrooms (canned or
  fresh)

Simmer the chicken in the cream on low heat. Melt the butter in a skillet. Add the flour and cook until bubbly. Pour in milk and cook until thick and smooth. Add egg yolks and cook over low heat. Mix *half* the sauce with the chicken and cream mixture; heat thoroughly. Season with salt and pepper. Pour into a shallow buttered 2-quart casserole.

Add the onion and *half* the cheese to rest of sauce. Cook until well-blended. Put the mushrooms on top of the chicken in the casserole. Pour the rest of the sauce over this. Sprinkle with remaining cheese and run under broiler to brown. Serves 10.

**Mrs. Gordon MacGregor (Mary Bacon Bland)**
**Brunswick**

# CHICKEN RITZ

12 pieces of boned chicken
    breast
2 cups Ritz cracker crumbs
¾ cup Parmesan cheese
¼ cup parsley, chopped

¼ teaspoon garlic salt
2 teaspoons salt
⅛ teaspoon pepper
1 cup butter, melted

Preheat oven to 350 degrees. Blend crumbs, cheese, parsley, garlic salt, table salt and pepper. Dip each piece of chicken in butter and then in the dry mixture. Coat well. Arrange in shallow open casserole in a single layer. Pour remaining butter over all. Place in preheated oven and bake for 1 hour. *DO NOT TURN!* Serves 12.

Mrs. Benjamin Davis Tyler (Elizabeth Golden)
Columbus

# OVEN BARBECUED CHICKEN

1 chicken, cut in quarters
½ cup butter, melted
1 tablespoon prepared
    horseradish mustard

salt and pepper
¼ cup Worcestershire sauce
juice of 2 lemons
¼ cup water

Salt and pepper chicken lightly. Mix melted butter, mustard, Worcestershire sauce, lemon juice, and water and pour over chicken in a baking pan. Bake in preheated oven 350 degrees for 60 to 90 minutes, depending on size of chicken. Baste often, but do not turn chicken while baking. May be cooked, then frozen and heated before serving. Chicken may be cut in halves, or in pieces as for frying.

Mrs. Warrington Maxwell Oliver (Mary Young Roberts)
Valdosta

# BAKED CHICKEN SALAD

2 medium chickens, cooked
    and diced
2 cups celery, diced
2 cups cooked rice
2 tablespoons lemon juice
4 tablespoons chopped onion

2 cans cream of chicken soup
1½ cups mayonnaise
4 tablespoons margarine
1 cup (small package) corn flakes
1 cup slivered almonds

Mix first seven ingredients and put in 2 two-quart casseroles. Bake covered at 300 degrees for 1 hour. Brown corn flakes and almonds in margarine and sprinkle on top. Bake fifteen minutes more uncovered. Freezes well.

Mrs. W. F. Barron (Mary Sue Jones)
Rome

# MISS MAGGIE'S CHICKEN CROQUETTES

1 large or 2 small chickens
1 pint oysters or
   sweetbreads*
1 tablespoon butter
1 cup milk
2 eggs

1 large onion (chopped)
3 ribs celery, chopped
salt, to taste
pepper, to taste
a little mace
cracker crumbs

Boil cut up chicken with salt and pepper. Pour off broth, remove skin and bones, grind chicken fine. Drain liquor from oysters and chop fine. Add chopped onion, put in stew pan with butter and let it come just to a boil. Make a thick custard of the milk and eggs in a double boiler, stirring constantly, then mix all together (custard, ground chicken, chopped oysters, celery and seasonings) and roll into shape. Put on ice for several hours, then roll in cracker crumbs and fry in hot oil till golden brown.

(*When sweetbreads are used, wash, soak and parboil as follows: cover with boiling, salted water, adding 2 tablespoons lemon juice or vinegar to each quart of water, simmer 15-20 minutes, and drain. Then chop fine, and proceed as with oysters.)

If chicken is 5 pounds or over, one is enough with 1 pound of sweetbreads; this will make about 25 croquettes. (Serves 6-8)

**Mrs. Thomas M. Johnson (Kathryn Twiggs)**
**Savannah**

# COMPANY CHICKEN

8 chicken breast halves
   (boned)
1 small jar dried beef
2 6-ounce jars sliced
   mushrooms
¼ cup of white wine

1 soup can milk
10¾ ounce can Campbell's Cream
   of Mushroom Soup
1 cup sour cream
4 tablespoons butter
1 can artichoke hearts

Wrap dried beef around chicken breasts and place them in buttered baking dish. Season with salt and pepper. Place drained mushrooms on chicken. In a separate pan, heat together soup thinned with the milk and butter. Add wine and pour over chicken. Cook uncovered at 300 degrees for one hour and 15 minutes. Add sour cream and artichoke hearts and cook 30 minutes more.

**Mrs. M. Felton Hatcher, Jr. (Beth Hall)**
**Fort Valley**

# CHICKEN AND RICE CASSEROLE

1 whole chicken (fryer)
½ cup celery, cut up
1½ teaspoons salt
1 cup sherry
1 cup water
1 small onion, cut up
1 pound or 8 ounce can mushrooms

1 6-ounce package wild and long
  grain rice
½ cup butter
1 cup sour cream
1 cup mushroom soup
slivered almonds

Bring chicken and first 5 ingredients to a boil, cover and simmer 1 hour. Skin, bone and cut chicken into bite sizes. Strain liquid and use to cook rice. Sauté mushrooms, mix with soup and sour cream. Add rice and chicken. Use 2½ or 3-quart casserole. Sprinkle with almonds. Bake at 350 degrees for 1 hour. Serves 8 or more.

**Mrs. Joel Guy Inman (Sara Phillips)**
**Albany**

# CHICKEN PILAU

3 cups rice
4½ cups chicken stock
liver from one chicken,
  chopped
gizzard from one chicken,
  chopped

1 cup white bacon, cut fine
1 cup onions, chopped fine
salt and pepper to taste
baking hen, baked

At low heat sauté bacon and onion together until fat of bacon is tender and onion is transparent. Do not brown. Add to rice, which has been mixed with chicken stock and liver and gizzard of hen. Cook in large double boiler 2 hours. When liquid has been absorbed by rice, lift from sides with fork. Repeat at least once during cooking. Serve with baked hen.

**Mrs. Howard Dasher (Mary McCulley)**
**Valdosta**

# DEVILED CHICKEN

4 tablespoons mayonnaise
3 tablespoons Durkee Sauce
½ cup butter

6 chicken breasts
1 8-ounce package Pepperidge
  Farm Herb Seasoned Stuffing

Bone and skin chicken. Mix mayonnaise, Durkee sauce and melted butter. Coat chicken with mixture. Crush Pepperidge Farm Stuffing. Roll chicken in stuffing. Place in casserole. Bake 1½ hours in 325 degree oven. Serves 6.

**Mrs. Lonnie Dunlap Ferguson (Georgia Boykin)**
**Thomasville**

# CHICKEN CURRY CRÊPES

| | |
|---|---|
| 12 prepared crêpes | ½ teaspoon curry powder |
| ¼ cup butter | 1 chicken bouillon cube |
| 1 cup celery, diced | 1½ cups milk |
| ½ cup onion, chopped | 2 cups cooked chicken, diced |
| 2 tablespoons flour | ½ cup pitted ripe olives, quartered |
| 1 teaspoon salt | Parmesan cheese |

Sauté celery and onion in melted butter until crisp-tender. Add flour and seasonings. Stir until well-blended. Gradually add milk; cook and stir until thickened. Fold in chicken and olives. Heat through. Put ⅓ cup filling in center of each crêpe. Fold two sides over filling and sprinkle with Parmesan cheese. Bake at 375 degrees for 10-15 minutes. Yield—12 crêpes.

## CRÊPES

| | |
|---|---|
| 1½ cups milk | 1½ cups all-purpose flour |
| 2 tablespoons vegetable oil | ⅛ teaspoon salt |
| 3 eggs | |

Put all ingredients into blender container in order listed. Cover and process at BLEND until smooth. Make crêpes according to instructions with your crêpe maker. Yield 18-20 crêpes.

**Mrs. Paul W. Reid (Kathleen Harper)**
**Madison**

# CHICKEN AND RICE

| | |
|---|---|
| 1 box Uncle Ben's Wild and Long Grain Rice | 1 can onion soup |
| | 1 can water |
| 6 tablespoons margarine | 6 chicken breasts (or other piece) |

Melt margarine in pyrex dish. Add rice. Arrange chicken on top. Add soup and water. Sprinkle seasoning from rice on top. Bake at 350 degrees for 1 hour covered with foil. Remove foil after 45 minutes if all liquid is not absorbed. Canned, drained mushrooms may be added when rice is added. Serves 4.

**Mrs. Ray Lowell Peacock, Jr. (Margaret Anne McGowan)**
**Augusta**

## CHICKEN LIVERS DIVINE

1 pound chicken livers
1½ cups brown rice
3 tablespoons white wine
½ pound or more fresh
    mushrooms
½ cup onions, chopped

1 10¾-ounce can mushroom soup
⅓ cup milk
⅓ cup parsley, chopped
½ cup almonds, slivered
3 tablespoons margarine

Cook rice. Brown chicken livers in butter; add mushrooms, soup, milk, wine, parsley and onions. Cook slowly for 20 minutes. Add rice and place in casserole with almonds on top. Cook in 350 degree oven for 30 minutes. This can also be made with chicken breasts. Serves 8.

**Mrs. Michael Justice Taylor (Mary Bothwell Burdell)**
**Augusta**

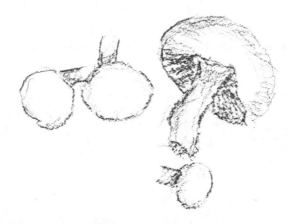

## CHICKEN LIVERS HUGO

1 tablespoon butter or
    margarine
1½ cloves garlic
½ pound chicken livers, halved
1 teaspoon salt
tiny pinch ground cloves

½ can consommé
½ pound mushrooms
¼ cup red wine
1½ teaspoons cornstarch
1 tablespoon water
freshly ground black pepper

Melt butter with garlic that has been put through press. Add livers and cook until no red juice runs from them. Add salt, consommé, cloves, mushrooms and wine. Cover and simmer for 10 minutes. Stir in cornstarch mixed with water. Cook 5 minutes, stirring constantly. Serves 3.

**Mrs. Henry M. Marks, Jr. (Virginia Clark)**
**Augusta**

# BASIC STUFFING FOR CHICKEN OR TURKEY

½ cup butter or margarine
1 cup chopped celery with
    leaves
½ cup chopped onion
2 cups chicken or turkey broth

6 to 8 cups cornbread and white
    bread crumbled
¼ cup chopped parsley
¼ teaspoon each basil, rosemary,
    and thyme

Melt butter in skillet; add celery and onion and cook until tender but not brown. Add broth; bring to a boil. Add crumbled bread, parsley, and herbs. Mix lightly. Add more broth or water if stuffing is too dry. Yield—approximately 3 quarts, enough for 12 to 16 pound turkey.

OYSTER STUFFING

Substitute liquid from 1 pint of oysters for part of the broth; add ½ teaspoon Tabasco. Coarsely chop oysters and add to stuffing mixture.
**Mrs. Henry D. Green (Fran Yates)**
**Brunswick**

# OYSTER STUFFING FOR TURKEY

12 cups bread cubes
⅓ cup bacon fat
¼ cup onions, chopped
1 cup celery, diced
2 tablespoons parsley, minced

1 teaspoon poultry seasoning
½ cup butter, melted
2 cups small oysters
1 teaspoon salt
¼ teaspoon pepper

Cut bread slices into half-inch cubes; brown in the fat heated in a frying pan. (Cook celery in a little butter till slightly softened), mix onion and celery into bread cubes. Cover and simmer 5 minutes. Add other ingredients, mixing lightly. Sufficient for a 10 pound turkey; make half the amount for a 5 pound duck or chicken.
*Note:* One of "Miss Maggie" Garmany's recipes.
**Mrs. Thomas M. Johnson (Kathryn Twiggs)**
**Savannah**

# TURKEY AND HAM BAKE
*(Serves 6)*

½ cup onion, chopped
2 tablespoons butter
3 tablespoons flour
½ teaspoon salt
¼ teaspoon pepper
1½ cups fine, soft bread
   crumbs
3 tablespoons melted butter
1 cup grated Swiss cheese

1 3-ounce can sliced mushrooms
   (undrained)
1 cup half & half cream
2 tablespoons dry sherry
2 cups cooked turkey, cubed
1 cup cooked ham, cubed
1 5-ounce can water chestnuts,
   drained

Cook onion in 2 tablespoons butter until tender. Add flour and cream. Stir until thick and bubbling. Add mushrooms and sherry. Add turkey, ham and water chestnuts. Pour into 1½-quart casserole. Sprinkle with cheese. Top with blended butter and bread crumb mixture. Bake in pan of boiling water in 400 degree oven until firm and lightly brown (30 minutes).

**Mrs. Forman Dismukes (Florence Barber)**
**Brunswick**


# MAMA'S TURKEY BOUDINE

4 cups turkey, chopped
2 cups mushroom soup
2 cups sharp cheese, grated
1 5-ounce can slivered almonds
salt and pepper to taste
1 5-ounce can whole
   mushrooms (drained)

½ cup pimento, chopped (drained)
¼ cup cooking sherry
½ cup turkey broth
1 cup egg noodles, cooked and
   drained

Mix all ingredients together and place in casserole. Top with additional grated cheese. Bake for 30 minutes, or until bubbly, at 350 degrees. May be prepared ahead of time and kept in refrigerator overnight. Serves 12.

**Mrs. James M. Treadwell, Jr. (Lynn Gibbs Walker)**
**Madison**

# GOURMET GAME HENS

6 Cornish game hens
1¼ cups cornflake crumbs
¾ cup English walnuts,
  chopped
¼ cup celery, finely chopped
2 teaspoons salt
2 tablespoons onion salt

4-5 grinds fresh black pepper
½ cup butter
½ cup bell pepper, thinly sliced
¼ cup fresh ginger root*, grated or
  sliced
1 cup soy sauce
1 cup pale, dry sherry

Defrost game hens, remove giblets, rinse with salted water, wipe dry. Mix cornflake crumbs, nuts, celery and seasonings. Melt butter in frying pan; toss cornflake mixture in melted butter, stirring till well coated. Use two to three tablespoons of the mixture to stuff each game hen, securing openings with toothpicks or small skewers. Arrange hens, backs down, close together in baking pan (about 9"x12"x2"). Scatter ginger and bell pepper over hens. Mix together sherry and soy sauce and pour over. Bake in 350 degree oven for 1¼ hours, basting occasionally. Reduce oven setting to 250 degrees, cover pan tightly with foil, and bake ½ to ¾ hour longer. Baste just before removing to serving dish. Serve hot, accompanied by white rice, with the sauce as gravy. (If desired, ginger root and bell pepper may be strained out of the sauce.) Serves 6.

*Fresh ginger root is available in Oriental specialty food shops, and in some supermarkets. It will keep unpeeled in freezer, for 2-3 months. Be sure to peel before grating or slicing.

**Mrs. Albert Sidney Britt, Jr. (Annie McIntosh)**
**Savannah**

# ORANGE CORNISH HENS

4 Cornish hens
½ cup butter or margarine
1 can frozen orange juice
  (undiluted)
¾ cup water

2 tablespoons honey or may
  substitute orange marmalade
2 tablespoons soy sauce
1 teaspoon salt
1 teaspoon rosemary, crushed

Cut hens in half; marinate in sauce (all but butter) for 3 or 4 hours or overnight. Brown hens in butter; sprinkled with flour. Remove hens and pour sauce in pan and stir to get crumbs loose. Put hens into pan and pour sauce over them. Cover and cook for 1 hour, ten minutes in a 350 degree oven until tender. Serves 6 to 8.

**Mrs. Herbert Chandler (Anne Paine)**
**Milledgeville**

## CORNISH HENS VERONIQUE

4 1-pound Cornish hens
salt
¼ cup melted butter
1 8-ounce can light seedless
    grapes
3 tablespoons sugar
¼ cup sauterne

2 tablespoons lemon juice
1 tablespoon cornstarch
¼ teaspoon salt
¼ teaspoon grated orange peel
¼ teaspoon grated lemon peel
fresh seedless grape clusters
    (optional)

Sprinkle cavity of hens with salt; truss hens, and place breast side up in a shallow roasting pan. Cover loosely with aluminum foil; bake at 375 degrees for 30 minutes. Remove foil. Bake at 375 degrees for an additional 15 minutes, basting frequently with butter. Drain grapes, reserving liquid. Set grapes aside. Heat sugar in a heavy saucepan over medium heat until melted and golden brown. Remove from heat, set aside. Bring reserved grape liquid to a boil in a small saucepan; gradually stir into caramelized sugar. Place over medium heat; cook stirring constantly until caramel dissolves. Combine sauterne, lemon juice, cornstarch, ¼ teaspoon salt, and citrus peel. Stir into syrup mixture. Cook, stirring constantly until mixture thickens and bubbles; stir in reserved grapes. Bake hens at 375 degrees an additional 15 minutes, basting frequently with syrup mixture. Garnish with fresh grape clusters. Serves 4.

**Mrs. John H. Cheatham, Jr. (Lelia Gillian Barnes)**
**Griffin**

## CORNISH HENS WITH WILD RICE
## AND ALMOND STUFFING

1 cup wild rice
3 tablespoons butter
6 slices bacon, halved
6 Cornish hens
½ cup chopped onion

½ cup toasted almonds, chopped
½ teaspoon salt
½ teaspoon marjoram
½ teaspoon crushed thyme leaves

Wash and cook wild rice by package directions. Drain. Sauté ½ cup chopped onion in 3 tablespoons butter. Mix with rice; add ½ cup chopped almonds. Add ½ teaspoon marjoram, ½ teaspoon thyme, and ½ teaspoon salt. Makes about 3½ cups.

Wash and prepare hens for roasting. Sprinkle cavities lightly with salt. Stuff hens with rice mixture and truss. Lay 2 half-slices bacon over each hen. Roast at 350 degrees, uncovered, for 1 to 1½ hours or until tender, basting occasionally with butter added to pan drippings. Serves 6.

**Mrs. Henry Turner Brice, Sr. (Sarah Mary Tillman)**
**Thomasville**

# RASPBERRY-GLAZED CORNISH HENS
## FOR 3 CORNISH HENS

MARINADE

GLAZE

⅓ cup vermouth
juice of one lemon
1 cup chopped onion
1 large clove garlic,
    peeled and crushed
1½ teaspoons thyme

2 tablespoons lemon juice
2 tablespoons vermouth
½ cup raspberry jelly
½ teaspoon grated lemon rind

Whirl marinade in blender until smooth. Remove package containing giblets from breast cavity of hen, tie legs together for better presentation, wipe dry, then pour 2 tablespoons of marinade inside birds. Place in roasting pan only large enough to contain the birds and pour remaining marinade on top. Turn birds frequently and marinate for 4 to 12 hours. Roast 2 hours in a preheated 325 degree oven. Blend ingredients for glaze together and baste birds liberally with glaze. Return to oven for another 15 minutes. Serve ½ bird to each person. May be served hot or cold. Serves 6.

**Mrs. Patrick Ross Bynum (Helen Lee Wright)**
**Americus**

# JIM'S DOVES

8 doves
¼ cup butter
1 3-ounce can sliced
    mushrooms and juice
½ onion, minced
1 tablespoon flour
several sprigs parsley and
    thyme, chopped

½ cup dry sherry
2 cups game bird stock (or
    Swanson's Chicken Broth)
½ cup sliced stuffed green olives
salt and pepper to taste

Brown birds on all sides in a skillet with the butter. Season lightly and remove to a casserole. In the same butter, brown the onion, herbs and drained mushrooms for five minutes. Add flour and stir until it is slightly brown and bubbly. Lower heat, add stock and mushroom juice, and stir until sauce is smooth. Add sherry and olives, simmer an additional minute or so and check seasoning. Pour sauce over doves in casserole, cover, and bake at 350 degrees until doves are tender, about 1½ hours. Serves 4.

**Mrs. James W. Knox (Katherine Richards)**
**Columbus**

## DOVES

8 doves
6 tablespoons butter
½ teaspoon coarsely ground
   black peppercorns

½ cup white wine
½ cup chopped onions
1 cup mushrooms
1½ cups bouillon or beef stock

Rinse and dry doves, split down the back. Pepper inside of doves. Sprinkle each lightly with flour and brown in butter in heavy skillet. Remove to baking dish and sprinkle drops of lemon juice over each breast. Turn breast down, add ¼ cup wine and roast uncovered for 1 hour or more until tender in 350 degree oven. Baste often with pan juices. While doves are roasting, sauté ¼ cup onions in same skillet used to brown doves. Scrape pan bottom and stir onions. If not enough browned bits of flour for gravy base, add more and brown in butter. Add ¼ cup wine and 1½ cups bouillon or stock. Add salt and pepper to taste and set aside. When doves are tender, remove from oven and cover with gravy. Add 1 cup sautéed mushrooms and simmer all gently a few minutes. Keep hot for an hour or more before serving.

**Mrs. Jesse W. Walters (Lucy Yancey)**
**Albany**

## DOVES

12 doves
¼ cup butter
2 tablespoons olive oil
juice of 1 lemon
2 tablespoons Worcestershire
   sauce

seasoned tenderizer
⅓ cup orange juice
2 tablespoons plum jam
3 lemon slices, quartered
parsley flakes
paprika

Sprinkle birds with tenderizer then brown in butter and oil, using heavy large frying pan. While birds are browning, cover with lemon juice and Worcestershire. With breast side up, place quarter of lemon slice on each bird, sprinkle with paprika and parsley flakes. Add orange juice and plum jam to pan, with just enough water to steam. Cover pan and steam on low heat two or three hours, adding water if needed to keep steaming.

**Mrs. Henry Sholars Brown, Jr. (Patti W. Smith)**
**Rome**

# SLOW AND EASY DOVES

dove—split down back
bacon strips—½ per bird
butter—1 pat per bird

Worcestershire sauce—1 teaspoon
    per bird
salt and pepper

Place 1 pat butter, 1 tablespoon Worcestershire sauce, salt and pepper in back cavity of each bird. Wrap half strip of bacon around breast and hold together at back with toothpick. Place birds breast down in roasting pan, place tin foil tightly over top. Roast at 250 degrees for 3½-4 hours. Just before serving, run birds under broiler, breast up to crisp bacon. Easy cooking for a large crowd!

**Mrs. Roland Wetherbee (Diane Waller)**
**Albany**

# DUCK SUPREME

Stuff duck with orange, apple, onions and celery pieces. Brown 5 tablespoons flour in 1 cup butter. Add 1 tablespoon Worcestershire sauce, 2 tablespoons lemon juice, salt and pepper to taste. Cook covered at 350 degrees for one hour, reduce heat and cook 3 more hours at 250 degrees or until done. Refrigerate overnight. In morning—remove stuffing from duck, discard all congealed fat, and strain gravy slowly while tearing meat from duck in bite size pieces.

SAUCE FOR FOUR DUCKS

5 cups cream sauce
3 diced apples
one sliced onion

½ pound fresh mushrooms, sliced
⅓ package ginger, grated
salt, pepper, sherry to taste

I usually cook at least 15 ducks when making this, which makes it necessary to make more sauce. Fifteen ducks in this sauce served over parsleyed rice will make four quarts and serve 24 people amply. This can be made ahead, frozen and sherry added at least minute when reheating.

**Mrs. Hoyt Whelchel, Jr. (Alice Erwin)**
**Moultrie**

# SOUTHAMPTON COUNTY, VIRGINIA, QUAIL

2 pounds fresh sausage meat
6 to 8 quail

flour, salt, pepper, butter
¼ cup water

Stuff cavities of birds with sausage. Save enough sausage for 2 patties. Use a paper bag with mixture of flour, salt and pepper. Place stuffed birds in bag and shake well. Place birds breast side down in casserole. Place extra sausage patties in casserole with quail. Dot backs of birds with butter, add ¼ cup water. Place top on casserole. Place in preheated oven at 450 degrees for 15 minutes. Turn oven to 200 degrees for 2 hours. Serve birds on platter, breast side up. Serves 4.

**Mrs. William W. Chisholm (Armin Cay)**
**Savannah**

# HAUNCH OF VENISON

haunch of venison
1½ gallons buttermilk
1 cup margarine or butter

1½ cups Cointreau
½ cup orange juice
1 lemon

Soak venison in buttermilk to cover overnight. Drain and pat dry when ready to put in oven. Preheat oven to 350 degrees. Insert meat thermometer. Put 1 cup margarine (or butter) on top of venison. (Use more margarine or butter if it is a very large piece of venison.) Put in oven and allow margarine to melt. Make sauce of Cointreau, orange juice and juice of 1 lemon. Pour over venison. Baste frequently until meat thermometer registers rare.

**Mrs. B. H. Hardaway, III (Sarah McDuffie)**
**Columbus**

# Vegetables

Mary F. Passalaigue

## SQUASH AND CORN CASSEROLE

2 cups cooked summer squash
2 cups cooked corn or
  uncooked
¼ cup butter

2 eggs
1 cup half & half cream (or milk)
salt to taste and pepper

Mix all ingredients. Bake in casserole in 350 degree oven for 45 minutes. Serves 8.

**Mrs. Shelby Myrick (Mary Robinson)**
**Savannah**

## SQUASH CASSEROLE

6 cups sliced yellow squash
½ cup grated Cheddar cheese
½ cup mayonnaise
¼ cup butter
1 egg
2 tablespoons butter

3 tablespoons sugar
salt and pepper to taste
½ cup Pepperidge Farm Herb
  Seasoned Stuffing
½ cup pecans, chopped

Cook squash in salted water until tender. Drain well and mix with mayonnaise, butter, egg, and sugar. Salt and pepper to taste. Pour in lightly greased two-quart casserole. Crush stuffing and brown in butter. Add pecans and cover top of casserole. Bake at 400° for 20 minutes. Serves 8.

**Mrs. John F. Shackleford (Lucy Eason)**
**Albany**

## EMILY NEEL'S SQUASH CASSEROLE

2 pounds squash
½ cup butter
½ package Pepperidge Farm
  Herb Stuffing
1 can cream of chicken soup

1 onion, chopped fine
1 small carton sour cream
1 can water chestnuts, sliced thin
salt and pepper to taste

Steam squash not too done (you do not want it soft), mix ½ cup of butter with ½ package Pepperidge Farm Stuffing—put ½ stuffing in buttered casserole. Mix all other ingredients and add to casserole. Sprinkle other half of stuffing on top. Bake at 350 degrees in oven for 30 minutes. Serves 8.

**Mrs. Thomas Lyle Williams, Jr. (Marguerite Neel)**
**Thomasville**

## YELLOW SQUASH WITH WHITE WINE

2 pounds yellow squash, sliced
1 teaspoon salt
1¼ cups Cheddar cheese, cubed
⅓ cup Parmesan cheese
salt and black pepper to taste

1 cup onion, chopped
¼ cup butter
1 cup sour cream
¼ cup dry white wine

Boil the squash and onion with the teaspoon of salt until barely tender. Drain and add the sour cream, Parmesan cheese, Cheddar cheese, wine and butter. Salt and pepper with freshly ground black pepper to taste. Butter an 11-inch gratin dish and pour the squash into it. Top with buttered crumbs. Bake at 350 degrees until bubbling hot and light brown, about twenty to thirty minutes. Serves six.

**Mrs. Robert R. Segrest (Laura Ann Phinizy)**
**Athens**

## SHREDDED ZUCCHINI

fresh zucchini
lemon juice to taste

salt to taste

Wash and shred zucchini on a coarse grater. Put in a large skillet on high heat. Cover for 1-2 minutes. Stir. Recover. Stir again after 1 to 2 minutes. Repeat until zucchini is just heated through and still crisp and green. Stir in salt and lemon juice to taste just before serving. Butter may be added but is not necessary.

**Mrs. Alvin M. Ratliff (Frances Lott)**
**Blackshear**

## FRESH CORN, TOMATO, ZUCCHINI POT

4 ears fresh corn
5 medium fresh tomatoes,
    unpeeled
6 or 7 small zucchini
2 medium onions

2 cloves garlic, minced
salt and pepper to taste
lemon pepper to taste
½ cup butter

Using a very sharp knife, cut the corn from cob into a large earthenware casserole. Wash the tomatoes and zucchini and pat dry. Slice the tomatoes into ¼-inch slices. Slice zucchini lengthwise into quarters. Add the onions which have been sliced into thin rings, tomatoes and zucchini to corn in casserole. Add the garlic, salt, pepper and lemon pepper and mix the vegetables carefully. Dot with butter. Cover and bake in preheated oven for 45 minutes at 325 degrees. Serves 6.

**Mrs. Julius Marshall Vann (Mary Porter Phinizy)**
**Augusta**

# ZUCCHINI FRITTATA

5 medium zucchini, sliced
2 tablespoons minced onion
1 small clove garlic, chopped
3 tablespoons olive oil

3 tablespoons butter
5 slightly beaten eggs
½ cup grated Parmesan cheese

Cook first 5 ingredients in heavy saucepan until almost done. Transfer to oiled casserole and add eggs and cheese. Bake in 300 degree oven for about 30 minutes until slightly brown. Garnish with buttered crumbs. Serves 6.

**Mrs. James Benjamin Kay, Jr. (Lois Anderson Sullivan)**
**Augusta**

# HOT STUFFED TOMATOES

6 firm medium-size tomatoes,
   in season
2 ripe tomatoes, peeled and cut
6 to 8 strips bacon

½ to 1 clove garlic, minced
1 cup finely chopped celery
2 raw eggs
salt and pepper to taste

Fry bacon and drain. Set pan aside. Remove inside of the 6 tomatoes and add to the 2 ripe tomatoes, along with garlic, celery, salt and pepper. Simmer on top of stove in pan in which bacon was cooked until all juice has cooked out. Stirring rapidly, add raw eggs, cooking about a minute, or less. Mixture should be rather stiff. Add crumbled bacon, saving a small amount to "top" stuffed tomatoes. Stuff the 6 tomato shells with the mixture and place in pan with ½ inch water. Bake in 350 degree oven for 45 minutes. These are both delicious and colorful. Serves 6.

**Mrs. Walter E. Lee, Jr. (Betty Monroe)**
**Waycross**

# ASPARAGUS SOUFFLÉ

4 eggs, beaten
1 cup mayonnaise
1 teaspoon salt
1 15½-ounce can chopped
   asparagus, drained

1 10½-ounce can mushroom soup,
   undiluted
1 cup sharp Cheddar cheese,
   grated

Blend eggs in a large mixing bowl, add other ingredients, mixing well. Pour into a buttered casserole and set in a pan of water. Cook in a 350 degree oven for one hour or until a knife inserted in the center comes out clean. Serves six.

**Mrs. Bolling Dubose (Mary Neilson Atkinson)**
**Athens**

# ASPARAGUS CASSEROLE

2 cups sweet milk
1 cup butter or margarine
2 tablespoons flour (sifted)
1 teaspoon salt
½ pound strong New York
  cheese (grated)
red pepper

2 large cans of tender asparagus
  tips
½ cup slivered blanched almonds
½ cup pimentoes
cup of cracker meal
paprika

Melt ½ cup of butter in saucepan over low heat. Add milk and 2 tablespoons of flour, stirring in slowly to prevent lumping. When sauce is smooth, slowly pour in grated cheese, stirring mixture as cheese is added. Add salt and dash of red pepper. Cook over low heat for ten minutes. Add juice from one can of asparagus to mixture and cook another five minutes. Grease casserole dish with butter. Pour a thin layer of sauce into dish; add a layer of asparagus from can without juice. Add almonds and pimentoes. Add second layer of sauce. Pour juice from second can of asparagus and add second layer of asparagus (not the juice). Add remaining sauce to cover vegetables. Sprinkle full layer of cracker meal over mixture. Top with butter and paprika. Bake 25 to 30 minutes in 350 degree oven. Serves 8.

**Mrs. W. Graham Ponder (Adelaide Wallace)**
**Madison**

# ASPARAGUS MOUSSE

½ pint whipping cream
2 tablespoons butter
4 egg yolks
juice of 1 lemon
1 can asparagus and liquid
1 cup almonds (slivered)

2 tablespoons flour
2 tablespoons gelatin
1 tablespoon onion juice
season to taste with salt and
  paprika

Melt butter in double boiler. Stir in flour. Mix thoroughly. Add asparagus juice, stirring constantly until thick. Pour over eggs which have been beaten lightly. Stir. Put back in double boiler and cook until eggs are done. Add dissolved gelatin, seasonings, onion juice and lemon juice. Cut up asparagus with scissors. When mixture is cool, fold in asparagus, nuts, and whipped cream. Pour into mold. Serve topped with mayonnaise. Serves 8.

**Mrs. R. G. Fleetwood (Mary Brandon)**
**Thomasville**

# SPINACH SUPREME

2 10-ounce packages frozen
  chopped spinach
3 slices bacon, cooked and
  crumbled
1 6-ounce can sliced
  mushrooms, drained

¼ teaspoon marjoram
1 8-ounce carton sour cream
1 cup grated sharp cheese

Cook spinach by package directions. Combine all ingredients except cheese. Put into greased 1½ quart casserole. Bake at 325 degrees for 20-25 minutes. Sprinkle with cheese and return to oven for 5 minutes. Serves 8.

**Mrs. John D. Powell (Laura Wise Powell)**
**Americus**

# SPINACH CASSEROLE

4 1-pound 15-ounce cans
  spinach
12 ounces sharp yellow cheese,
  grated

3 1-pound cans tomatoes
cracker crumbs

Drain the spinach but not the tomatoes. In a buttered casserole put a layer of spinach, a layer of tomatoes, a layer of cheese and a layer of cracker crumbs. Dot with butter and repeat ending with a layer of buttered crumbs. Add the tomato juice. Bake at 325 degrees for 25 minutes or until browned. Serves 10.

**Mrs. Edward Gordon Dudley (Caro Lamar DuBignon)**
**Athens**

# SPINACH AND ARTICHOKE CASSEROLE

½ cup butter
1 small can water chestnuts
½ cup chopped onion
2 10-ounce packages frozen
  chopped spinach

1 14-ounce can artichokes
8 ounces sour cream
½ cup Parmesan cheese

Sauté onions in the butter. Drain and slice the water chestnuts. Combine all ingredients and turn into a buttered casserole. Bake at 350 degrees for twenty minutes or more.

**Mrs. Thomas Hamilton Milner (Agnes Rosena White)**
**Athens**

# BAKED SPINACH

2 10 ounce packages spinach
  (frozen or fresh)
½ cup grated sharp cheese
2 tablespoons melted butter
½ teaspoon salt
½ teaspoon paprika
3 eggs hard-boiled and chopped
  finely

2 cups milk
¼ teaspoon pepper
⅛ teaspoon nutmeg
½ cup cornflakes (or buttered
  bread crumbs)
2 tablespoons minced onions
1 tablespoon flour

Cook spinach and drain. Sauté onions in butter, stir in flour, add milk slowly, stirring until mixture thickens. Next fold in spinach and eggs. Add the four remaining seasonings. Put in greased casseroles or individual ramekins. Combine bread crumbs melted butter and cheese and sprinkle over the top. Bake in a 375 degree oven for about 20 minutes. Serves 6.

**Mrs. Robert O. Arnold (Florence Turner)**
**Covington**

# POTATOES IN THE STYLE OF THE FRENCH ALPS

6 medium red potatoes (about
  2¼ pounds), pared, thinly
  sliced
2 teaspoons salt
½ teaspoon ground white
  pepper

½ teaspoon ground nutmeg
2 cups Swiss Gruyère cheese,
  shredded
2 tablespoons butter or margarine
¾ cup beef broth, boiling

Place potatoes in 4 layers in buttered two quart shallow baking pan, sprinkling each layer with ¼ of the salt, pepper, nutmeg, and cheese. Dot with butter. Pour boiling broth over potatoes. Bake at 350-375 degrees until potatoes are tender, top is brown, and broth is absorbed, about 1 hour.

**Mrs. Edward Wohlwender, Jr. (Mary Cooper)**
**Americus**

# GERMAN POTATOES

6 strips bacon
2 onions, chopped
2 stalks celery, chopped
1 green pepper, chopped
salt and pepper to taste
boiled new potatoes, enough
  for 6

2 tablespoons flour
½ cup sugar
½ cup vinegar
¾ cup water
dill weed, 2 tablespoons fresh or 1
  tablespoon dried

(Note: use small, whole, unpeeled new potatoes if possible. If not available, peel and cube the large potatoes.)

Slice bacon into ½ inch pieces, fry until brown, drain and reserve. In bacon grease, fry onions until golden, add celery and green pepper and cook gently until tender-crisp. Stir in flour, then sugar, salt and pepper. Slowly stir in vinegar and water, continue stirring until thickened. Add dill weed and pour this sauce on the hot, boiled potatoes. Mix gently and sprinkle reserved bacon on top.

**Mrs. John Angell (Ashby Lippitt)**
**Savannah**

# SWEET POTATO BALLS

2½ cups mashed sweet
  potatoes
2 tablespoons melted butter
¼ cup miniature
  marshmallows

1 tablespoon butter
⅓ cup honey
1 cup chopped pecans
¾ teaspoon salt
dash black pepper

Combine mashed sweet potatoes, salt, pepper, and 2 tablespoons melted butter. Stir in marshmallows. Chill mixture in refrigerator for easier handling. Shape into balls using ¼ cup mashed potato mixture for each ball. Heat one tablespoon butter and the ⅓ cup of honey is small heavy skillet. When syrup is hot add the potato balls one at the time. Carefully—with two forks—roll each ball in syrup for quick glaze. Lift out of syrup and roll in chopped nuts. Place on greased baking pan or foil-lined baking pan. *Be sure* they do *not* touch. Bake in 350° oven for 15 or 20 minutes. Makes 10 balls.

**Mrs. Joe Britt Ehresman (Kay Weeks)**
**Brunswick**

# SCALLOPED POTATOES
## (gratin Dauphinois)

2 cups plus 2 tablespoons milk
1 large egg
salt and white pepper
1 clove garlic, peeled

5 tablespoons melted butter, plus
12 small nuts of butter
2 pounds boiling potatoes

In a bowl whisk together milk, egg, and salt and pepper to taste. Lightly rub a flat gratin dish with garlic. Pour melted butter into dish and spread around with your fingers. Peel and finely slice potatoes and dry in a towel. Line bottom of gratin dish with a layer of potatoes and alternate with egg-milk mixture. Dot surface with nuts of butter and bake for 45 minutes in a preheated 375 degree oven or until it is lightly brown on top. Serves 6.

**Mrs. Thomas A. McGoldrick (Dahlis Smith)**
**Savannah**

# PARMESAN SCALLOPED TOMATOES

2 16-ounce cans peeled
  tomatoes
1 teaspoon salt
1 medium onion, chopped

10 tablespoons seasoned bread
  crumbs
1½ cups sharp cheese, grated
Parmesan cheese

Mix tomatoes, salt and onion. Place ½ mixture in 1½ quart baking dish, cover with ½ bread crumbs and ½ sharp cheese. Add remaining tomato mixture, remaining bread crumbs and sharp cheese. Sprinkle all over generously with Parmesan cheese. Bake 30 minutes in 350 degree oven. Serves 4 to 6.

**Mrs. W. Claggett Gilbert, Jr. (Barbara Guild)**
**Savannah**

# SWEET POTATO CASSEROLE

2 eggs
1 cup sugar (granulated or
  brown)
2 cups grated raw sweet
  potatoes
1 cup evaporated milk
1 tablespoon vanilla

1 teaspoon lemon juice
¼ cup melted butter
½ teaspoon grated lemon rind
½ teaspoon salt
½ teaspoon nutmeg
1 teaspoon ginger (optional)

Beat eggs with sugar until light. Add melted butter, lemon juice, lemon rind, evaporated milk, salt, nutmeg, ginger, and vanilla, adding sweet potatoes last. Mix well and put into casserole dish. Bake at 350 degrees for 45 minutes. Half way through the baking process, stir mixture once.

**Mrs. Archibald Little Griffin (Alma Lee Whitfield)**
**Valdosta**

# YAM SOUFFLÉ

2 yams, approximately 1 pound
  each
1 stick butter
2 eggs
1 tablespoon cinnamon
1 teaspoon nutmeg

¼ teaspoon vanilla extract
1 tablespoon brown sugar
½ cup raisins
3 ounces chopped pecan meats
marshmallows sufficient to cover
  top of soufflé

Bake yams wrapped in foil for two hours at 300 degrees. Cream yams with potato masher and large spoon. Fold in eggs, slightly beaten; add butter, melted. Add nutmeg, cinnamon, raisins, vanilla, sugar, nut meats (save 1 ounce to sprinkle on top of soufflé). Place all in pie pan or baking dish. Put in 250 degree oven for 15 minutes, take out and dot top with marshmallows. Return to oven on "broil" heat, and quickly brown marshmallows. Serves 6.

**Mrs. Cyril Breitenbach (Mary Hatcher)**
**Atlanta**

# SCALLOPED CORN

4 ears fresh corn
¼ cup chopped onion
¼ cup chopped green pepper
2 tablespoons butter
2 tablespoons flour
1 teaspoon salt
½ teaspoon paprika

¼ teaspoon dry mustard
dash of pepper
¾ cup milk
1 egg, slightly beaten
⅓ cup cracker crumbs
1 tablespoon of butter or
  margarine

Shuck the corn and scrape off enough of the kernels to measure 2 cups. Cook and stir onion and green pepper in 2 tablespoons butter until onion is tender. Remove from heat. Stir in flour and seasonings. Cook over low heat, stirring until mixture is bubbly. Remove from heat. Gradually stir in milk. Heat to boiling, stirring constantly. Stir in corn and egg. Pour mixture into an ungreased, flat casserole (7x9). Combine crumbs and remaining butter; sprinkle over corn mixture. Bake uncovered in preheated oven 350 degrees for 30 to 35 minutes. Serves 6.

**Mrs. Olin T. McIntosh (Violet Nash)**
**Hilton Head Island, South Carolina**

# BAKED HALVES OF TOMATOES

¼ cup margarine
4 whole tomatoes (cut in halves
    or quarters)
1 teaspoon fresh parsley
    (chopped fine)
1 teaspoon sweet basil
1 teaspoon chopped chives

1 teaspoon curry powder
few drops Worcestershire sauce
1 teaspoon celery flakes
salt and pepper on tomatoes
(to taste)
bread crumbs

Grease 1½ quart Pyrex baking dish. Line with tomato halves or quarters. Salt and pepper. Sprinkle parsley, chives, basil, curry powder, and celery flakes over tomatoes—drizzle Worcestershire sauce over all. Melt oleo. Mix with bread crumbs. Spread over tomatoes. Bake at 400° 30 minutes. Watch, and don't let them burn. Serves 4 to 5.

**Mrs. Mary Maddox (Mary Oates)**
**Brunswick**

# MARINATED VEGETABLES

1 can small peas, drained
1 can French-cut beans,
    drained
1 sliced onion
1 cup sliced celery
1 can white whole corn

1 green pepper, sliced
¾ cup Wesson oil
¾ cup vinegar
6 tablespoons sugar
salt, pepper and garlic salt
    to taste

Combine all ingredients. Refrigerate 24 hours. Drain. Serve cold.

**Mrs. William R. Howard (Louise Alford)**
**Milledgeville**

# STEAMED LEEKS

15 tender leeks
salt and pepper

1 tablespoon butter

Wash and trim leeks, taking particular care to remove all grit from base of green leaves. Steam until tender to touch of fork (approximately 20 minutes). Pour off all water, dot with butter, and sprinkle salt and pepper over leeks. Toss until well coated with butter. Serves 3.

**Mrs. Robert D. Newcomb (Mimi Bland Pace)**
**Albany**

# BUFFET BROCCOLI RING

2 tablespoons butter or
  margarine
2 tablespoons flour
¼ cup milk
¼ cup sherry wine
1 bouillon cube
2 cups finely chopped, cooked
  broccoli

1 tablespoon minced onion
1 teaspoon lemon juice
3 eggs, separated
½ teaspoon salt
pepper to taste

Melt butter, stir in flour; slowly add milk, wine, then bouillon cube; cook, stirring constantly, until mixture boils and thickens and bouillon cube is completely dissolved. Remove from heat. Add broccoli, onion, lemon juice, slightly beaten egg yolks, salt and pepper; fold in stiffly beaten egg whites. Pour into a well greased one quart ring mold. Set mold in shallow pan of hot water. Bake at 375° for 45-50 minutes, or until firm. Remove from oven and let stand 5-10 minutes before unmolding. Unmold on a hot platter and top with rich cheese sauce:

SAUCE

2 tablespoons butter
2 tablespoons flour
1 cup milk

salt and red pepper to taste
1 cup sharp Cheddar cheese
1 teaspoon Worcestershire sauce

Cook as any cream sauce. Garnish with raw, or slightly cooked, broccoli flowerets if desired. Serves 8 to 10.

**Mrs. Felton Davis (Jeanne Wilson Redwine)**
**Valdosta**

# BROCCOLI CASSEROLE

2 packages chopped broccoli
1 can cream of chicken soup
½ cup mayonnaise
1 cup fine bread crumbs

½ teaspoon curry powder
¼ cup slivered almonds or chopped
  water chestnuts

Cook broccoli in small amount salted water for seven minutes. Make sauce of soup (undiluted), mayonnaise and curry. Add almonds or chestnuts. Mix all together. Place in covered, greased, casserole and cook 15 minutes in 350° oven. Remove covering. Sprinkle bread crumbs over soufflé. Cook uncovered for 15 more minutes.

**Mrs. Edward King (Pauline King)**
**Brunswick**

# PARTY BROCCOLI

2 tablespoons butter
1½ cups sour cream
1 teaspoon white vinegar
½ teaspoon paprika
dash cayenne pepper
½ cup cashew nuts

2 tablespoons minced onion
2 tablespoons sugar
½ teaspoon poppy seed
¼ teaspoon salt
3 packages frozen broccoli spears

Cook broccoli until just tender and drain. Melt butter in small saucepan; sauté onions. Remove from heat and stir in sour cream, sugar, vinegar, poppy seed, paprika, salt and cayenne pepper. Arrange broccoli on heated platter. Add cashew nuts to sour cream sauce just before serving and pour over broccoli spears. Serves 10.

**Mrs. Ben J. Tarbutton (Rosa McMaster)**
**Augusta**

# BROCCOLI-PEANUT CASSEROLE

2 10-ounce packages frozen
chopped broccoli
1 can cream of mushroom soup
1 cup mayonnaise
½ cup chopped roasted peanuts
4 strips bacon, cooked and
crumbled

2 well-beaten eggs
1 chopped onion
¼ cup butter
1 cup bread crumbs
1 cup sharp cheese, grated

Cook broccoli in salted water, according to directions on package. Drain well. Add mushroom soup, mayonnaise, chopped peanuts, and crumbled bacon, mixing well. Add eggs and onion. Mix well and pour into well-greased 1½ or 2 quart casserole. Sprinkle with grated cheese. Melt butter and pour over bread crumbs. Sprinkle over top of casserole and bake for 30 minutes in 350 degree oven. Serves 8 to 10.

**Mrs. Jack Williams, Jr. (Margaret Rogers)**
**Waycross**

# MIDDLEBURG PLANTATION CORN PUDDING

1 pint scraped corn
4 well-beaten eggs
salt and pepper to taste

2 cups cream
1 tablespoon butter

Mix all ingredients together and put in buttered baking dish. Place dish in pan of hot water and bake 30 to 40 minutes in a moderate 350 degree oven. Serves 6.

**Mrs. Leon Belk (Marsha Blackmar)**
**Columbus**

# ONION SOUFFLÉ

| | |
|---|---|
| 3 tablespoons butter | 3 tablespoons flour |
| 1½ cups milk | 4 eggs, separated |
| ¾ teaspoon salt | 6 medium onions |
| ¼ teaspoon white pepper | |

Peel and quarter onions. Cook in salted water until tender. Drain, chop fine, and drain again. Melt butter, stir in flour slowly to blend. Slowly add milk and cook over low heat until thick cream sauce consistency. Add salt and pepper. Cool slightly and add slightly beaten egg yolks. Stir in onion. Beat egg whites very stiff and fold into onion mixture. Turn into a buttered casserole and bake at 350 degrees for twenty-five to thirty minutes. Serves six to eight.

Boiled onions have a different flavor from sautéed ones. This is a different method of preparing if the sautéed flavor is preferred.

Mince onions fine. Melt butter and add onions. Cook over low heat covered, shaking or stirring occasionally until the onions are golden and wilted. Sprinkle over the flour and stir in. Slowly stir in the milk. Remove from heat and put mixture in blender and purée. Return to pan and over low heat cook until the cream sauce has thickened. Add salt and white pepper, or one teaspoon chicken bouillon granules and melt in. Taste to check for flavor. Add the egg yolks and blend in. Add the stiffly beaten whites and bake as above.

This is delicious—and different—with roast beef.

**Mrs. John Henry Terrell (Elinor Marie Tillman)**
**Athens**

# MUSHROOM SOUFFLÉ

| | |
|---|---|
| ½ pound fresh mushrooms | 4 tablespoons butter |
| ¾ cup water | 3 tablespoons flour |
| 1 teaspoon salt | 3 eggs, separated |
| 1 teaspoon pepper (or less) | |

Chop mushrooms (stems and all) fine; sauté in 2 tablespoons butter until brown. Cover with water and simmer for 10 minutes. Drain and add mushroom liquid to butter and flour. Cook until creamy in top of double boiler. Add mushrooms and salt and pepper. Remove from stove and stir in slightly beaten yolks of eggs. Let it cool. Beat whites of eggs until stiff and fold them into the mushroom mixture. Turn into well-greased baking dish, glass preferred. Set in pan of water and bake in pre-heated 350 degree oven for 45 minutes. Serves 6.

**Mrs. Russell Jones Brooke (Julia Anderson McClatchey)**
**Atlanta**

# AMBER GLAZED CARROTS

12 medium carrots, peeled and
    cut across and at angle into
    2-inch shapes
1½ cups beef stock, fresh or
    canned
4 tablespoons butter

2 tablespoons sugar
½ teaspoon salt
freshly ground pepper
2 tablespoons chopped parsley
    (fresh preferred)

In a heavy 8 to 10 inch skillet, bring the carrots, stock, butter, sugar, salt and a few grindings of pepper to boil. Cover and simmer over low heat, roll carrots occasionally. Check liquid and adjust heat if liquid is cooking away too fast. Carrots should be cooked only until tender, not soft. When tender, the braising liquid should be a brown, syrupy glaze. If it is not reduced enough, then remove carrots and boil down over high heat. Replace carrots and roll them around to coat with glaze. Serve with chopped parsley. Serves 4 to 6.

**Mrs. Frank Jarrell (Marion Elizabeth Ellis)**
**Atlanta**

# HOT CARROTS WITH MINT SAUCE

1½ cups carrots, diced
2 tablespoons butter
1 teaspoon cornstarch
1 tablespoon sugar

1 tablespoon mint leaves, shredded
⅓ cup water
few drops lemon juice
grated rind ¼ lemon

Cook carrots in small quantity slightly salted water. When tender, put carrots to one side of pan. Put in butter and melt over low fire. Blend cornstarch with sugar, add water, mint leaves, lemon juice and rind. Add this to the butter and cook, mixing in the carrots as the sauce cooks. Nice with lamb.

**Mrs. Benjamin T. Youmans (Sue Potts)**
**Rome**

# CARROTS PHILADELPHIA

8 carrots (diced)
6 ounces Philadelphia cream
    cheese
4 ounces green chili peppers
    (chopped)

¼ cup heavy cream
¼ cup parsley

Steam carrots for 7 minutes. Immediately add cream cheese, green chili peppers, cream, and place in casserole. Garnish with parsley. Bake at 325 degrees for 10 minutes before serving. Serves 6 to 8 .

**Mrs. Martha M. Dykes (Martha Marshall)**
**Americus**

# MUSHROOM STROGANOFF

2 medium onions, chopped
3 tablespoons minced parsley
1 cup butter
1 beef bouillon cube
3 shakes each of garlic powder,
   salt, and pepper

1½ pounds fresh mushrooms
1½ pints sour cream
¾ cup red wine
¼ cup minced celery

In a small saucepan melt bouillon cube in wine and set aside. Melt butter in a large pot such as a dutch oven. Add parsley, celery, and three shakes of garlic powder, salt, and pepper. Add mushrooms. As soon as they show color, add onion. Stir often until onion is transparent. Add wine. Remove from heat and fold in sour cream until thick. If too thick, stir in more sour cream and heat, not boil, until desired consistency, not soupy. Serve mushrooms sliced or quartered over rice, toast or noodles. For a nice party dish, leave mushrooms whole, or if very large, halved and serve from a chafing dish with toothpicks. Serves 15.

**Mrs. George Wilmer Williams (Minnie Keller Roberts)**
**Savannah**

# SCALLOPED MUSHROOMS

6 cups fresh mushrooms
1 cup packaged prepared
   stuffing
¾ cup heavy cream

½ cup chicken stock
2 tablespoons butter
2 tablespoons sherry

Slice mushroom stems and leave caps whole. Place layer of uncooked mushrooms in a buttered shallow casserole; scatter half of the stuffing over them. Repeat with another layer of mushrooms and top with remainder of stuffing. Place a few mushroom caps fill side up, on top with a little butter inside. Pour cream and stock over the top, dot with butter, cover with foil and bake. Before serving, remove foil. Turn mushrooms on top right side up and cook a few minutes longer. Pour sherry over at the very last. Bake at 350 degrees for 40 minutes. Serves 8.

This is good with chicken, beef and turkey.

**Mrs. John Hayes Sherman (Katherine Card)**
**Augusta**

# EGGPLANT CASSEROLE

1 eggplant
1 or 2 tomatoes
1 or 2 onions
1 bell pepper

salt and pepper
2 tablespoons or more of melted
  butter

Peel and cut up eggplant, tomatoes and onions in bite size pieces. Take seeds out of pepper and cut it up. Put in layers in a greased casserole, putting salt and pepper on each layer. Pour over all at least 2 tablespoons of butter. Cover tightly and bake for 40 minutes in a 350 degree oven. (Miss Isabelle Harrison)

**Mrs. Hugh H. Gordon (Mary Elliott Barrow)**
**Bluffton, South Carolina**

# BAKED EGGPLANT & GROUND BEEF CASSEROLE

1 large eggplant or 2 medium
  (peeled and cubed)
1 pound hamburger
1 large onion, chopped
½ green pepper, chopped
½ teaspoon salt
½ teaspoon paprika

¼ teaspoon pepper
1½ cups tomatoes (fresh)
1½ cups buttered bread crumbs or
  Pepperidge Farm Bread Crumbs
1 teaspoon basil
1 teaspoon oregano

Cook eggplant in boiling water or better, steam it. Brown meat, onions and green pepper in skillet. Drain eggplant; combine all ingredients except bread crumbs in a buttered casserole. Top with buttered crumbs. Bake at 350 degrees for 30 minutes. Serves 6.

Easy—freezes well.

**Mrs. Guion Haskell (Judith Gracey)**
**Augusta**

## BAKED STUFFED EGGPLANT WITH HAM

1 medium eggplant
1 small onion, chopped
2 cups diced cooked ham
½ cup Cheddar cheese,
    shredded

2 tablespoons margarine or butter
1 egg, well beaten
¼ cup bread crumbs

Cook eggplant (whole and unpeeled) in enough boiling water to cover. Cook for 10 minutes. Drain and cool slightly. Cut in half lengthwise. Scoop out pulp leaving a one-inch shell. Cut pulp into small pieces. Cook in butter or margarine with onion until heated through. Combine this mixture with the ham and egg. Pack lightly into eggplant shells and top with bread crumbs and cheese. Bake at 375 degrees for ½ hour. Serves 4.

**Mrs. Eugene Mitchell Long (Jane Bush)**
**Augusta**

## STUFFED EGGPLANT WITH SHRIMP

1 medium eggplant
½ pound shrimp, chopped
¼ cup celery, chopped
½ cup parsley, chopped
1 clove garlic, minced
3 green onions, finely
    chopped

1 tablespoon butter or margarine
3 slices bread, crumbed in
    processor or blender
1 egg, beaten
salt
pepper
Parmesan cheese, grated

Cut eggplant in half lengthwise and scoop out inside part. Boil it in water until tender, drain and mash. Fry onions, celery and garlic in butter; add shrimp and cook until pink. Add eggplant, parsley and crumbs and season to taste with salt and pepper. Put in shells and sprinkle with cheese. Bake 20 to 25 minutes at 400 degrees.

**Mrs. Thomas Clay (Anita Lippitt)**
**Savannah**

# EGGPLANT CASSEROLE

2 medium-size eggplants
¾ cup butter
1 large onion, chopped
1½ cups grated cheese
2 whole eggs

1 to 2 tablespoons sugar
1½ tablespoons celery salt
1½ cups Pepperidge Farm bread
    crumb stuffing

Peel eggplants. Slice in circles. Boil in salt water in covered pot. Cook 15 to 20 minutes or until greenish brown and fork tender. Drain. Add butter, onion, cheese, eggs, sugar, celery salt and bread crumbs. Mix well. Bake in buttered shallow baking dish at 350 degrees for 45 minutes. Serves 6 to 8.

**Mrs. John Walter Wright, Jr. (Joanne Werner)**
**Atlanta**

# CAULIFLOWER SUPREME

1 whole head cauliflower
½ cup mayonnaise
¼ cup grated Parmesan
    cheese

2 tablespoons chopped parsley
1 tablespoon lemon juice
¼ teaspoon salt
2 egg whites, beaten stiff

Cook cauliflower about 10 minutes in boiling salted water. Drain. Mix together mayonnaise, cheese, parsley, lemon juice, salt. Fold in beaten egg whites. Frost cauliflower with this mixture. Bake in moderate 350 degree oven until brown, about 20 minutes. Serves 6.

**Mrs. Wilder G. Little (Peggy Elder)**
**Marietta**

## CROATIAN GREEN BEANS

1½ pounds string beans
1 stick butter
2 tablespoons bread crumbs

½ bunch parsley, snipped
½ cup sour cream
1 clove garlic, crushed

Cook beans in rapidly boiling water until tender. In a separate pan, melt butter over low heat; stir in bread crumbs and let them brown. To this, add snipped parsley leaves and crushed garlic. Mix the herbs with buttered crumbs and combine with drained beans. Put mixture in Pyrex dish, pour sour cream over the top and bake in moderate oven for 15 minutes.

**Mrs. Osborne S. Mackie (Katharine Phinizy)**
**Augusta**

## SWISS BEAN CASSEROLE

2 cans French green beans
2 cups sour cream
4 tablespoons butter
4 tablespoons flour
2 teaspoons salt

½ teaspoon pepper
2 teaspoons sugar
1 teaspoon grated onion
1 teaspoon dry mustard
½ pound Swiss cheese, grated

Melt butter and blend in dry ingredients. Add sour cream slowly. Add part of cheese and stir until melted. Drain and wash beans in colander. Butter a casserole dish and put a layer of beans, then some sauce. Repeat and top with remaining cheese. Cook in oven until bubbly and cheese is melted. Serves 8-10.

**Mrs. John D. Powell (Laura Wise)**
**Americus**

## GARLIC CHEESE GRITS

1 cup of uncooked grits
1 teaspoon salt
4 cups of boiling water
¼ cup margarine or butter
2 tablespoons Worcestershire
   sauce

1 6-ounce roll garlic cheese,
   cubed
½ pound sharp Cheddar cheese,
   shredded

Gradually stir grits into boiling water. Add salt. Cook until thick, stirring constantly. Add margarine, garlic cheese, shredded Cheddar cheese and Worcestershire sauce; mix until margarine and cheese have melted. Pour into greased 2½-quart casserole. Sprinkle with paprika. Bake 15-20 minutes in 350 degree oven. Serves 8-10.

**Mrs. Carey S. Johnson (Julia Osborne)**
**Albany**

# HOMINY SOUFFLÉ

¾ cup uncooked hominy
1 cup boiling water
2 cups milk
¼ cup melted butter

4 egg yolks, well-beaten
salt
white pepper
6 egg whites

Preheat oven to 350 degrees. Grease a 2½-quart soufflé dish and dust with flour. Pour the hominy into the rapidly boiling water into a 1½-quart saucepan. Cook over medium heat for 2 minutes, stirring constantly. Stir in 1 cup of the milk and set the saucepan over boiling water. Cook for 30 minutes. Remove from heat and stir in the remaining cup of milk and the melted butter. Place this again over boiling water and stir until the mixture is smooth and heated through. Add salt and pepper to taste. Remove from the fire and stir in the well-beaten egg yolks. Cook to lukewarm. Meanwhile, in a large bowl, beat the egg whites until stiff but not dry. Fold the whites into the hominy mixture. Pour into the prepared dish and bake 45 minutes. Serves 6 to 8.

**Mrs. John Leitch (Anne Douglas)**
**Savannah**

# BAKED GRITS
## (Georgia Ice Cream)

6 cups boiling water
1½ cups grits
½ cup butter
1 pound sharp cheese

2 teaspoons salt
3 beaten eggs
½ cup milk

Cook grits in boiling water for 10-15 minutes. Remove from heat and add butter, salt, milk and grated cheese. Mix well. When slightly cool add beaten eggs. Pour into 8 inch by 10 inch dish. Refrigerate overnight. Bake at 300 degrees for 1½-2 hours. Corn flakes may be sprinkled over top. Good brunch dish.

**Mrs. William R. Howard (Louise Alford)**
**Milledgeville**

## ARTICHOKES MILANESE

6 artichokes
boiling salted water
6 teaspoons salt
12 teaspoons grated Parmesan
   cheese

6 tablespoons water
8-10 teaspoons butter

Cut the stems from 6 artichokes and with scissors cut ½ inch from top of each leaf. Parboil the artichokes for 7 minutes in boiling salted water to cover. Drain them, spread the center leaves apart slightly, and remove the chokes with a spoon or knife. In the center of each artichoke place a generous teaspoon of butter and 2 teaspoons of grated Parmesan cheese. Place the artichokes in a heavy buttered casserole and sprinkle 1 tablespoon of water over each. Cover the casserole and steam over very low heat for about 50 minutes. Add a few drops of water should the artichokes become too dry. Serves 6.

**Mrs. Crawford Burgard (Augusta Crawford)**
**Columbus**

## PINEAPPLE CASSEROLE

½ cup butter, melted
6 slices bread
3 eggs

1¼ cups sugar
1 large can crushed pineapple

Melt butter in pie pan in oven. Cut crust from bread and cube. Remove butter from oven, add bread cubes and toss. Beat eggs with sugar until well blended. Pour over bread cubes, add pineapple (not drained) and toss. Bake at 350 degrees for one hour.

**Mrs. Rudolph Fredrick Wagner (Margaret Plaub Hatcher)**
**Valdosta**

# Rice

Mary F. Passailaigue

## CHARLESTON RICE AND SHRIMP SUPPER

2 cups long grain rice,
   uncooked
2 cups water
salt
parsley

½ cup butter
2 pounds cooked, cleaned shrimp
16 strips cooked, crisp bacon
16 small link sausages, cooked
4 eggs, hard-boiled

Cook the 2 cups of long grain rice in 2 cups of water that has had salt added. Use a Charleston Rice Cooker or steamer if you have one. The rice should be dry and fluffy when done. Have a large warmed platter ready. First put the rice on it. Then place the strips of crisp, cooked bacon around the edges. Next place the cooked link sausages in between the bacon strips. The 4 hard-boiled eggs should be sliced and heated in the butter along with the 2 pounds cooked shrimp. Pour all of this hot mixture over the rice. Grind whole black peppercorns over the entire platter. Garnish with parsley. Serves 8.

**Mrs. James F. Crist (Elizabeth)**
**Atlanta**

## BAKED RICE

1 medium onion, diced
1 beef bouillon cube
1 can consommé
1 can water
1 cup rice, raw and rinsed
salt and pepper to taste

¼ pound margarine
1 bay leaf
parsley
1 small can mushrooms
dash of Worcestershire sauce

Sauté onions in margarine. Crumble bouillon cube in water, stirring well. Add this to sautéed onion. Add consommé, rice and other ingredients. Bake in covered casserole for 1 hour in 350 degree oven. Serves 8.

**Mrs. Chenault Hailey (Mary Louise Strickland)**
**Atlanta**

# RICE DRESSING FROM LOUISIANA

1 pound ground beef
giblets from 1 hen
1 large green pepper
1 large onion
4 stalks celery
3 pods garlic
1 teaspoon red pepper

1 teaspoon black pepper
salt to taste
chopped onion tops
chopped parsley
4 tablespoons cooking oil
2 tablespoons flour
4 cups cooked rice

Brown beef in cooking oil with flour. Grind and add giblets, green pepper, onion, celery and garlic. Add salt and pepper. Cook until vegetables are mushy. Mix with rice. Add chopped onion tops and parsley before serving.

**Miss Alice Hall**
**Milledgeville**

## BROWN RICE

2 cups of cooked rice
1 can Chinese vegetables
1 medium onion
2 stalks of celery

4 strips of bacon
½ of a fresh green pepper
soy sauce

Broil bacon until crisp. Crumble and set aside to cool. Add chopped celery, onion, and green pepper to bacon drippings and brown. Add Chinese vegetables and cooked rice to this mixture with enough soy sauce to turn the rice a rich golden brown. Add bacon. Serves 6 and is delicious with barbequed ribs, broiled chicken, etc. You will need a large frying pan.

**Mrs. James Henry Campagna (Katherine Mixson)**
**Atlanta**

## YELLOW RICE

2½ cups carrots, grated
8 ounces cheese, grated
2 cups cooked rice
   (Uncle Ben's)
2 eggs, beaten

¼ cup milk
1 tablespoon butter, melted
1 tablespoon onion, grated
1 teaspoon salt
⅛ teaspoon pepper

Mix carrots, cheese, and rice. Combine eggs, milk, melted butter, grated onion, salt, and pepper. Slowly add combined ingredients to carrot mixture. Turn into greased 1½-quart casserole, cover and bake in 350 degree oven for 40 minutes. Serves 6.

**Mrs. Alva Wallace Barrett, Jr. (Anita Champion)**
**Albany**

## CHINESE RICE

3 tablespoons oil
1 cup rice
¼ cup onion, chopped
¼ cup celery, chopped

4 tablespoons soy sauce
2 cups chicken broth
½ cup pine nuts—or almonds

Heat oil in heavy skillet, add rice and stir until golden. Add onion, green pepper and celery. When vegetables are limp, add soy sauce. Add chicken stock and nuts. Cover and cook until rice is fluffy and the moisture is absorbed; or this can be baked in a 350 degree oven for 45 minutes. This freezes well. Serves 4.

**Mrs. James Lawton Riley (Ethel Worthington)**
**Brunswick**

## CHEESE AND RICE DISH

2 cups cooked rice
2 cups grated sharp cheese
1 cup cut up fresh parsley
  leaves
2 medium-size onions, chopped
1 clove garlic, minced

⅓ cup Wesson oil
2 eggs, beaten
2 cups milk
1 teaspoon salt
dash red pepper

Simmer onion and garlic in Wesson oil until limp. Combine all ingredients and put in uncovered casserole dish. Bake in 350 degree oven for 40 minutes to 1 hour. Serves 6.

**Mrs. Henry Cabaniss (Elizabeth Marshall)**
**Savannah**

## CHUTNEY RICE

1 cup chopped onion
1 cup sliced celery
4 tablespoons butter
3 cups cooked rice

½ cup flaked coconut
¼ cup mango chutney
½ teaspoon ground ginger
1 teaspoon curry powder

Sauté onion and celery in butter. Add remaining ingredients and toss with a fork over low heat. Serves 6-8.

**Mrs. Arthur B. Simkins (Lisa Marshall)**
**Savannah**

# RICE CASSEROLE

2 cups long grain rice
1 stick butter
1 can chicken broth
1 can frozen orange juice

½ teaspoon curry powder
½ cup white raisins, soaked in
   sherry and drained

Put in casserole and bake at 350 degrees until done.

**Mrs. Harold Cooledge (Rebecca Clark)**
**Clemson, South Carolina**

# RICE-PEPPER CASSEROLE

4 cups cooked rice (1 cup
   uncooked makes 4 cups)
2 cups sour cream
1 cup small curd cottage cheese

2 4-ounce cans green chilies,
   drained and chopped
1 bay leaf, crushed fine
salt and pepper to taste

Mix together. Grate sharp cheese on top. Heat until bubbly in 350 degree oven. Makes one large casserole or two smaller ones. Serves 8-10.

**Mrs. William Bell (Caroline L. Hull)**
**Augusta**

# SHERRIED RICE

1 cup Uncle Ben's rice
½ cup sherry
1¾ cups water
1 tablespoon dehydrated
   minced onion
dash Tabasco

2 teaspoons instant beef bouillon
   or 2 bouillon cubes
½ stick butter
½ pound sliced fresh mushrooms
   or 1 8-ounce can

Combine all ingredients but butter and mushrooms in top of double boiler. Cook over boiling water 1½ to 2 hours. Sauté mushrooms in butter and stir into cooked rice. Serve hot as accompaniment to roast beef. Brown rice is delicious also. Adjust liquid to 2 cups to 1 cup brown rice and cook 2 hours in double boiler. May be prepared ahead and reheated in a casserole dish. Serves 6.

**Mrs. Marvin Reynolds McClatchey (Sally Bruce Blackford)**
**Atlanta**

## PICNIC PRIDE RICE

1½ cups rice
1½ cups water
2 bouillon cubes
2 tablespoons bacon grease
½ cup chopped peanuts

½ cup raisins, chopped
½ cup cut up celery
1 teaspoon concentrate beef
  extract
salt and pepper to taste

Dissolve bouillon cubes in water. Combine water and rice in rice steamer. Add bacon grease, salt and pepper to water and rice. Cook until rice has soaked up all the water. Add chopped peanuts, raisins, celery and beef extract. Cook 30 minutes more or until rice is no longer hard. Serves 6.

**Mrs. Jesse Fulenwider, Jr. (Leonora Atkinson)**
**Savannah**

## WILD RICE MIX CASSEROLE

1 package wild rice mix
1 medium onion, chopped
1 can cream of mushroom soup
½ cup milk
2 pounds ground beef

1 large can mushrooms
1 can cream of chicken soup
salt, pepper to taste
buttered crumbs

Cook rice according to directions on package. Brown beef and onion. Mix rice, beef, onion, mushrooms, soups, milk and seasonings and place in buttered casserole. Top with buttered bread crumbs and bake at 350 degrees for one hour. Serves 8 to 10. Freezes well.

**Mrs. Kenneth H. Merry (Gena Callaway)**
**Augusta**

## MARINATED COLD RICE

2 packages Uncle Ben's Wild
  and White Rice mixture
1 large can mushrooms or 6 or
  7 large fresh mushrooms,
  sliced
15 green olives, sliced

15 pitted black olives, whole
2 small onions, chopped
oil and vinegar dressing or bottled
  Caesar's dressing
herbs to taste, such as thyme,
  tarragon, parsley

Boil rice with packet of seasoning that comes with it. Drain. Add other ingredients and marinate in dressing in refrigerator for 24 hours. Serve as a cold casserole along with shrimp, chicken salad, or cold meat. Serves 14.

**Mrs. Allison W. Ledbetter, Jr. (Irby Lasseter)**
**Rome**

# Cheese, Eggs and Sauces

Mary F. Passailaigue

## SCOTCH PARTRIDGE EGGS

½ pound mild sausage
1 tin boiled partridge eggs
1½ ounces bread crumbs
½ tablespoon green onions,
  minced

1 egg, beaten
¼ teaspoon lemon rind, grated
¼ teaspoon oregano, thyme, sage,
  mixed

Fresh partridge eggs are difficult to obtain, but tins of hard-boiled bamboo partridge eggs may be obtained in an oriental grocery store. There are about thirty in a can. One half pound sausage covers 24 or 25 eggs, depending on the size, for they vary. The tinned ones have been boiled without salt and should be sprinkled with salt. Mix half the crumbs with the onion, lemon rind, and herbs into the sausage with the hands. Taking up a generous tablespoonful of the mixture, flatten it out with the fingers and bring it up about the tiny egg. Prepare ahead of time and set in the refrigerator. When ready to serve, dip each egg in beaten egg and then roll in other half of the crumbs. Fry in deep fat until light brown. The coating of sausage is so thin it takes only a few minutes. Drain on paper and serve hot, sliced in half.

**Mrs. John Michael Gregory (Helen Louise Theuss)**
**Athens**

## CURRIED EGGS

20 hard cooked eggs, cut
  lengthwise
3 10½-ounce cans mushroom
  soup
1 3-ounce can Kraft grated
  Parmesan cheese
4½ teaspoons curry powder

2 4½-ounce jars sliced mushrooms,
  drained
6 tablespoons Heinz Chili Sauce
1 4-ounce jar pimentos (chopped
  fine)
1 8-ounce can water chestnuts,
  sliced

Place 40 egg halves in buttered 3-quart pyrex flat baking dish. In saucepan mix mushroom soup, Parmesan cheese, curry powder, chili sauce and chopped pimentos. Heat mixture. Add mushrooms and water chestnuts. Mix well and pour over eggs. Top with coarse bread crumbs. Dot generously with butter. Bake at 350 degrees until brown and bubbly. About 20 minutes. Serves 18.

**Mrs. John Alston Bracey (Marie Brice)**
**Thomasville**

# QUICHE LORRAINE

12 slices bacon
¼ cup chopped chives
4 eggs
2 cups light cream
1 cup Cheddar cheese, grated

¼ teaspoon nutmeg
½ teaspoon salt
¼ teaspoon pepper
3 dashes cayenne pepper
1 teaspoon chopped onion

PASTRY FOR 9″ PIES (2) BOTTOM CRUST ONLY

2 cups flour
⅔ cup shortening

½ teaspoon salt
⅓ cup cold water

Mix flour and salt. Work in shortening. Add water. Roll out and line 2 pie plates—9″ size.

Fry bacon until crisp. Break into pieces and sprinkle over pastry. Sprinkle chives and onion over bacon. Beat eggs and cream. Add grated cheese and seasonings. Pour mixture into pie shells. Bake 15 minutes in 400 degree oven. Reduce heat to 325 degrees and bake 30 minutes longer. Give silver knife test. If it comes clean, quiche is done. Serve hot as main dish for lunch or supper. Allow 2 wedges per person. This recipe will serve 6.

**Mrs. Francis Willson Daily (Alice Hunt)**
**Savannah**

# HOT HARD-BOILED EGGS

8 eggs, hard-boiled
½ cup mayonnaise
salt and pepper
3 tablespoons flour
3 tablespoons butter

1 cup milk
1 4-ounce can mushrooms,
   drained
½ cup bread crumbs
½ cup grated Cheddar cheese

Peel eggs, cut in half. Remove yolks and mash thoroughly. Combine with mayonnaise, salt and pepper. Refill egg whites and arrange in buttered casserole, one layer deep. Make a cream sauce of flour, butter and milk; season with salt and pepper and add drained mushrooms. Pour over eggs. Sprinkle bread crumbs and cheese over all. Bake in 350 degree oven for 20 minutes.

To simplify: 1 can mushroom soup diluted with ⅛ cup water may be used in place of cream sauce and mushrooms.

**Mrs. Leo Jackson Allen (Janet Brantley)**
**Blackshear**

## EGGS DIJON

1 teaspoon Dijon mustard
¼ teaspoon salt
1 cup sour cream
3 tablespoons grated Gruyère
  cheese

1 tablespoon dry white wine
6 eggs
buttered bread crumbs

Mix together the Dijon mustard, salt, sour cream, grated cheese and wine. Break eggs into a greased shallow baking dish or two-egg ramekin. Cover eggs with sauce and sprinkle buttered bread crumbs over top. Place in a pan of hot water and bake in a 350° oven for fifteen minutes.
Substitute Swiss cheese, if you like. Serves 3.

**Mrs. George Welby Brantly (Wylma Jenkins)**
**Moultrie**

## EGG CROQUETTES

10 eggs, hard-boiled
1 can mushroom soup
1 tablespoon minced parsley
1 tablespoon minced onion

salt and pepper
2 eggs, slightly beaten
bread crumbs

Put hard-boiled eggs through meat grinder, or grate. Mix with next four ingredients and form into croquettes. Roll in slightly beaten egg and then bread crumbs. Chill in refrigerator two or three hours. Fry in deep fat.

**Mrs. Ellis Hale (Elizabeth Hand)**
**Rome**

## WELSH RAREBIT

1 teaspoon butter
1½ cups diced cheese
⅓ teaspoon salt
¼ teaspoon dry mustard

pinch cayenne pepper
1 teaspoon Worcestershire sauce
1 cup cream or half and half
1 egg yolk

Melt butter in pan over hot water. Stir in cheese and melt slowly. Add salt, dry mustard, cayenne, and Worcestershire sauce. Slowly, stir in the cream or half and half. Remove the pan from the heat and beat in egg yolk. Serve at once over hot, toasted crackers or bread. Serves 4.

**Mary Eugenia Lee**
**Augusta**

# CHEESE PUFF

4 tablespoons butter or
  margarine
4 tablespoons plain flour
1 cup milk
½ teaspoon salt

4 egg yolks
4 egg whites, stiffly beaten
1 cup grated American cheese,
  packed firmly (sharp or medium
  sharp)

Make a cream sauce of butter, flour and milk, adding salt and cheese, stirring until cheese is melted. Remove from heat, allow to cool slightly and add egg yolks which have been beaten slightly. Set aside and allow to cool until lukewarm and gently fold in stiffly beaten egg whites, combining thoroughly. Pour into 1-quart glass baking dish. Preheat oven to 300 degrees. Place dish in a pan of water and bake 40 minutes. Remove from oven and allow to cool. It may be kept in refrigerator overnight or frozen for several days. Before serving, thaw thoroughly and return to 300 degree oven, again in a pan of water, and bake for 20 minutes more. Serve immediately. Serves 4 to 6.

This dish is great for brunch, breakfast or lunch. It may be served as is or with creamed chicken, ham or seafood. It is similar to a soufflé, but the second cooking makes the top crunchy and easier to serve to a crowd.

**Mrs. S. William Clark (Susan Lott)**
**Waycross**

# CHEESE SOUFFLÉ

6 slices white bread, trimmed
2½ cups milk
2 cups sharp cheese, grated
butter

4 eggs
1 teaspoon prepared mustard
little onion salt

Butter the bread slices and cut in small cubes. Butter a casserole and layer the bread in it, alternating layers of the cheese with the bread cubes. Beat the eggs in the milk with the mustard and the onion salt. Pour over the bread and cheese. Set in the refrigerator overnight. One hour before baking, remove from the refrigerator. Set in a pan of hot water and bake in a 350 degree oven for one hour, or until puffed and browned on top. Serve at once.

**Mrs. Cuyler Trussell (LaGrange Robeson Cothran)**
**Athens**

## FREEZER CHEESE SOUFFLÉ

2 tablespoons finely chopped
   shallots OR 1 small onion,
   chopped
⅓ cup flour
1 teaspoon salt

1½ cups milk
1 tablespoon prepared mustard
1½ cups shredded Cheddar cheese
6 eggs, separated

Butter 6-cup soufflé dish. Sauté shallots or onion in butter until soft. Stir in flour and salt; cook, stirring constantly, until mixture bubbles. Gradually stir in milk; continue cooking and stirring for one minute. Stir in mustard and cheese. Remove from heat. Beat egg whites until stiff in a large bowl. Beat yolks well in a metal bowl. Beat hot cheese sauce into yolks. *Fold* yellow mixture into white. Pour into prepared dish. Cover with foil. LABEL, DATE, FREEZE. To bake: place unwrapped frozen soufflé in *cold* oven; set temperature at 350 degrees. Bake for one hour or until puffed and golden.

(One cup finely diced ham may be substituted for one cup cheese. Swiss cheese may be used instead of Cheddar.)

Must be cooked immediately after removing from freezer.

**Mrs. Heard Robertson (Mary Barrett)**
**Augusta**


## CHEESE SOUFFLÉ

4 egg yolks
3 tablespoons margarine
3 tablespoons cornstarch
½ teaspoon salt
⅛ teaspoon white pepper

1 cup milk
1 cup shredded sharp Cheddar
   cheese (about 4 ounces)
4 egg whites

Beat egg yolks until thick and lemon colored. Melt margarine in saucepan. Remove from heat, blend in cornstarch, salt and pepper. Gradually add milk, mixing until smooth. Cook over medium heat stirring constantly until mixture thickens and comes to a boil. Remove from heat. Gradually stir cheese mixture into beaten egg yolks. Beat egg whites until stiff but not dry. Gently fold cheese mixture into egg whites. Pour into 1½-quart soufflé dish or casserole. With a teaspoon or spatula make a shallow path in cheese mixture all around casserole one-inch from edge. Place dish in pan of warm water one-inch deep. Bake in 350 degree oven for 1¼ hours. Makes 4 servings.

**Mrs. Lewis J. Hubbard (Alice Brinson)**
**Moultrie**

# QUICK CHEESE SOUFFLÉ

2 slices of bread
1 cup of milk
5 eggs
2 to 3 pats of butter

8 ounces extra sharp Cheddar
  cheese
½ teaspoon salt

Trim the edges of two slices of white bread and break into small pieces. Pour one cup of sweet milk over bread and let dissolve. While bread and milk are dissolving, beat 5 whole eggs and grate cheese. Pour the eggs and grated cheese into soaked bread. Put 2 or 3 pats of butter on top. Bake in pre-heated oven at 350 degrees for 35 to 40 minutes.
Serves 4.

Mary Page Walker
Madison

# CLASSIC CHEESE FONDUE

1 pound Swiss cheese
1 box Gruyère cheese
  (6 ounces)
2 tablespoons cornstarch
1½ cups dry white wine

1½ tablespoons lemon juice
dash nutmeg
dash pepper
dash garlic powder
1½ loaves crusty French bread

Grate Swiss and Gruyère cheese. In top of double boiler, heat wine and lemon juice until air bubbles just begin to rise. Mix cornstarch with cheese and stir in cheese, a handful at a time. Add seasonings. When well-blended and smooth, transfer to fondue pot and keep warm over simmering water. Serve with French bread. Serves 6 for supper.

Mrs. Francis Willson Daily (Alice Hunt)
Savannah

# CHEESE CASSEROLE

10 slices white bread, buttered
  and crust removed
2 cups milk
3 eggs

½ pound cheese, grated
1 teaspoon salt
1 teaspoon dry mustard

Cut bread in small pieces. Place alternate layers of bread and cheese in 1½-quart casserole. Pour over that a mixture of the eggs, salt and mustard. Place in refrigerator at least 12 hours. Bake about 45 minutes or until brown in a 350 degree oven. Serve immediately. Serves 6.

Mrs. James P. Champion, Jr. (Jane Luthy)
Albany

# BREAKFAST STRATA

½ pound hot sausage
½ pound bacon
8 pieces bread, each slice cubed
    into 4 pieces
1½ cups sharp cheese, grated

4 eggs
½ teaspoon salt
½ teaspoon dry mustard
1 pint milk
Worcestershire sauce to taste

Cook both the sausage and bacon. Drain, then crumble the sausage and break the bacon into small pieces and mix together. Butter a 3-quart casserole dish. Cover with half of the bread cubes, half the cheese and all the sausage-bacon mixture. Cover with remaining bread cubes and cheese. Beat eggs, Worcestershire sauce, salt, dry mustard and milk. Pour over casserole and refrigerate overnight. Bake about 45 minutes at 325 degrees.

Dilute one can mushroom soup with ¼ to ½ cup milk and spread on casserole. Bake 15 to 30 minutes longer at 300 degrees.

**Mrs. Tom Huston (Minnie Bullock)**
**Coral Gables, Fla.**

# RAISIN SAUCE

1 cup sugar
½ cup water
1 cup seedless raisins, white if
    possible
1 cup oranges cut fine, rind
    left on
2 tablespoons butter
2 tablespoons vinegar

2 teaspoons cornstarch
⅛ teaspoon Worcestershire sauce
½ teaspoon salt
¼ teaspoon ground cloves
⅛ teaspoon mace
1 cup currant jelly
¼ cup ham drippings, if available

Mix together all the ingredients except ham drippings and cornstarch and bring to a boil. Cook until raisins are plump. Add drippings and cornstarch dissolved in a little water. Cook until clear.

Sauce for ham should be light-bodied and thin. This is a good sauce to keep in the refrigerator. Use it on ham, corned beef, Canadian bacon, or smoked tongue. Makes 4 cups.

**Mrs. Edward S. Shorter (Mildred Watts)**
**Columbus**

## BASIC MUSHROOM SAUCE

1 tablespoon butter or
  margarine
1 onion 1½-inch diameter,
  diced
8 ounces fresh mushrooms,
  rinsed and sliced

4 ounces sherry wine
2 teaspoons flour
1 beef or chicken bouillon cube

In 8-inch skillet, melt butter. Add diced onion. Cook slowly until onion is transparent. Add mushrooms. Cook until the mushroom juice starts coming out. Add bouillon cube. Mix thoroughly the flour into the wine. Add this to the mushroom and onion mixture. Cook slowly until liquid thickens.

Use this as a sauce, as an additive to gravy or serve as mushrooms on toast. Serves 2 as a dish or, of course, more as a sauce.

**Mrs. Robert Hatcher (Josephine Stetson)**
**Macon**

## BROWN SAUCE WITH MUSHROOMS

2 tablespoons butter
2 tablespoons flour
1½ cups turkey stock
1 teaspoon salt

dash red pepper
⅓ cup white wine
8 medium fresh mushrooms, sliced
1½ tablespoons green onions

Cook butter and flour until brown. Add turkey stock, salt, red pepper and simmer until reduced ⅓. Add white wine and reduce more while you sauté sliced mushrooms and green onions. Add to sauce. Makes about 1½ cups. Serve over rice, sliced turkey, or dressing.

**Mrs. James Dickson Maddox (Rebecca Wall)**
**Rome**

## MIDWINTER CHILI SAUCE

3 large cans of tomatoes
6 large bell peppers (fresh or
  frozen)
6 large onions
1½ cups sugar
1½ cups vinegar

2 teaspoons cinnamon
1 teaspoon nutmeg
1 teaspoon allspice
1 teaspoon celery seed
2 teaspoons salt

Cook until vegetables are tender, simmer. If a thickened relish is desired, dissolve about 2 tablespoons of cornstarch in cold vinegar.

**Mrs. Mercer Sherman (Ernestine Walker)**
**Albany**

# HOLLANDAISE SAUCE

2 egg yolks
juice of one large lemon
¼ pound butter

salt
white pepper
Tabasco sauce

In the top of a double boiler beat well with a fork the 2 egg yolks. Add the juice of 1 large lemon and mix well. Cut the ¼ pound of butter into about 6 pieces. Spear 1 piece of butter at a time with a fork and stir into lemon mixture until melted. Hold the pan over, not in, the boiling water and don't be in a hurry to cook too fast or it will curdle. It takes only a few minutes anyway. Season with salt, white pepper, and a couple of drops of Tabasco sauce.

This may be made ahead of time and rewarmed in a jar set in a pan of warm (not hot) water.

**Mrs. Archibald Little Griffin (Alma Lee Whitfield)**
**Valdosta**

# HENRIETTA'S SAUCE FOR BIRDS

1 jar currant jelly
2 teaspoons dry mustard
2 tablespoons Worcestershire
   sauce

1 stick butter
juice of 1 orange
juice of 1 lemon
dash of cayenne pepper

Melt butter in double boiler with currant jelly. Add juice of orange and lemon. Add dry mustard, cayenne pepper and Worcestershire sauce. Bring to a boil. Serve with quail.

**Mrs. Bernard F. Williams (Celia Howell Jones)**
**Savannah**

# MIGNONNETTE SAUCE
## (A superb sauce for raw or roasted oysters)

½ cup white wine vinegar or
   herb vinegar
½ teaspoon grated onion
½ teaspoon lemon juice
2 teaspoons shallot, chopped

2 teaspoons chives, chopped
2 teaspoons parsley, chopped
2 teaspoons freshly ground pepper
   corns
salt to taste

Shake well and chill over night. Serve in ramekins to dip oysters in.

**Mrs. Thomas Clay (Anita Lippitt)**
**Savannah**

## RIPE TOMATO SAUCE (For Pork)

4 quarts tomatoes, peeled and
  cut up
8 cups sugar
2 cups vinegar
4 cups chopped onion
½ teaspoon salt

4 sticks cinnamon
1 teaspoon nutmeg
1 teaspoon allspice
1 teaspoon ground cloves
pepper to taste

Combine all ingredients in large preserving kettle or heavy boiler (8 to 10-quart). Cook slowly over medium heat, stirring quite often to prevent sticking. Cook until fairly thick and dark brown, about one hour. Store in regular canning jars—any size. Top with hot melted paraffin ¼-inch deep and seal tightly. Of course you may cook ½ or ¼ this recipe if you only want a small amount.

**Mrs. Walker S. Reid (Maud Winter Hack)**
**Madison**

## WIENER SAUCE
*Special sauce for wieners—quick and different*

1 cup tomato catsup
1 cup boiling water
3 tablespoons diced onion
1 tablespoon sugar
1 tablespoon vinegar

1 tablespoon prepared mustard
½ teaspoon salt (optional)
⅛ teaspoon pepper
½ pound or more wieners

Mix catsup, water, and vinegar. Add sugar, mustard, salt, pepper and diced onion. Simmer 20 minutes. Store in refrigerator until ready to use. Cut wieners into bite sized pieces. Add sauce and simmer 12 to 15 minutes until well-seasoned. Serve with macaroni and cheese and tossed salad.

**Mrs. John Winn Shinholser (Hallie McHenry)**
**Madison**

# BARBECUE SAUCE

½ cup oil
¾ cup chopped onion
¾ cup tomato catsup
¾ cup water
⅓ cup lemon juice
3 tablespoon sugar

3 tablespoons Worcestershire
  sauce
2 tablespoons prepared mustard
2 teaspoons salt
½ teaspoon pepper

Cook onions in oil until tender. Add all other ingredients. Simmer together 7 minutes. Sufficient for 2 chickens.

**Mrs. William McCollum (Carolyn Eidson)**
**Thomasville**

# BEEF KABOB MARINADE

½ cup olive oil
¼ cup soy sauce
½ cup claret or Burgundy

2 tablespoons ketchup
1 tablespoon curry powder
½ teaspoon black pepper

Mix together. Add no salt. Marinate beef covered with sauce in refrigerator twelve to sixteen hours. Cook on grill.

**Mrs. Hilliard Burt (Henrietta Carlisle)**
**Albany**

# PARTY FLANK STEAK MARINADE

4 tablespoons olive oil
6 tablespoons soy sauce
¼ teaspoon black pepper

3 tablespoons lemon juice
1 grated onion

Marinate flank steak in sauce for 3 hours or more. Broil meat until cooked to desired doneness. Slice steak on the bias—across the grain. Serve in strips.

**Mrs. William Q. Walker (Ida MacGregor)**
**Brunswick**

# Salads and Salad Dressings

Mary F. Passailaigue

# RUSSIAN BEET MOLD

1 can (1 pound) Julienne beets
  (drained) (save juice)
⅓ cup wine vinegar
3 tablespoons sugar

dash of Tabasco
½ small onion, grated
1 envelope gelatin
½ teaspoon seasoned salt

Soften gelatin in beet juice. Combine with other ingredients and beat until gelatin is dissolved adding beets last. Pour in oiled mold and chill until firm. Serve with sour cream topped with spoon of caviar. Make a large mold for a buffet by alternating layers of Russian Beet Mold with Horseradish Mold.

HORSERADISH MOLD WITH RUSSIAN BEETS

1½ tablespoons horseradish
1 teaspoon anchovy paste
1 teaspoon onion juice
2 teaspoons white vinegar
½ teaspoon each of sugar and
  dry mustard

1 teaspoon salt
1 cup sour cream
½ cup mayonnaise
1 envelope gelatin
½ cup cold water

Blend horseradish, anchovy paste, onion juice, and white vinegar until smooth. Mix thoroughly with sour cream and mayonnaise. Soften gelatin in water—dissolve over hot water and beat in mayonnaise. Soften gelatin in water, dissolve over hot water and beat into mixture. Pour into mold on top of Russian Mold. If doing in small molds, garnish with avocado and parsley.
**Mrs. Jane Huckabee Miller (Marjorie Jane Huckabee)**
**Albany**

# CUCUMBERS AND SOUR CREAM

2 cucumbers
¾ cup sour cream
½ teaspoon salt
3½ tablespoons sugar

3 tablespoons vinegar
¼ teaspoon dry mustard
2 tablespoons onion, chopped

Remove peel from cucumbers and slice very thin. Salt to remove some moisture, drain and rinse before adding to dressing.

DRESSING

Add a few drops of vinegar to dry mustard and cream thoroughly. Blend all ingredients, add cucumbers and let stand in refrigerator at least one day.
**Mrs. Silas Mason Hearne (Louise Scott)**
**Marathon, Florida**

## CHINESE VEGETABLE SALAD

1 16-ounce can mixed Chinese
vegetables, drained
1 8-ounce can small green peas,
drained
1 16-ounce can seasoned green
beans, drained

1 8-ounce can water chestnuts
drained, sliced
1 medium onion, sliced
1 cup celery, diced
pinch red pepper
1 pound fresh mushrooms

Slice fresh mushrooms and mix all vegetables together. Spread in a shallow pan. Pour over the vegetables the following marinade.

MARINADE

½ cup tarragon vinegar
½ cup salad oil

½ cup sugar

Put sugar and vinegar in a saucepan and heat until sugar is dissolved and the mixture is hot but not boiling. Stir in salad oil. When cool, pour over vegetables. Cover and refrigerate at least overnight. (This is a very sweet dressing and for many tastes the sugar should be reduced.)

**Mrs. Edward Davison Burch (Julia Devereux Cain)**
**Athens**

## SPINACH AND SOUR CREAM SALAD

6 packages frozen chopped
spinach (cooked)
1 cup sour cream
1 cup minced celery
¼ cup finely chopped onion

1 tablespoon lemon juice
3 teaspoons salt
⅛ teaspoon pepper
¼ teaspoon Tabasco

Drain and cool the spinach. Add sour cream, celery, and onion. Season with lemon juice, salt, pepper and Tabasco. Pack in oiled mold and chill. Serve with sour cream dressing. Serves 8.

**Mrs. John Searcy (Martha Triplett)**
**Thomasville**

# MOLDED SPINACH RING

3 packages, 12 ounces each, of
  Stouffers frozen Spinach
  Soufflé
4 envelopes, 19 ounces each, of
  MBT instant
  chicken-flavored broth
2½ envelopes, ¼ ounce each, of
  Knox unflavored gelatin

⅓ cup cold water
lettuce leaves
sliced fresh mushrooms (enough to
  fill center of ring when
  unmolded)

DRESSING

2 cups of mayonnaise

1 cup crabmeat

*Salad:* Completely defrost spinach soufflé in a large mixing bowl. Soften gelatin in cold water. Dissolve the chicken broth powder in hot water and bring again to boiling point. Add boiling broth to softened gelatin and stir until gelatin is completely dissolved. Add broth-gelatin mixture to defrosted spinach. If spinach is still cold, this will set very quickly so fill the mold before the mixture congeals. This exactly fills an 8½-inch ring mold. Refrigerate but do not freeze. To assemble, unmold spinach ring onto a platter. Surround with lettuce leaves. Fill center with sliced mushrooms. Serve crab, mayonnaise separately. Serves 6.

*Dressing:* Use your own judgment in this quantity, according to the consistency of the mayonnaise. If canned crabmeat is used, it must be thoroughly drained.

**Mrs. Richard Crosby Glass (Sally Ainsworth)**
**Atlanta**

# SPINACH SALAD

½ pound raw spinach
2 hard-boiled eggs
1 tablespoon vinegar
4 tablespoons oil
½ teaspoon salt

⅛ teaspoon black pepper
⅛ teaspoon thyme
⅛ teaspoon basil
⅛ teaspoon marjoram

Cut leaves of spinach in large pieces in mixing bowl. Reserve hard-boiled eggs for garnish. Make a dressing of the remaining ingredients. Shake dressing thoroughly; pour over spinach and toss. Serves 4.

**Mrs. Lucian Lamar Daniel (Jean Paullin)**
**Moultrie**

## GREEN BEANS WITH SOUR CREAM
### (Cold)

2 cans cut Blue Lake green
  beans
1 thinly sliced medium sized
  onion

1 tablespoon salad oil
1 tablespoon vinegar
salt—cracked pepper to taste

Marinate the above items 1½ hours. Drain. Remove onion. Serve with horseradish sour cream dressing:

1 cup sour cream
1 teaspoon lemon juice
1 tablespoon prepared
  horseradish

½ cup mayonnaise
¼ teaspoon dry mustard
¼ teaspoon onion juice

Pour dressing over marinated bean mixture and chill before serving.

**Mrs. Charles V. Smith (Betty Allen)**
**Tennille**

## KOREAN SALAD

½ pound fresh spinach, washed
  and drained
1 6-ounce can water
  chestnuts
½ cup sugar
1 medium onion, minced
¼ cup good wine vinegar

salt to taste
2 eggs, hard boiled and sliced
5 strips bacon, fried crisp
1 cup salad oil
½ cup catsup
2 teaspoons Worcestershire
  sauce

Tear spinach in bits. Drain and slice thin the water chestnuts. Crumble bacon. Put all in a salad bowl with the sliced eggs and pour over all the following dressing.

Mix the sugar, oil, onion, catsup, Worcestershire sauce, salt, and vinegar in a blender until well combined. Taste and check for sugar and salt. Vinegar varies a great deal in acidity.

**Mrs. Thomas F. Gerdine (Florida Hill)**
**Athens**

## GREAT GRANDMOTHER HAMILTON'S CHICKEN SALAD

2 hens, about 6 or 7 pounds
8 ounces Spanish olive oil
1 cup good apple cider vinegar
1 tablespoon butter
2½ tablespoons dry mustard

6 eggs
6 hard boiled eggs
2 tablespoons sugar
3 cups celery, cut in crescents
salt and cayenne pepper

Boil hens until tender in stock reserved and frozen from last boiled chickens. If there is not sufficient stock add water to cover, parsley, carrot, half of lemon, salt, pepper, and a small onion. When tender, cool chicken in stock and then dice meat.

Place the yolks of the six raw eggs in a bowl and slowly beat in the oil. (Spanish olive oil is hard to find. If Italian oil must be used, use half olive oil and half salad oil. The Italian oil is much heavier.) As the oil is added the mayonnaise will, of course, thicken. Mash yolks of the 6 hard boiled eggs and mix with one cup of good vinegar. Add dry mustard and a pinch of cayenne pepper. Pour the vinegar mixture into the raw egg mixture very slowly, beating all the time. Melt the butter in a sauce pan and add the egg mixture. Heat until the mixture thickens, stirring constantly. Set aside to cool.

Add the chicken and celery to the boiled dressing. Chill. To serve arrange Boston lettuce on a platter, mound salad in center and sieve over it the hard boiled egg whites.

**Mrs. David Robert Cumming (Elizabeth Hamilton Hall)**
**Athens**

## CHICKEN SALAD

2 cups cooked chicken, diced
1 large can water chestnuts,
    sliced
1 large can chunk pineapple
2 cups toasted, slivered
    almonds

2 cups diced celery
3 cups mayonnaise
1 tablespoon curry powder
2 tablespoons soy sauce
2 tablespoons lemon juice

Mix thoroughly and refrigerate over night.

**Mrs. Robert Henry Humphrey (Josibel Christopher)**
**Swainsboro**

# CHICKEN MOLD

4 cups diced chicken
4 hard boiled eggs, diced
1 cup celery, diced
1 cup *tiny* English peas
½ cup almonds, diced
salt and pepper to taste

2 cups chicken stock
2 envelopes Knox gelatin
1 cup mayonnaise
1 tablespoon lemon juice
2 tablespoons relish, drained
1 teaspoon onion juice

Soak gelatin in ½ cup cold water. Dissolve in 2 cups hot chicken broth. Let cool slightly and add mayonnaise. Add other ingredients to gelatin and mayonnaise. Pour into mold and congeal.

**Mrs. George Ellis (Edith Morgan)**
**Americus**

# HAM MOLD

2 cups cooked ground ham
1 hard boiled egg, diced
6 Spanish olives, sliced
1 envelope gelatin
1 teaspoon lemon juice

½ cup celery, finely chopped
½ small onion, finely chopped
½ cup crushed saltine crackers
¼ cup mayonnaise
½ cup cold water

Dissolve gelatin in ½ cup cold water placed over boiling water. Break saltine crackers with fingers. Don't roll. Combine above ingredients and add ½ cup mayonnaise last. Turn into a greased mold to get cold and firm. Serve on lettuce as a salad or use as a main dish for a hot day.

**Mrs. Kenneth F. Luthy (Mildred Hollis)**
**Albany**

# MARINATED VEGETABLE SALAD

2 heads cauliflower
2 pounds carrots
1 pound mushrooms
1 bunch broccoli

3 green peppers
1 bunch celery
3 zucchini
2 cucumbers

Cut the above fresh vegetables into bite-sized pieces. Then combine and stir until well mixed:

½ cup salad oil
3 cups tarragon vinegar
3 cloves garlic, minced
1 tablespoon prepared mustard

½ cup olive oil
½-¾ cup sugar
1 tablespoon salt
2 teaspoons tarragon leaves

Pour oil mixture over vegetables. Cover and chill at least 12 hours (better overnight), stirring occasionally. Makes 30 servings.

**Mrs. David Draper Garrison (Augusta Benning Burgard)**
**Augusta**

## STUFFED TOMATOES LOUIS

½ pound frozen shrimp
1 can tuna (6½ ounce)
¼ cup mayonnaise
¼ cup sour cream
1 tablespoon chili sauce
1 tablespoon salad oil
1 tablespoon lemon juice

1 teaspoon horseradish
2 tablespoons chopped chives
½ to ¾ teaspoon salt
dash cayenne pepper
4 large tomatoes
crisp salad greens

Cook shrimp according to package directions. Drain and chill. Drain and flake tuna. Chill. Prepare dressing by combining remaining ingredients except tomatoes and salad greens. Add dressing to shrimp and tuna; toss lightly. Chill an hour or more. Core tomatoes and cut into eighths almost to the bottom. Sprinkle with salt and pepper. Gently pull apart and fill with seafood mixture. Serve on salad greens.

**Mrs. Thomas G. Moore (Janet Fitzhugh Knox)**
**Atlanta**

## GAZPACHO ASPIC

1 large ripe tomato
1 cucumber
⅓ cup bell pepper
1½ envelopes unflavored
   gelatin
12 ounces tomato juice
⅛ teaspoon Tabasco
¼ cup cold water

⅛ teaspoon celery salt
1 tablespoon olive oil
1½ tablespoons red wine vinegar
white pepper to taste
1 tablespoon green onion, chopped
1 tablespoon lemon juice
freshly ground black pepper to
   taste

Peel the tomato and cucumber and chop fine along with the bell pepper. Put aside. Dissolve gelatin in the cold water. Heat tomato juice to which the chopped green onion has been added, and stir in the gelatin. Add the seasonings and cool until mixture begins to congeal. Add the chopped vegetables and pour into individual molds. Chill until firm. Serve on garden lettuce with fresh homemade mayonnaise.

**Mrs. Francis Norman (Virginia Illges)**
**Columbus**

## RAW MUSHROOM SALAD

8 to 10 mushrooms
1½ teaspoons prepared
    mustard
1 tablespoon chopped onion
½ lemon, juiced
salt

pepper
½ teaspoon prepared horseradish
6 tablespoons olive oil
1 egg yolk
1 tablespoon chopped parsley
2 teaspoons sour cream

Wash and dry mushrooms. Remove tips from stems and slice. Mix remaining ingredients together. Add mushrooms at the last and serve chilled mixture on lettuce leaves. Serves 2.

**Mrs. Bogan Nathaniel Gist, Jr. (Marguerite)**
**Atlanta**

## FRENCH BEAN SALAD

2 cans green beans
½ cup Wesson Oil
3 tablespoons vinegar
½ teaspoon salt
½ teaspoon pepper
6 tablespoons mayonnaise

2 teaspoons wet mustard
4 teaspoons vinegar
salt and pepper to taste
4 hard-boiled eggs, finely
    chopped

Cook beans about 3 minutes and drain well. Combine beans with Wesson Oil, 3 tablespoons vinegar, salt and pepper. Chill overnight or longer. Mix mayonnaise, mustard, remaining vinegar, salt and pepper. Before serving, drain beans and mix with the sauce. Put a layer of chopped eggs in the middle and on top. Serves about 6.

**Mrs. Jack Passailaigue (Mary R. Flournoy)**
**Columbus**

## GRAPEFRUIT AND SHRIMP

2 grapefruit
1 pound shrimp, cooked and
    cleaned

2 cups Hellman's mayonnaise
4 tablespoons catsup
1 small bottle stuffed olives

Halve grapefruit. Remove seeds and core. Fill center with shrimp and pour sauce made of mayonnaise, catsup and sliced olives, over grapefruit and shrimp. Serves 4.

**Mrs. John Dickey Boardman (Gene Allen)**
**Augusta**

# SHRIMP MOLD

2 tablespoons plain gelatin
1 cup consommé
8 ounces cream cheese
2 cups boiled shrimp, chopped
1 cup celery, chopped
2 pimentos, chopped
    tle capers, drained
    lespoons grated onion

¾ cup mayonnaise
½ cup chili sauce
¼ cup chopped parsley
¼ teaspoon pepper
2 tablespoons lemon juice
2 teaspoons Worcestershire sauce
1 teaspoon salt
2 drops Tabasco sauce

Soften gelatin in ¼ cup consommé. Heat remaining consommé, add softened gelatin, and dissolve. Cool. In a bowl, beat cream cheese and mayonnaise with a wooden spoon until well blended. Add cooled consommé and all the other ingredients. Place in a lightly greased 2 quart ring mold or fish mold. Chill. Serve on lettuce with French dressing. Can be prepared a day in advance. Serves 8.

**Mrs. George W. Cross (Eleanor Irene Calley)**
**Covington, Louisiana**

# CURRIED SHRIMP SALAD

2 pounds picked shrimp
   (cooked)
1 cup diced celery
1 cup sliced water chestnuts

1 cup mayonnaise
2 tablespoons curry powder
2 tablespoons soy sauce

Mix curry and soy sauce into mayonnaise, fold into shrimp, celery and water chestnuts. Serve on bed of Boston lettuce with slices of avocado. Serves 4.

**Mrs. Gerrard Haines, Jr. (Harriette Johnson)**
**Savannah**

# CRAB SALAD

1 pound crabmeat
1¼ cups celery
2 tablespoons mild onion
3 tablespoons light olive oil
1 tablespoon lemon juice

salt, Tabasco, tarragon, parsley to
taste
enough mayonnaise to hold all
together

Mix together all ingredients except mayonnaise. Let stand at least 30 minutes in cool place. Drain off any excess liquid. Mix in mayonnaise. Serves 4.

**Mrs. Kenneth Lasseter (Christine Thesmar)**
**Savannah**

# AVOCADO AND CRABMEAT RING

1½ cups water
3 envelopes unflavored
  gelatin
2 6½ ounce cans crabmeat
  (drained)
1 large ripe avocado
1 cup sour cream
1 cup mayonnaise

3 tablespoons onion, grated
¼ cup thinly sliced celery
1½ teaspoons salt
⅛ teaspoon pepper
⅓ cup lemon juice
2 large tomatoes, sliced
salad greens

Sprinkle gelatin over 1½ cups water in top of double boiler, let stand 5 minutes to soften. Place over hot water and stir until gelatin dissolves. Refrigerate until consistency of unbeaten egg white—about 30 minutes. Remove membranes and flake crabmeat into medium bowl. Peel avocado and cut into chunks that can be pressed through a sieve. Measure 1 cup. Gently toss and mix well the crabmeat with avocado, sour cream, mayonnaise, onion, celery, salt, pepper, and lemon juice. Fold mixture into gelatin until well combined. Turn into 6½ cup ring mold and refrigerate about three hours or until firm. Unmold and surround with salad greens and tomato slices. Serve with mayonnaise or cooked salad dressing if desired. Makes 6 to 8 servings.

**Mrs. John Alston Bracey (Marie Brice)**
**Thomasville**

# MOBILE CRABMEAT SALAD

1 pound crabmeat
¼ cup finely chopped onions
½ teaspoon salt
¼ teaspoon pepper

½ cup Wesson oil
½ cup vinegar
½ cup cold water

Mix all ingredients together and let marinate in refrigerator before using. 4 good servings.

**Mrs. James D. F. Evans (Margaret Bracey)**
**Thomasville**

## CRAB-SHRIMP MOUSSE

1 can Campbell Cream of
  Shrimp Soup
1 cup mayonnaise
2 3-ounce blocks of cream
  cheese
½ teaspoon Worcestershire
  sauce

½ teaspoon salt
1 tablespoon grated onion
¼ pound boiled, deveined shrimp
7 ounces crab meat
2 envelopes plain gelatin
red food coloring

In blender, blend together until smooth, first 6 ingredients. Put in double boiler and add chopped shrimp and crab meat (or shrimp and crab meat can also be blended in blender with other ingredients). Dissolve 2 envelopes of plain gelatin in ¼ cup water, let stand 5 minutes. Dissolve gelatin over low heat and mix with other ingredients. Add few drops of red food coloring. Pour into 5½ cup oiled fish mold. Refrigerate at least 3 hours, preferably over night. Unmold on lettuce. Serve with crackers.

**Mrs. Isaac M. Aiken Jr. (Louise McNeel)**
**Savannah**

## SALMON MOLD

2 cups canned red salmon
½ teaspoon salt
1½ tablespoons sugar
½ tablespoon flour
1 teaspoon mustard
few grains red pepper

2 egg yolks
1½ tablespoons melted butter
¾ cup milk
¼ cup vinegar
¾ tablespoon gelatin
soaked in 2 tablespoons water

In top of double boiler, over hot water, cook the dry ingredients which have been mixed with egg yolks, butter, milk and vinegar. Cook, stirring constantly until thickened. Remove from heat, add soaked gelatin, then flaked salmon. Fill greased mold and chill well. Serve masked with sour cream sprinkled with dill and surrounded with thinly sliced cucumbers.

**Mrs. John Zantzinger Speer (Frances Carter Tanham)**
**Augusta**

# OYSTER MOUSSE

2 envelopes plain Knox gelatin
½ cup water
1 cup mayonnaise
1 8-ounce package cream
  cheese
1 can mushroom soup
1 can smoked oysters, drained
  and mashed

1 teaspoon Worcestershire sauce
2 teaspoons chopped parsley
few drops Tabasco sauce
½ teaspoon garlic powder
few drops red food coloring
  (optional)

Dissolve gelatin in water. Heat mayonnaise and cream cheese in saucepan until cheese melts. (Do not boil as the mayonnaise will separate.) Add all other ingredients and mix well over low heat until gelatin is melted and blended. Pour into greased mold. Chill several hours or over night. Serve with crackers. Makes two small molds or one large one.

**Barbara Bunn Vereen**
**Moultrie**

# SHRIMP NEW ORLEANS

2½ pounds shrimp
¾ cup wine vinegar
1½ tablespoons celery seed
2 slices from a red onion
  in rings

½ cup salad oil
3 tablespoons capers
1½ teaspoons salt
3 drops Tabasco

Cook shrimp in boiling salted water until the shell draws from the curve of the back, about three minutes. Shell, devein, and marinate for several days in a sauce made from the salad oil, vinegar, onion, capers, celery seed, salt, and Tabasco. Serve very cold in the marinade.

**Mrs. Joseph Kenneth Morris (Ann Montgomery Orr)**
**Athens**

## LAYERED LUNCHEON SALAD

6 slices whole wheat bread
3 ounces cream cheese
1 tablespoon anchovy paste
3 medium tomatoes

¼ cup mayonnaise
¼ cup sour cream or plain
　yogurt
6 hard-boiled eggs

Cut bread into rounds. Mix cream cheese and anchovy paste and spread on bread. Top with thick slice of tomato. Mix together mayonnaise, sour cream (or yogurt) and diced whites of eggs. Top tomatoes with this mixture and sprinkle with crumbled egg yolks. Garnish with paprika, parsley and marinated asparagus spears. Serves 6.

**Mrs. Heeth Varnedoe (Claire Flowers)**
**Thomasville**

## CONGEALED HAM SALAD

2 envelopes plain gelatin
½ cup cold water
1½ cups hot chicken stock
1 8-ounce block cream cheese
3 tablespoons lemon juice

1 cup mayonnaise
3 cups ham, chopped
1½ cups celery, diced
1½ cups bell pepper, diced
2 tablespoons onion, grated

Soften gelatin in cold water, dissolve in hot chicken stock. Blend cream cheese with lemon juice and combine. Beat until smooth. Add mayonnaise, ham, celery, bell pepper, and onion. Pour in 6 cup mold and chill until firm. Serves 6.

**Mrs. Alvin M. Ratliff (Frances Lott)**
**Blackshear**

# AVOCADO MOLD

2 cups hot water
½ cup lemon juice
1 very large or 2 small
    avocados
4 fresh tomatoes cut in
    wedges
2 tablespoons sugar

paprika
1 scant tablespoon salt
3 tablespoons gelatin in cold water
    to cover
1 tablespoon grated onion
1 cup chopped onion

Place avocado and tomato wedges artistically around in a mold. Heat the gelatin which has been softened in cold water in the hot water. Add lemon juice, paprika, sugar, salt and onion. Pour this mixture over the avocado and tomato wedges and put in refrigerator to congeal.

Serve with fresh homemade mayonnaise.

**Mrs. Wilbur H. Glenn (Nell Gardiner)**
**Columbus**

# TEA GARDEN SALAD

1 cup hot tea, strong
1 3-ounce package orange Jello
1 8-ounce can crushed
    pineapple

1 11-ounce can mandarin orange
    plugs
1 8-ounce can water chestnuts

Dissolve orange Jello in hot tea. Drain pineapple and oranges, saving the juice. If the juice does not make a cup, add water. Add this cup of liquid to the hot Jello. Cool to consistency of raw egg white. Thinly slice the water chestnuts. Add orange plugs, pineapple and water chestnuts to the cooled Jello mix. Put into mold ( 1 or 1½ quart size) or into individual molds. Chill. Unmold onto lettuce. Serve with mayonnaise or with a dressing of mayonnaise made by adding 1 teaspoon grated orange rind and a little whipped cream to mayonnaise.

**Elise C. Shover**
**Atlanta**

## QUEEN ANNE CHERRY FRUIT SALAD

1 cup Queen Anne cherries,
   pitted
½ cup crushed pineapple
1 3-ounce size box lemon Jello
1 cup hot pineapple juice

1½ cups gingerale
½ envelope plain gelatin
1 tablespoon crystallized ginger
½ cup slivered almonds
¼ cup cold water

Dissolve the plain gelatin in ¼ cup cold water. Add the hot pineapple juice to the lemon Jello and the dissolved plain gelatin. Stir until well mixed. Cool. Add the cherries, pineapple, crystallized ginger, almonds and gingerale. Pour into an 8 cup mold and chill. Especially good served with chicken salad. Serves 8.

**Mrs. James H. Lawrence (Virginia Sheppard)**
**Waycross**

## FROZEN FRUIT SALAD

4 egg yolks
4 tablespoons vinegar
4 tablespoons sugar
1 pound marshmallows
4 slices canned pineapple

1 bottle maraschino cherries
4 bananas
1 package dates
1 cup pecans, chopped
1 pint of whipped cream

Cook first three ingredients in double boiler until creamy. Add marshmallows and stir until blended. When cool add the fruit and nuts. Add whipped cream and freeze. Serve on lettuce.

**Mrs. Marvin Perry, Jr. (Ellen Gilliam)**
**Atlanta**

# CIDER MOLD SALAD

3 3-ounce packages orange
   Jello
2 large apples, cored and
   cubed

6¼ cups apple cider (divided)
½ cup seedless white raisins
½ cup chopped walnuts or pecans

Dissolve Jello in 2 cups of boiling apple cider, mixing well. Then add 4 cups cold cider. Chill until gelatin mixture is slightly congealed. Soak raisins in ¼ cup cider for 30 minutes, drain. Add raisins, apples, and nuts to gelatin mixture; mix lightly. Pour into a 2½ quart mold and chill until firm. Yields 10 to 12 servings.

**Mrs. Jesse Lyle Parrott (Nancy Rutledge Wainer)**
**Hahira**

# MAYONNAISE

1 quart safflower (or corn) oil
5 egg yolks
2 whole eggs
½ cup lemon juice (can use
   Minute Maid frozen lemon
   juice)

1 tablespoon salt
2 teaspoons paprika
¼ teaspoon Tabasco sauce

This must be an uninterrupted process of continuous beating in a mixer or with electric hand beater. Have all ingredients measured and available before beginning.

Beat egg yolks and whole eggs until light yellow. Add paprika, salt, Tabasco. Add 1 teaspoon of the measured lemon juice. Beat until blended. Add oil, drizzling slowly, about ¼-⅓ cup at a time. Continually use a rubber spatula to scrape mixture off sides into the mixing bowl. When all oil has been added and blended thoroughly in a smooth, glossy mixture, add remaining lemon juice all at once. Do not panic over the change in consistency. Keep beating until mixture is once again thick and glossy. This recipe is less thick in hot weather, but is nevertheless delicious. Makes about 1 quart plus 1 cup.

**Mrs. Lloyd Guyton Bowers (Effie Campbell Siegling)**
**Columbus**

## COOKED DRESSING FOR CHICKEN SALAD

2 eggs, well-beaten
⅔ cup sugar
2 level tablespoons flour
½ cup vinegar

½ cup water
½ teaspoon salt
¼ stick of oleo or butter

Beat eggs, mix with sugar. Dissolve flour in water, add along with vinegar to the eggs and sugar. Add salt. Cook over medium heat, stirring constantly until it thickens. Remove from heat—add butter. Cool before mixing with chicken.

**Mrs. John Franklin Beard (Mary Huber)**
**Moultrie**

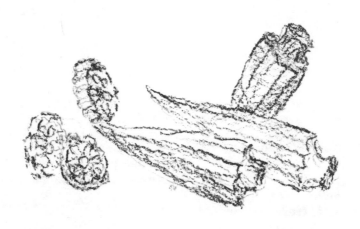

## "GRETA" SAUCE FOR GREEN SALAD

1 large bud garlic, minced
1 tablespoon salt
1 tablespoon black pepper
2 tablespoons sugar

¼ cup vinegar
½ cup catsup
½ cup salad oil

Mix and store in refrigerator indefinitely.

**Mrs. Frank Turpin, Jr. (Sarah Walker Wise)**
**Americus**

## RECTOR'S FRENCH DRESSING

2 teaspoons salt
1 teaspoon black pepper
1 teaspoon paprika
½ teaspoon confectioners'
  sugar

1 shake cayenne pepper
½ teaspoon onion juice
1 cup olive oil
⅓ cup vinegar

Rub a wooden bowl with a clove of garlic. Rub together all ingredients except oil and vinegar into the bowl. Drip oil slowly into the bowl, stirring all the time until all ingredients are thoroughly emulsed. Drip the vinegar into the bowl slowly, stirring vigorously. Best if used the same day you make it.

**Mrs. Wilder G. Little (Peggy Anne Elder)**
**Marietta**

## TOMATO FRENCH DRESSING

1 teaspoon dry mustard
2 teaspoons salt
2 teaspoons paprika
1 can condensed tomato
  soup
1½ cups Wesson oil

¾ cup sugar
¾ cup vinegar
2 teaspoons minced onion
2 garlic cloves
1 lemon, juiced

Put all ingredients in jar and shake well. Makes one quart.

**Mrs. Charles H. Werner (Elizabeth Cox)**
**Atlanta**

## SEA ISLAND FRENCH DRESSING

½ cup sugar (or a little less)
½ cup vinegar
1 teaspoon salt
1 teaspoon dry mustard

1 small onion, grated
1 cup Wesson oil
1 tablespoon poppy seed

Combine and chill. This is good on fruit salads.

**Mrs. Henry D. Green (Fran Yates)**
**Brunswick**

# SALAD DRESSING

½ cup mayonnaise
¼ cup sour cream
2 tablespoons wine vinegar
1 tablespoon lemon juice

2 teaspoons anchovy paste
¼ cup chopped parsley
½ cup chopped green onion

Mix ingredients thoroughly with a fork and refrigerate.

**Mrs. Julian A. Space (Margaret McGowan)**
**Savannah**

# ANCHOVY DRESSING FOR WATERCRESS

4 ounces cream cheese
½ cup mayonnaise
1 tablespoon vinegar
1 tablespoon olive oil

salt and pepper to taste
2 flat fillets of anchovy
¼ cup minced celery

Mix everything but celery in blender. Add celery, stirring by hand. Serve over fresh watercress. Pick your own if possible. Serves 4-6.

**Mrs. James Dickson Maddox (Rebecca Wall)**
**Rome**

# Breads and Sandwiches

Mary F. Passailaigue

## WHOLE WHEAT-BRAN MUFFINS

1 cup water, boiling
1 cup All-Bran cereal
1 cup vegetable shortening
¾ cup sugar
1½ teaspoons salt

2 packages yeast
1 cup warm water
2 eggs
6 cups flour (3 cups plain white and
    3 cups whole wheat—sifted)

Pour one cup boiling water over 1 cup All-Bran cereal, 1 cup vegetable shortening, ¾ cup sugar and 1½ teaspoons salt. Stir mixture until shortening is well distributed and melted. Let mixture cool. Dissolve 2 packages yeast in 1 cup warm water. Add yeast to mixture. Add 2 eggs, slightly beaten. Stir in flour. Both regular white flour and whole wheat flour should be sifted prior to measuring. Grease the top of mixture with melted margarine and refrigerate four hours or overnight. Remove about ⅓ of mixture from bowl. Knead on floured board until dough is elastic, and not sticky. Roll out to about ⅓ inch thick and cut into rounds. Form into rolls. Place on buttered cookie sheet. Cover with tea towel and allow to rise in warm place for approximately 2 hours. Bake in preheated oven at 400 degrees about 8 minutes until partially done. Remove from oven, allow to cool. Place in Ziploc freezer bags and freeze, if desired. If to be served immediately, allow rolls to bake until brown and serve.

**Mrs. Candler Shumway (Frances Candler)**
**Madison**

## NUT BREAD

1 cup nuts, chopped
2 cups flour
1 cup milk
½ cup water
3 teaspoons baking powder

1 teaspoon butter
¼ teaspoon salt
1 cup raisins
1 cup sugar
2 eggs

Beat sugar, eggs, butter together. Add nuts, then milk, flour and water. Put in well-greased loaf pan. Bake in slow oven (300 degrees) for 45 minutes.

**Martha Miller**
**Augusta**

# BLUEBERRY PANCAKES

| | |
|---|---|
| 1 egg | ¼ teaspoon salt |
| 1 cup milk | ½ teaspoon mace |
| 2 tablespoons sour cream | 1 tablespoon sugar |
| 1 cup flour | 1 tablespoon baking powder |
| 2 tablespoons butter, melted | 1 cup blueberries |

In a small bowl, whisk together egg, milk, and sour cream. Into a larger bowl, sift together flour, salt, mace, sugar, and baking powder. Into this flour mixture pour the liquid and beat well with wire whisk or eggbeater. Add the two tablespoons of melted and cooled butter and stir until mixed. If you like pancakes thin, add a bit more milk, perhaps ¼ cup. Fold in blueberries. Drop batter by large spoonfuls onto hot, lightly greased griddle. Brown on one side, turn and brown on the other; turn only once.

The batter is light and delicious even without the blueberries. Serve with plenty of fresh butter and maple syrup in generous pitcherfuls. This recipe makes about a dozen pancakes.

**Mrs. Archibald Little Griffin (Alma Lee Whitfield)**
**Valdosta**

# BLUEBERRY MUFFINS

| | |
|---|---|
| ¼ cup shortening (part butter) | ⅓ cup sugar |
| 1 egg | ½ teaspoon salt |
| 1½ cups flour, sifted before measuring | 3 teaspoons baking powder |
| ½ cup milk | 1 cup blueberries |

Cream shortening and sugar. Beat well. Add egg and beat well again. Sift together flour, baking powder and salt and add alternately with the milk. Grease and flour lightly two 2-inch muffin tins of twelve muffins each. Spoon batter into the tins. Bake in a pre-heated oven of 375 degrees for about twenty minutes.

**Mrs. Greene Flournoy Johnson (Caroline Lovell)**
**Athens**

# CRANBERRY BREAD

2 cups flour
½ teaspoon salt
½ teaspoon soda
1½ teaspoons baking
  powder
1 cup sugar
1 egg beaten

2 tablespoons butter, melted
½ cup orange juice
2 tablespoons hot water
½ cup pecans, chopped
grated rind ½ orange
1 cup cranberries, chopped

Sift dry ingredients. Add egg, butter, orange juice, hot water, and mix until moistened. Fold in pecans, cranberries, and orange rind. Bake in greased loaf pan for 1 hour and 10 minutes in a 350 degree oven. Ripen 24 hours.

**Mrs. Shelby Myrick Jr. (Alice Barrow)**
**Savannah**

# SPOON BREAD

1 cup cooked hominy (grits)
1 cup corn meal
2½ cups milk
1 teaspoon salt

1 teaspoon sugar
1 teaspoon bacon grease
3 eggs, separated

Melt bacon grease in baking pan in oven preheated to 400 degrees. Sift meal, salt and sugar into milk and boil a minute or two until meal thickens. Stir in hominy grits. Add beaten egg yolks and fold in stiffly beaten egg whites. Bake 40 minutes in oven at 350 degrees. Serves 6.

**Mrs. Lee Adler (Emma Walthour Morel)**
**Savannah**

# CORN LIGHT BREAD

2 cups meal
1 cup flour
¼ teaspoon soda
½ cup sugar
1 egg

½ cup cooking oil
1 teaspoon baking powder
1 teaspoon salt
2 cups buttermilk

Grease loaf pan (9¾x5¾x2¾). Sprinkle with meal. Mix ingredients in the order given. Cook 1 hour at 350 degrees.

**Mrs. J. Mack Barnes (Betty Newton)**
**Jekyll Island**

## LETTY'S CORN BREAD, MUFFINS OR CORN STICKS

1 cup corn meal
⅓ cup plain flour
½ tablespoon sugar
1 teaspoon baking powder
½ teaspoon salt

½ cup milk
½ cup water
1 egg
2 tablespoons bacon drippings

Sift meal and flour together. Mix all ingredients and pour into well greased muffin molds or stick molds. Bake in hot oven 450 degrees for 15 to 20 minutes.

**Mrs. Ralph B. Willis, Jr. (Lillian Neely)**
**Augusta**

## BATTER BREAD

2 cups milk
2 eggs
1 cup corn meal

3 tablespoons butter
1 teaspoon salt
1 teaspoon sugar

Warm milk in double boiler. Add meal and stir until thick mush. Add sugar and salt. Break egg yolks and whites separately. Pour batter into beaten yellows. Fold in beaten whites. Pour batter into greased baking dish. Bake at 375 degrees for 45 minutes. Serves 3.

**Mrs. Lawrence Hand (Nell Hammond)**
**Thomasville**

## SALLY LUNN

2 cups flour
4 teaspoons Rumford baking
   powder
2 eggs

1 cup sweet milk
½ cup margarine
½ cup sugar
¾ teaspoon salt

Cream margarine and sugar together, until well blended. Beat the eggs and then add beaten eggs and milk, gradually, alternating with flour which has been sifted with baking powder and salt.

Bake in oblong 10-inch pan at 350 degrees for 20 minutes. Grease and flour pan—or use PAM. Cut in squares to serve.

**Mrs. James I. Garrard (Sarah Hearn)**
**Milledgeville**

# CUISINART ITALIAN RYE BREAD

3½-4½ cups unbleached flour
1 cup rye flour
1 tablespoon salt
1 tablespoon sugar
½ stick butter
½ teaspoon fennel or caraway
 seeds

2 packages active dry yeast
1¾ cups very warm water
cornmeal
corn or vegetable oil
1 tablespoon cold water
1 egg
1 teaspoon dill weed

With metal blade in place, add rye flour, 2 cups unbleached flour, and next five ingredients to bowl of food processor. Turn machine on and off rapidly 2 or 3 times until butter is thoroughly cut into dry ingredients. Add half the water and turn the processor on and off 4 times. Add 1½ cups flour and remaining water. Repeat on/off turns 4 times, then let processor run until a ball of dough forms on the blades. If the dough is too sticky (wet), add remaining water. Turn dough on to lightly floured board and knead several times to form a smooth ball. Cover with plastic wrap and a towel. Let rest for 20 minutes. Divide dough in half. Roll each half into an oblong 15x20 inches. Beginning at wide side, roll tightly. Pinch seam to seal and taper ends by rolling gently back and forth. Place on greased baking sheets sprinkled with corn meal. Brush dough with corn oil. Cover loosely with plastic wrap. Refrigerate 2 to 24 hours.

When ready to bake, remove from refrigerator. Uncover dough carefully and let stand at room temperature for 10 minutes. Make 3 or 4 cuts on top of each loaf with edge of metal blade or knife. Brush with egg beaten with cold water and dill weed and bake in 420 degree oven for 25 to 30 minutes until golden brown. Cool on wire rack. Makes 2 loaves.

**Mrs. Lloyd Summer, Jr. (Virginia Barron)**
**Rome**

# OATMEAL MUFFINS

| | |
|---|---|
| 1 cup oatmeal | ½ cup salad oil |
| 1 cup buttermilk | 1 cup unbleached flour |
| 1 egg | ½ teaspoon soda |
| ½ cup brown sugar | 1 teaspoon baking powder |
| ¼ teaspoon salt | |

Soak oatmeal in milk for 5 minutes. Add egg and beat. Add sugar and oil and beat. Add other ingredients and stir only until mixed. Batter should be lumpy. Fill greased 12-cup muffin tin ⅔ full and bake at 400 degrees for 15 to 20 minutes.

**Mrs. William Willis Anderson, Jr. (Sallie Gaillard Mixon)**
**Atlanta**

# WHOLE WHEAT MUFFINS

| | |
|---|---|
| ⅓ cup flour | 1 egg |
| ⅔ cup whole wheat flour | ¾ cup milk |
| 2 teaspoons baking powder | 3 teaspoons sugar |
| ½ teaspoon salt | 3 tablespoons oil |

Mix white flour and whole wheat flour, sugar, baking powder and salt together. Beat egg. Add milk and dry ingredients alternately to egg. Mix thoroughly with egg beater. Add oil and mix thoroughly again. Fill greased muffin pans ⅔ full and bake in 450 degree oven for 12 minutes for small muffins—15 minutes for large muffins.

**Mrs. Remer Lane (Louise Harris)**
**Savannah**

# WHEAT GERM MUFFINS

| | |
|---|---|
| 1½ cups sifted flour | ¼ cup brown sugar |
| 3 teaspoons baking powder | 1 egg |
| ½ teaspoon salt | 1 cup milk |
| ¾ cup wheat germ | ¼ cup salad oil |

Into mixing bowl, sift flour, baking powder and salt. Add wheat germ and mix well. In another mixing bowl, beat sugar and egg until frothy. Add milk and salad oil; mix well. Pour this mixture into flour mixture. Stir lightly until just mixed *(do not beat)*. Fill 18 well-greased muffin cups ½ full. Bake in 375 degree oven for 15 minutes or until brown.

**Mrs. James Clyde Mixon (Elizabeth Edwards Gaillard)**
**Atlanta**

# CORN PONES

¼ teaspoon soda
1 teaspoon salt
1 cup buttermilk

1½ cups cornmeal
1½ tablespoons fat
1½ teaspoons sugar

Mix together and let stand for at least one hour. Shape into pones with spoon. Place on hot greased skillet and bake in 350 degree oven until golden brown.

**Mrs. John Archie Cauble (Florence Horkan)**
**Canton**

# SOUR CREAM CORNBREAD

1 cup self-rising cornmeal
½ cup creamed corn
2 eggs, slightly beaten

¼ cup cooking oil
1 cup sour cream

Mix cornmeal and oil. Beat in eggs. Beat in sour cream. Add creamed corn. Turn into a very hot iron skillet, generously greased with bacon grease. Bake at 350 degrees for a half hour or more until well done. This is a very good cornbread, half way between the very crisp, very brown usual cornbread and spoonbread, since it is very light but can be cut in slices.

**Mrs. Aaron Newton Bowers (Mary Stark Davison)**
**Athens**

# WAFFLES DE LUXE

1 cup flour, sifted
¼ teaspoon salt
½ cup milk
½ cup water
4 teaspoons baking powder

1 tablespoon sugar
6 tablespoons oil
1 egg yolk
1 egg white

Beat together flour, salt, milk, water, sugar, oil and egg yolk. Fold in beaten egg white (until stiff). And lastly beat in 4 teaspoons baking powder. If batter seems too thick add a little cold water.

**Mrs. N. Nesbit Teague (Claire Ellis)**
**Augusta**

# SWEET POTATO BISCUITS

1½ cups sweet potatoes,
  mashed
6 rounded tablespoons of
  shortening

2½ cups flour
2 teaspoons baking powder
⅓ cup of sugar
1 teaspoon of salt

In a medium-sized bowl stir together the flour, baking powder, salt, and sugar. Add the sweet potato blended with shortening. If dough is very sticky, add flour sparingly. Roll out biscuits on floured board ½ inch thick. With a floured round 2-inch cutter, cut out biscuits. Place slightly apart on an ungreased cookie sheet. Bake in a preheated 450 degree oven until browned—15 to 18 minutes. Serve with butter.

**Mrs. T. Miesse Baumgardner (Lauretta King)**
**Brunswick**

# WHIPPED CREAM BISCUITS

2 cups all-purpose flour
3 teaspoons baking powder

1 cup heavy cream, stiffly whipped
¾ teaspoon salt

Sift the flour, baking powder, and salt together in a bowl. With a fork, mix in the whipped cream. Turn out the mixture on a lightly floured board, and knead it lightly for about 1 minute. Pat or roll the dough out about ⅓ inch thick, and cut with a 1½ inch biscuit cutter. Prick each biscuit with the tines of a fork. Put the biscuits on an ungreased baking sheet, and bake in a hot (425 degree) oven for 10 to 12 minutes, or until they are pale gold.

**Miss Frances Huguenin Ellis**
**Columbus**

# POPOVERS

1 cup Wondra flour
1 cup milk
2 eggs

½ teaspoon salt
1 tablespoon melted butter

Mix flour, milk, eggs, salt and butter in a bowl. Do not be concerned about lumpiness. Grease 5 custard cups with unsalted shortening. Place on cookie sheet and distribute mixture equally between cups (approximately ⅔ full). Place in cold oven. Turn oven to 425 degrees and cook 40 to 50 minutes, until brown. Serve immediately.

**Mrs. Alexander Lawrence Cann (Mary Gatewood)**
**Savannah**

# BISCUITS

2 cups flour
4 teaspoons baking powder
1 teaspoon sugar
1 teaspoon salt

½ teaspoon cream of tartar
½ cup butter or margarine
½ cup milk

Sift dry ingredients. Add butter and cut in until mixture resembles coarse crumbs. Add milk all at once and stir together. Pat out on a floured surface ½ inch or more thick. Cut and bake at 325-350 degrees for 15 minutes.

**Mrs. William B. Hardagree (Eleanor Glenn)**
**Columbus**

# CREAM CHEESE BISCUITS

½ cup butter
1 cup Bisquick

¼ pound cream cheese

Let stand at room temperature to soften. Mix and roll out thin using ¼ cup flour on bread board to keep from sticking. Cut size of 50¢ piece. Bake until brown, about ½ hour at 350 degrees. Serves 8.

**Mrs. Henry D. Stevens III (Ann Stovall)**
**Savannah**

# CRUMPETS OR FEATHER BEDS

2 eggs
3 tablespoons sugar
2 cups milk
1 package yeast

½ cup margarine or butter
1 tablespoon salt
4½ to 5 cups flour

Beat eggs well. Melt butter or margarine. Warm milk a little. Dissolve yeast in warmed milk, add sugar and salt. Add eggs, then add flour a little at the time, using a wooden spoon. Use enough flour to make dough stiff enough to drop from spoon. Add melted margarine or butter last. Cover dough in large bowl and let rise in warm place until doubled. When doubled push the dough down and put in greased muffin tins. Let rise again. Bake in 425 degree oven until browned.

**Mrs. Carlus Howard Griffin (Katherine Martica Saunders)**
**Valdosta**

# REFRIGERATOR ROLLS

6 cups flour
2 packages yeast
2 eggs
2 cups water

½ cup sugar
1 teaspoon salt
½ cup shortening (Crisco)

Dissolve yeast in 1 cup lukewarm water. Boil 1 cup water and dissolve sugar, salt and shortening in it. Cool until lukewarm. Add yeast mixture and well beaten eggs. Stir in flour and beat well. Refrigerate over night, or several hours. Shape into rolls and let rise 1 hour before cooking. Bake at 400 degrees for about 15 minutes. Makes 140 rolls.

You can partially cook rolls, cool, then freeze. Take out and brown before serving. Sometimes, I use half whole wheat flour and half white flour for whole wheat rolls.

Sometimes, I put half the dough in a regular size bread pan, let rise until doubled, bake at 400 degrees for a nice loaf of bread.

**Mrs. Henry Green (Mary Frances Yates)**
**Brunswick**

# CRUSTY FRENCH BREAD

5 to 5½ cups unbleached
 flour
1 tablespoon sugar
3 teaspoons salt

2 packages dry yeast
2 cups warm water
2 tablespoons shortening
1 tablespoon baking powder

Combine 2 cups flour, sugar, salt and dry yeast. Add warm water and shortening. Beat with fork until smooth. Stir in remaining flour to form stiff dough. Knead about 5 to 10 minutes. Place in greased bowl, turn dough to coat all sides. Cover with a damp cloth and let rise in warm place for 1 to 1½ hours; or until doubled in bulk. Punch down and then form into loaves; 2 long loaves, 2 bread pan size or 16 small loaves. Let rise about 45 minutes. Brush with 1 tablespoon water mixed with 1 egg white, slightly beaten.

Bake in 375 degree oven for 45 minutes for large loaf; 25 minutes for small loaf.

**Mrs. Quealy Walker (Lucile Gillican)**
**Brunswick**

# BANANA BREAD

1 cup sugar
½ cup butter/margarine
2 eggs
3 ripe bananas
1 teaspoon soda (level)

1½ cups flour
¼ teaspoon salt (optional)
1 teaspoon vanilla
1 cup nuts (optional)

Cream butter and sugar. Add eggs one at a time. Add vanilla and flour. Beat together bananas, soda, and nuts. Add this mixture last. Bake slowly at 325 degrees for 45 minutes. Use 2 loaf pans (4½-inch by 9-inch) greased and lined with waxed paper.

**Mrs. John L. Wright, Jr. (Frances H.)**
**Atlanta**

# BANANA FRITTERS

2 or 3 bananas
1 egg
1 cup flour

½ teaspoon baking powder
pinch salt
⅔ cup milk

Beat egg with milk. Stir into flour, which has been mixed with baking powder and salt. Cut bananas into halves lengthwise, then into pieces about 1½ inches long. Drop banana into batter to coat thoroughly. Drop by spoonfuls into deep, hot oil.* Fry until golden brown, drain on paper towel, serve piping hot. These may be used as a vegetable, or, sprinkled with powdered sugar, as a dessert. Serves 3-4.

*If cooked in a frying pan have oil at least 1½ to 2 inches deep; follow directions for a deep-fat fryer.

**Mrs. Albert Sidney Britt, Jr. (Annie McIntosh)**
**Savannah**

# ST. HELENA WHOLE WHEAT BREAD

3 packages yeast
2 tablespoons sugar
2 tablespoons salt
4 tablespoons honey
2 tablespoons bacon grease
1 quart warm (not hot) water

2 eggs, beaten
100% whole wheat flour, approximately 3 pounds (may take a little more in damp weather)

In a large (several gallon) mixing bowl, put yeast, sugar, salt, honey, bacon grease, water and eggs. Beat with French whip. Add flour gradually. 2 cups at a time, beating after each addition. As batter becomes too stiff for a whip, change to a large spoon. When batter is stiff enough to form a ball, remove to a large flat area for kneading (I use a large cutting board, but a clean counter-top is adequate). Place dough on 1 cup of flour and cover with one cup of flour. Knead, adding flour as necessary until dough is no longer sticky and can be handled. Place in greased bowl and cover with a damp dish towel. Allow to rise in a draft-free area until doubled in bulk (1½ to 2 hours). Divide into four pieces, shape and place in four, 1 pound bread pans, greased. Cover and let rise for 45 minutes. Bake at 350 degrees for 45 minutes. Makes 4 loaves.

**Mrs. John Angell (Ashby Lippitt)**
**Savannah**

# FLUFFY PANCAKES

3 eggs
1½ cups buttermilk
1 teaspoon soda

1½ cups self-rising flour
1 teaspoon sugar
3 tablespoons margarine, melted

Separate 3 eggs. Whip whites and set aside. Beat yolks until thick and fluffy, then add buttermilk and soda. Sift and beat in self-rising flour. Add sugar. Beat in margarine. Fold in beaten egg whites. Cook on preheated griddle. Left-overs may be frozen and reheated.

**Mrs. William E. Johnson (Nancy Hale)**
**Rome**

## CHEESE PIMENTO BREAD

1½ cups milk
2 tablespoons sugar
¼ cup butter or margarine
2 teaspoons salt
1 teaspoon coarse pepper
2 packages dry yeast
1 teaspoon sugar
½ cup warm water

2 eggs plus 1 egg yolk
1½ cups sharp Cheddar cheese,
  shredded
½ cup pimento, finely chopped
1 teaspoon powdered thyme
½ teaspoon powdered marjoram
about 7 cups plain flour

Scald the milk, cook to lukewarm. Dissolve the yeast in the warm water. Add 1 teaspoon sugar. Let stand in a warm place until bubbling. Put into large bowl 3 cups flour, 2 tablespoons sugar, milk, yeast mixture. Beat well. Add two eggs, the soft butter, pimento and spices. Mix well. Add enough flour to make a soft dough. Stir until the dough clears the bowl. Spread a cup of flour on the pastry board. Knead well, adding flour as needed. Flatten the dough with the hands. Spread ½ cup of cheese over the dough. Roll up and flatten again. Repeat until all cheese is worked into dough. Knead again to evenly distribute the cheese. Return the dough to the bowl. Grease the top of the dough. Cover and let rise until doubled.

Turn out, knead down and cut into 6 equal pieces. Roll into even strips, tapering at each end. Lay 3 strips of each on two greased cookie sheets. Start in the middle and braid the strips to each end, pressing the ends down lightly. Cover with a light barely damp towel and let rise again until light.

Brush tops of braids with egg yolk beaten with 2 tablespoons water. Preheat oven to 350 degrees. Cook for 20 minutes. Reduce heat to 325 degrees and continue to bake for 25 minutes. Brush again with egg wash about 5 minutes before end of baking period. Immediately turn out of pans on to wire rack. Let cool completely before slicing.

This bread may also be baked in two 5 inch x 9 inch loaf pans. Bake at 375 degrees for 35 minutes. Brush the tops of the loaves with egg wash before baking and just before removing from the oven.

**Mrs. Leo Smith (Dorothy Quillian)**
**Waycross**

## GEORGIA RAMBLE PIMENTO CHEESE SPREAD

8 ounces sharp Cheddar cheese
1 cup mayonnaise
1 teaspoon grated onion

½ teaspoon Worcestershire sauce
⅛ teaspoon salt
2 tablespoons chopped pimento

Grate and mash cheese. Mix with other ingredients. Enough for 7½ healthy sandwiches.

**Mrs. Langdon Strong Flowers (Margaret Powell)**
**Thomasville**

# BENEDICTINE CUCUMBER SANDWICHES

1 large package Philadelphia
cream cheese
1 large cucumber or 2 small
cucumbers

1 large onion
4 drops of green food coloring
mayonnaise (preferably
home-made)

Peel cucumber and slice thin. Peel onion and slice thin. Place them in salted, vinegar water for 2 hours, then remove from water. Grind or put in blender and then pour off all liquid. Add this mixture to softened cream cheese to which has been added about 4 tablespoons of home-made mayonnaise. Color this mixture with green food coloring—not too much color.

Cut slices of bread with round cutter. Spread both sides with mayonnaise and spread filling on bottom half.

**Mrs. Gordon MacGregor (Mary Bacon Bland)**
**Brunswick**

# ASPARAGUS ROLL UP SANDWICH

1 loaf very thin sliced sandwich
bread
1 can small green asparagus
1 8-ounce package cream
cheese

1 6-ounce jar Roquefort cheese or
1 6-ounce package Roquefort
cheese
1 tablespoon Hellman's
mayonnaise
1 whole egg (beaten)

Cut crusts from slices of bread and roll each slice, smooth with rolling pin. Mix two cheeses and mayonnaise well. Add beaten egg—mix well. Drain asparagus on towel paper. Spread mixture on each slice of bread. Spread all the way to edges. (This will make roll stick.) Place 1 asparagus spear on each slice. Roll like jelly roll. Smooth edges of rolls and ends. Cut each roll into 3 pieces. Brush with melted butter. Toast in 350° oven until light brown.

Note: These freeze well in tupperware box. Do not toast until ready to serve.

**Mrs. Forman Dismukes (Florence Barber)**
**Brunswick**

# SPUTNIK SANDWICH

2 slices bread                    soft butter or margarine
1 egg                             1 slice tomato
sharp Cheddar cheese

Put cheese between 2 slices of bread. Butter outside of top slice and cut middle out of sandwich with biscuit cutter. Place sandwich with hole in it in skillet in which has been melted 2 tablespoons butter. Break egg and place in hole. When egg sets on bottom, flip. Fry until soft set. Small circle may be fried the same way and placed on a tomato slice to be served beside large sandwich.

**Mrs. Lloyd Langston Summer, Jr. (Virginia Gordon Barron)**
**Rome**

# SHRIMP SANDWICHES

1 loaf sandwich bread cut in      milk to soften cheese
   rounds                         dash of Tabasco
1 pound package of frozen         dash of Worcestershire sauce
   shrimp                         salt to taste
1 8-ounce package cream           paprika
   cheese                         parsley (fresh)
1 teaspoon grated onion

Cook shrimp. Start cooking in cold water, let boil one minute. Drain and put in bowl of ice. Put in blender when cold and grind fine. Mix cream cheese with milk until it is the consistency of cream soup. Season with salt, onion, dash of Tabasco and Worcestershire sauce. Mix well. Add shrimp to cream cheese mixture. Mix well. Spread on bread rounds. Spread rather thick. Put dash of paprika on each sandwich and sprig of parsley in middle of each sandwich. Serve open face.

**Mrs. Forman Dismukes (Florence Barber)**
**Brunswick**

## SANDWICH SPREAD

8-ounce package cream
   cheese, softened

½ cup grated pecans or almonds
orange marmalade

Mix softened cream cheese with nuts and enough marmalade to give spreading consistency (about 3 ounces). Use as much rind as possible for flavor. Drain off some of the jelly part or it may be too runny. Spread on very thin bread (trimmed). Cut in finger sandwiches.

**Mrs. Dan M. Hicky (Hattie Mina Reid)**
**Madison**

## HOT TUNA SANDWICH

4 English muffins, split (not
   cut)
¼ pound Swiss cheese, cubed
1 cup tuna chunks
2 tablespoons green pepper,
   diced

2 hard-boiled eggs, chopped
2 tablespoons onions, diced
3 tablespoons olives, chopped
¼ cup chopped celery
½ cup mayonnaise
¼ cup mustard (Dijon)

Mix all ingredients together (except English muffins). Spread on the muffins and bake in 425 degree oven until hot and cheese is melted. Serves 4 for lunch.

**Mrs. Clayton Pierce Boardman, Jr. (Ann Carter Burdell)**
**Augusta**

# WAFFLES

2 cups flour
4 teaspoons baking powder
2 teaspoons sugar
1 teaspoon salt

1 cup water
⅓ cup sweet milk
1 egg
½ cup Wesson oil

Sift dry ingredients together, add milk and water. Break in egg and mix, then add oil.

**Mrs. Edward Vason Jones (Maria Martin)**
**Albany**

# JASMINE TEA BREAD

2 cups sugar
½ cup butter or margarine
2 eggs, lightly beaten
grated rind of two oranges
grated rind of one lemon
grated rind of one lime
6 cups flour

2 teaspoons baking powder
2 teaspoons baking soda
1 teaspoon salt
½ teaspoon cinnamon
1½ cups orange juice
1 cup jasmine tea
1 cup chopped pecan nuts

In a bowl combine the sugar and butter until light. Add eggs and the orange, lemon and lime rinds. Into a bowl sift together the flour, baking powder, baking soda, salt and cinnamon. Add the flour mixture to the butter mixture alternately with the orange juice and jasmine tea combined, beating well after each addition. Add the nuts and combine the batter well. Turn into four well buttered 7x3x2 inch pans or two well buttered 9x5x3 inch pans. Bake the loaves in 350 degree oven until skewer comes out clean, which is approximately forty minutes for the smaller pans. Allow bread to cool in pans for 10 minutes, then turn out on wire rack to cool. Freezes well.

**Ellen Merry**
**Augusta**

# Desserts and Pies

Mary F. Passailaigue

## ALMOND PUDDING

3⅓ cups confectioners' sugar
5 eggs, beaten well
1 teaspoon vanilla extract
1 cup almonds, toasted and
    chopped

1 cup butter
1½ teaspoons almond extract
½ pound graham cracker crumbs
vanilla ice cream

Mix crumbs and almonds. Spread one-half of the mixture in a nine-by-fifteen-inch pan. Cream the sugar and butter and eggs with the extracts. Press the mixture onto and over the crumbs. Spread the remaining graham cracker crumbs and almonds over the top. Press in firmly. Place in refrigerator for at least twenty-four hours or in the freezer for eight hours. Serve topped with vanilla ice cream with a few crumbs sprinkled on top.

**Mrs. George Burnley Vest (Roberta Selph Henry)**
**Athens**

## FLOATING ISLAND

1 quart whole milk
4 eggs
6 tablespoons sugar
1 tablespoon rum

½ gallon vanilla ice cream
1 cup crumbled almond
    macaroons, or
½ cup toasted crushed almonds

Put milk in top of double boiler. Heat over medium-low heat until warm. Beat eggs and sugar in a large bowl. Pour the warm milk into the eggs and sugar mixture while stirring. Return the milk, eggs, and sugar mixture to the top of the double boiler. Cook while stirring constantly until it coats a spoon. Remove from heat at once and put the top boiler in cold water to cool quickly. Continue stirring until cold. Add 1 tablespoon of rum. Serve the custard over a scoop of vanilla ice cream topped with toasted (crushed) almond macaroon cookies. Or top with crushed toasted almonds. Serves 10 to 12 people.

**Mrs. William Wallace Gravely (Frances Poole)**
**Thomasville**

## ERLINE'S FOUR-LAYER DESSERT

1 stick margarine
1 cup flour
¼ teaspoon salt
1 cup chopped pecans
1 8-ounce package cream
 cheese
2 small cartons Cool Whip, or
 ½ pint cream, whipped
½ cup roasted, salted, diced
 almonds (optional)
1 cup confectioners' sugar

1 teaspoon vanilla
pinch of salt
chocolate pudding as follows:*
½ cup sugar plus 1 tablespoon
3 tablespoons cornstarch
⅓ cup cocoa
¼ teaspoon salt
2½ cups milk
1½ teaspoons vanilla

1st layer:
Melt margarine, add flour, salt (¼ teaspoon) and nuts. Spread over bottom of 13-inch x 9-inch pan. Bake 15 minutes in 350 degree oven. Cool.

2nd layer:
Cream cheese and sugar with mixer until fluffy, adding 1 teaspoon vanilla and pinch of salt. Add one small Cool Whip and spread on 1st layer.

3rd layer:*
Prepare chocolate pudding for this layer as follows: mix sugar, cornstarch, cocoa and salt; add milk gradually to blend. Cook over medium heat until mixture thickens, stirring constantly. Add vanilla. Allow to cool slightly and spread on 2nd layer.

4th layer:
Cover with 1 small carton of Cool Whip and refrigerate.
Optional: before serving, sprinkle the top with roasted, salted, diced almonds. This adds a nice touch.
This recipe serves 15-18. It will keep several days.

*If desired two small packages of an instant chocolate or butterscotch pudding mix may be substituted, using instructions on box, but substituting 3 cups of milk and ½ cup of half and half, and adding 2 teaspoons vanilla.

**Miss Virginia Watts**
**Waycross**

## STRAWBERRIES IN CREAM

1 quart strawberries
½ cup orange juice or ½ cup
 Cointreau

⅔ cup brown sugar
1 pint sour cream

Wash and remove stems from strawberries. Either leave whole or slice. Marinate in orange juice or Cointreau for 1 hour. Mix brown sugar with sour cream and blend with the marinated strawberries. Serves 6 to 8.

**Mrs. Freddie Wood (Emily Reynolds)**
**Atlanta**

## CHOCOLATE SOUFFLÉ (AN OLD FAMILY FAVORITE)

2 squares unsweetened
    chocolate
2 cups milk
½ cup sugar
⅓ cup flour

2 tablespoons butter
1 teaspoon vanilla
4 egg yolks, beaten
4 egg whites, stiffly beaten

Add chocolate to milk and heat in top of double boiler. When chocolate is melted, beat with beater to blend. Combine sugar, flour and salt; add dry ingredients to chocolate mixture and continue cooking for 5 minutes. Remove from boiling water and add butter and vanilla. Let cool while beating eggs. Add yolks and mix well. Fold in whites and turn into greased 2-quart souffle dish. Place in pan of hot water and bake in 350 degree oven for 1 hour or until firm. Serve with whipped cream to 6 or 8.

**Mrs. William Schweigert Burdell (Marguerite Bothwell)**
**Augusta**

## COFFEE CONGEALED CUSTARD

2 tablespoons instant coffee
¼ teaspoon salt
⅔ cup sugar
2 envelopes gelatin
3 cups milk

¼ cup cognac
2 cups heavy cream, whipped
grated semi-sweet chocolate
1 cup whipped cream (optional)

Combine coffee, salt, sugar, and gelatin in saucepan. Add milk and stir over low heat until sugar and gelatin are dissolved. Remove from heat and stir in cognac. Chill until mixture mounds slightly. Fold in whipped cream. Serve as preferred in spring form pan lined with lady fingers, or graham cracker crumb crust, or sherbet glasses. Chill until set. Serve with grated semi-sweet chocolate on top with or without whipped cream.

You may substitute Sweet and Low for sugar, skim milk for homogenized, and Cool Whip for whipped cream, which will lower calories, and serve as a custard. May be made day before.

**Mrs. Stephen D. Smith (Joyce Cooper)**
**Rome**

# CHOCOLATE SOUFFLÉ

1½ squares chocolate
1 cup sugar
2 tablespoons hot water
2 tablespoons butter
2 tablespoons flour

¾ cup milk
3 egg yolks, beaten until thick
½ teaspoon vanilla
3 egg whites, beaten until stiff

Melt 1½ squares chocolate, add 1 cup sugar and 2 tablespoons hot water. Stir until smooth. When this mixture is prepared, set it aside. Make a white sauce by melting 2 tablespoons butter and adding 2 tablespoons flour and ¾ cup milk. Bring this to a boiling point and boil for 3 or 4 minutes, stirring all the time to prevent its becoming lumpy. Combine the two mixtures and add egg yolks beaten until thick. Then add vanilla and egg whites beaten until stiff. Turn at once into a buttered baking dish, set in a pan of hot water, and bake in a 375 degree oven for 45 minutes.

**Mrs. Robert Clark (Alice Corbin)**
**Savannah**

# STRAWBERRY MOUSSE

1 envelope plain gelatin
1 10-ounce package frozen
   strawberries, sliced
½ cup whipping cream
1 tablespoon fresh lemon juice

½ cup wine
1 egg white
⅛ teaspoon salt
¼ cup sugar

Soften gelatin in wine and lemon juice and dissolve over hot water. Stir in thawed strawberries. Cool until slightly thickened. Beat egg white and salt until barely stiffened. Beat sugar into egg white gradually. Whip cream stiff and fold into egg white. Fold all into strawberry gelatin and pour into lightly greased mold or six dessert glasses and chill.

**Mrs. Thomas McKey Tillman, Sr. (Louise Phinizy)**
**Athens**

# CHERRY MOLD

1 3-ounce package cherry
   gelatin
1½ cups hot water
½ cup Cherry Heering liqueur

½ pint whipping cream, whipped
1 cup diced pineapple, drained
1 cup white seedless grapes (can
   use canned grapes)

Dissolve gelatin in hot water. Add Cherry Heering. Chill until the consistency of unbeaten egg whites. Fold in fruits. Mold and chill. Serve with whipped cream. Serves 6.

**Mrs. Malcolm McKinnon (Sara Crowell Bullock)**
**Columbus**

# LEMON CHARLOTTE RUSSE

1 envelope plain gelatin
1½ cups sugar, divided
4 eggs, separated
½ cup fresh lemon juice
⅛ teaspoon salt
3 tablespoons butter
1½ teaspoons grated fresh
   lemon rind

1 teaspoon vanilla
Ladyfingers
½ pint whipping cream, whipped
whipped cream for garnish
   (optional)

Mix gelatin and 1 cup sugar in top of double boiler. Beat egg yolks with lemon juice and salt; stir into gelatin mixture. Cook over simmering water, stirring constantly, until thickened (about 10 minutes). Stir in butter, lemon rind and vanilla. Chill until mixture mounds slightly when dropped from a spoon. Line bottom and sides of a 9 inch spring form pan with split Ladyfingers. In large mixing bowl beat egg whites until soft peaks form. Gradually add remaining ½ cup sugar and beat until very stiff. Fold egg whites and whipped cream into lemon mixture. Turn into spring form pan. Chill several hours, or until firm. Garnish with whipped cream, if desired. Makes 10 servings.

**Mrs. G. Stuart Watson (Nell Martin)**
**Albany**

# FRUIT PIZZA

1 package (1 pound 2 ounces)
   refrigerated sugar cookie
   dough
8 ounces cream cheese,
   softened
⅓ cup sugar
½ teaspoon vanilla
banana slices
blueberries, fresh, frozen or
   canned drained and rinsed

mandarin orange sections,
   drained
strawberry halves, fresh or frozen
pineapple chunks
green grape halves, etc.
¼ cup apricot preserves
1 tablespoon water

Cut dough in ⅛ inch slices and line 14 inch pizza pan with slices slightly overlapping. Bake at 375 degrees for 12 minutes. Cool.

Blend softened cream cheese, sugar and vanilla. Spread over cookie crust. Arrange fruit over that. Choice of fruits is limited only by imagination. Just be careful that the fruit is not the kind that will darken.

Mix preserves and water. Glaze pie. Chill.

**Mrs. Michael Clay (Edwina Whitaker Moore)**
**Dearborn, Michigan**

# DEVIL'S FOOD PUDDING

3 squares chocolate  
1½ cups sugar  
1½ cups milk  
½ teaspoon salt  

½ cup shortening  
2 eggs  
2 cups flour  
1 teaspoon vanilla  

Melt chocolate; add ½ cup sugar and ½ cup milk and cook until thick. Mix shortening, 1 cup sugar and eggs. Add to flour alternately with 1 cup milk, salt and vanilla. Bake in greased ring mold for 60 minutes in a 325 degree oven. Serve with whipped cream. Serves 4.

**Mrs. J. A. Redfearn (Elleighfare Muse)**
**Albany**

# MOCHA NUT TORTONI

½ cup almonds, sliced and  
   toasted  
½ cup semi-sweet chocolate  
   drops  
2 egg whites  

¼ cup sugar  
2 cups heavy cream  
2 tablespoons instant coffee  
2 egg yolks  
2 teaspoons vanilla  

Toast ½ cup sliced almonds. Melt chocolate drops over hot water. Cool slightly. Beat egg whites stiff. Add sugar. Whip heavy cream, add instant coffee, egg yolks, slightly beaten, and vanilla. Add chocolate and nuts. Fold in beaten egg whites. Spoon into paper baking cups. Freeze in muffin pans. When frozen, remove to a covered tin box or container. Keeps well. Makes 24.

**Mrs. Sam McArthur Duggan (Virginia Carlton)**
**Moultrie**

# ORANGE CHARLOTTE

1⅓ tablespoons plain gelatin  
⅓ cup cold water  
⅓ cup boiling water  
1 cup sugar  

3 tablespoons lemon juice  
1 cup orange juice and pulp  
3 egg whites, stiffly beaten  
½ pint cream, whipped  

Soak gelatin in cold water, dissolve in boiling water, strain, and add sugar, lemon juice, orange juice and pulp. Chill in pan of ice water; when quite thick, beat with wire whisk until frothy, add stiffly beaten egg whites and fold in whipped cream. Rinse in cold water a 6 cup melon mold (or other decorative mold). Turn in mixture and chill several hours or overnight. Turn out on chilled serving dish and garnish with orange slices and sprigs of mint or green grapes. Serves 6.

**Mrs. Rudolph John Thiesen (Mary Couper Traylor)**
**Atlanta**

## MARGARITA CHARLOTTE

| | |
|---|---|
| 10 eggs, separated | 1 teaspoon salt |
| 1 cup sugar | ½ cup tequila |
| 1 cup lime juice | ½ cup Triple Sec |
| grated peel of 4 limes | 2 cups heavy cream, whipped |
| (2 tablespoons) | 2 envelopes plain gelatin |

In a large mixer bowl on high speed, beat egg yolks until light and fluffy. Gradually add sugar and beat until smooth and light yellow. Mix in lime juice, peel, and salt. Cook in top of double boiler over boiling water until mixture thickens, about 10-15 minutes, stirring constantly. In small saucepan sprinkle gelatin over tequila and Triple Sec. Cook over low heat until the gelatin is dissolved, stirring constantly. Gradually stir the gelatin mixture into the hot custard. Chill. Butter a two quart soufflé dish. Wrap a folded wax paper collar around the dish extending 3 inches above the rim. Secure the collar with tape. Beat egg whites until stiff. Fold egg whites into custard mixture with the whipped cream. Pour into dish and chill for 3 hours.

**Mrs. Clarence Butler (Sarah Louise Turner)**
**Columbus**

## APRICOT FLOAT

| | |
|---|---|
| 4 ounces dried apricots | 3 eggs (or 2 whole eggs & 2 yolks) |
| ½ cup sugar | ⅓ cup sugar |
| water to cover apricots | ½ teaspoon vanilla |
| 3 egg whites | ¼ teaspoon almond extract |
| 1 pint milk | ½ pint whipping cream |

Cover apricots and sugar with enough water to cover and simmer until tender. Put in blender and purée, add more sugar to taste if necessary. Refrigerate until cold. (I do it the day before). Beat 3 egg whites until stiff and fold in apricots.

Beat 3 eggs (or 2 whole eggs and 2 yolks) thoroughly with ⅓ cup of sugar, add 1 pint of milk and cook in double boiler, stirring constantly until thickened. Remove from fire and add a pinch of salt, ½ teaspoon vanilla, ¼ teaspoon almond extract. Whip cream and sweeten to taste. Before serving, assemble in individual compotes. Pour custard over apricots and top with sweetened whipped cream.

**Mrs. Alva Wallace Barrett, Jr. (Anita Champion)**
**Albany**

# CHOCOLATE ANGEL TORTE

2 egg whites
⅛ teaspoon salt
⅛ teaspoon cream of tartar
½ cup sugar
1½ teaspoons vanilla

½ cup chopped pecans
4 ounces Baker's German Sweet
   Chocolate
3 tablespoons water
½ pint whipping cream

Meringue shell: beat egg whites with salt and cream of tartar until foamy. Add sugar, 2 tablespoons at a time, beating well after each addition, then continue beating to very stiff peaks. Fold in ½ teaspoon vanilla and nuts. Spoon into lightly greased 8 inch pie pan to form a nest like shell, build sides up ½ inch above edge of pan. Bake in slow oven 300 degrees 50 to 55 minutes. Cool.

Chocolate cream filling mixture: stir chocolate in the water over low heat in double boiler until chocolate is melted. Cool until thickened. Add 1 teaspoon vanilla. Whip cream, fold in chocolate mixture. Pile in meringue shell. Chill 2 hours. Serves 6 to 8.

**Mrs. Alexander Sullivan (Sarah Kirk Heyward)**
**Savannah**

# GRAPE SHERBET

2 cups frozen grape juice
2 cups pineapple juice
½ cup lemon juice

2 cups sugar
1 pint whipping cream (or ½ pint
   cream, ½ pint milk)

Boil pineapple juice and sugar for 1 minute. Cool 5 minutes. Add grape and lemon juices. Place in a 2 quart electric freezer and chill. Stop freezer, add cream, or cream and milk. Finish freezing, put in 2 quart plastic cartons for freezer storage.

Allow to soften a little before serving. Beautiful in the spring with a garnish of fresh purple violets and green violet leaves.

**Mrs. Frank Willingham (Mary Watson)**
**Macon**

# PAVLOVA

2 egg whites
½ teaspoon vanilla
1 teaspoon cornstarch
½ pint cream, whipped,
    sweetened

1 teaspoon white vinegar
1 cup sugar
¼ cup water, boiling
fresh, canned or frozen fruit in
    quantity desired

Put sugar, cornstarch, egg whites, vanilla and vinegar in a large mixing bowl and add the boiling water as you begin to beat the ingredients with an electric beater. Beat for ten minutes. The mixture will become very stiff and shiny. On a well greased oven proof dish, form the meringue into a seven inch round. Bake in the oven at 300 degrees for seventy-five to ninety minutes. It is normal for cracks to form while in the oven. Remove from the oven. Beat the cream stiff and beat in sugar to taste. Pour over meringue. Top with fruit. Makes six servings.

Pavlova is the national dessert of New Zealand and Australia and always served on special occasions.

**Mrs. Hubert B. Owens (Anna Torian)**
**Athens**


# PLUM PUDDING FROM GRANDMOTHER McLAIN

4 eggs beaten separately
1 loaf bread (1¼ pounds)
    crumbed
2 cups milk, scalded
1 cup butter
2 cups sugar
½ cup lemon juice
1 box raisins (15 ounce)

1 box currants (11 ounce)
½ pound crystallized citron
1 tablespoon nutmeg
1 tablespoon ground cinnamon
1 tablespoon ground cloves
1 tablespoon allspice
2 cups slivered almonds

Mix raisins, currants, citron and almonds with small amount of bread. Pour milk over remaining bread crumbs. Cream butter. Add sugar gradually. Add egg yolks, bread mixture, lemon juice and spices. Add fruit-nut mixture, then egg whites. Place in gauze bag and steam over boiling water two hours. Serve hot on a silver tray with butter sauce made by creaming 2 cups powdered sugar with 1 cup butter and sherry or brandy for flavor. Serve pudding flaming by pouring ½ cup 80 to 100 proof brandy over it just before serving. Light by heating a silver teaspoon of brandy until it flames. Use flame to light pudding. May be stored in refrigerator in jars for months, then reheated. Serves 20 to 25.

**Mrs. William Lee Wood, Jr. (Frances Elizabeth Bush)**
**Macon**

# CHOCOLATE CHARLOTTE

1 envelope gelatin
3 tablespoons cold water
2 ounces unsweetened
   chocolate
½ cup confectioners' sugar
1 cup milk

¾ cup granulated sugar
¼ teaspoon salt
1 teaspoon vanilla
2 cups whipping cream—whipped
   stiff

Soften gelatin in water. Set aside. Melt chocolate in double boiler over hot, *not* boiling water. Stir in confectioners' sugar and blend until smooth. Scald milk; stir into chocolate mixture. Cook, stirring constantly, until mixture reaches boiling point. *Do not boil.* Remove from heat and mix in softened gelatin, granulated sugar, salt and vanilla. Chill until slightly thickened. Beat until light and airy. Fold whipped cream carefully into chocolate mixture. Pour into soufflé dish or serving bowl. Refrigerate 2-3 hours, or until firm. Serves 6-8.

**Mrs. Eugene McNeel (Louise Inman)**
**Brunswick**

# CHOCOLATE MOUSSE

2 tablespoons cold strong
   coffee
2 tablespoons brandy
10 ounces bittersweet
   chocolate

8 eggs, separated
½ pint cream, whipped
almond flakes, roasted

Combine chocolate, coffee and brandy in top of double boiler and melt over low heat. Beat egg yolks in a bowl and stir hot chocolate mixture well into them. Put aside to cool. Beat egg whites in bowl until stiff and fold in cooled chocolate mixture. Put in serving dish and refrigerate for 4 hours. Serve with whipped cream and almond flakes.

**Mrs. Joseph E. Birnie (Octávia Riley)**
**Atlanta**

# FRUIT CRUNCH

1 cup flour
1 cup white sugar
½ teaspoon salt
½ teaspoon soda

½ pint whipping cream
½ cup pecans, chopped
¾ cup light brown sugar
1½ cups fruit cocktail and juice

Mix flour, white sugar, salt, soda, fruit cocktail and juice. Grease an 8x10-inch pyrex dish. Place mixture in dish. Sprinkle top with light brown sugar and then with the pecans. Bake in 350 degree oven for 35 minutes. Cut in squares and serve with topping of whipped cream. Serves 8 generously.

**Mrs. R. G. Fleetwood (Mary Brandon)**
**Thomasville**

# LEMON ANGEL FOOD DESSERT

1 angel food cake
1 pint whipping cream
1 can condensed milk

1 cup coconut, grated
½ cup sugar
juice of 4 lemons

Break cake into 1 inch pieces, and put one half of them in a 9x13-inch pan. Mix condensed milk, lemon juice, and cream which has been whipped. Pour one half of mixture over cake pieces. Put remaining pieces of cake in the pan and pour other half of whipped cream mixture over the cake. Sprinkle freshly grated coconut over the top. Refrigerate or freeze.

**Mrs. Donald Neil Wilson (Eulalie Converse Pickett)**
**Cedartown**

# LADY FINGER DELIGHT

9 lady fingers (split)
9 ounce carton Cool Whip
⅓ cup chopped nuts

⅓ cup sherry, rum or bourbon
¼ cup tart jelly

Use 8½x4½-inch pan or bowl of equal capacity. Make layer of lady fingers in pan. Using pastry brush, dampen with sherry, rum, or bourbon. Add half of Cool Whip. Sprinkle with half the nuts and dots of jelly. Repeat layers. Refrigerate overnight. Sweetened whipped cream may be used.

**Mrs. Charles Ferguson (Jean Davis)**
**Thomasville**

# LEMON CUSTARD PUDDING

1 cup sugar
4 tablespoons flour
¼ teaspoon salt
2 tablespoons butter or
　margarine

3 eggs
1½ cups milk
5 tablespoons lemon juice
2 teaspoons grated lemon rind

Separate eggs. Melt butter. Mix sugar and flour, pour melted butter over this mixture and mix well. Beat egg yolks, add milk, and add this to the mixture. Add lemon juice and rind. Add well beaten egg whites. Bake in a casserole at 350 degrees for 45 minutes. Serves 4 to 6.

**Mrs. Calder W. Payne (Eugenia Coleman)**
**Macon**

# MAINE NUT TORTE

3 egg whites
1 cup sugar
1 teaspoon vanilla
whipped cream

1 teaspoon baking powder
20 Ritz crackers rolled into crumbs
¼ cup chopped nuts (pecans
　preferable)

Beat egg whites until stiff. Beat in sugar and vanilla. Fold in Ritz cracker crumbs, baking powder and nuts. Butter well a 9-inch pie pan. Spread mix to edges of pan as pie pan is filled. Bake at 350 degrees for 30 minutes. Allow to cool. Serve topped with whipped cream. Serves 8 people.

**Mrs. John M. Cutler (Helen Crump)**
**London, England**

# BAKED CUSTARD

6 whole eggs
1 cup sugar
1 quart milk

¼ teaspoon salt
1 teaspoon vanilla
6 plain ladyfingers

Beat eggs with wire whisk. Add sugar to eggs and beat again. Heat milk until hot but not boiling. Pour hot milk into egg and sugar mixture, beating with whisk constantly. Add salt and vanilla. Beat again. Arrange ladyfingers in a 2-quart soufflé dish and pour custard over them. Put dish in pan of hot water and cook in 325 degree oven for 45 minutes. Cool. Serves 8.

**Mrs. Merritt Dixon, III (Janet Barnett)**
**Savannah**

# NUT TORTE

2 cups pecans, ground
4 egg yolks
1 cup sugar
2 tablespoons flour
½ teaspoon salt
½ teaspoon baking powder

1 tablespoon orange juice
4 egg whites
1 cup cream
6 ounces semi-sweet chocolate
½ cup sour cream

Beat egg yolks well, add sugar, flour, baking powder, orange juice, salt, ground pecans—and egg whites, beaten stiff. Bake in two 8-inch greased cake pans, in which two sheets of greased and floured waxed paper have been placed, at 350 degrees for thirty minutes. Cool one to three hours. Whip cream to put between layers. Melt semi-sweet chocolate in double boiler. Stir in sour cream. Spread over cake and decorate with pecan halves.

**Mrs. Hoyt Henry Whelchel, Jr. (Alice Erwin)**
**Moultrie**

# MAPLE PARFAIT

12 egg yolks
1½ cups maple syrup

1 pint whipping cream, whipped

Cook egg yolks and syrup together in the top of a double boiler until a coating is formed on the spoon. Remove from the stove and cool. Beat whipping cream until thick. Combine with syrup mixture. The parfait can be frozen in the freezer compartment of the refrigerator in a large ice tray. Stir at least once while freezing.

**Mrs. William E. Johnson (Nancy Hale)**
**Rome**

# BUTTERSCOTCH SAUCE

1 egg yolk
5 tablespoons butter
4 tablespoons water
⅔ cup brown sugar

⅓ cup corn syrup
½ cup pecans, toasted and broken
   in pieces

Beat egg yolk slightly. Add remaining ingredients except nuts and cook over hot water, stirring frequently until thick. Add toasted pecans. Serve over ice cream.

**Mrs. Cason Callaway, Jr. (Nancy Hodges)**
**Columbus**

# CHOCOLATE SAUCE

2 ounces semi-sweet chocolate
2 ounces unsweetened
  chocolate
6 ounces German chocolate
⅔ cup water

1 cup sugar
½ teaspoon vanilla
2½ tablespoons butter
dash salt

Melt chocolate; add water and sugar. Boil for two minutes. Remove from heat. Add salt, vanilla, butter. Excellent topping for ice cream and pies. Keep refrigerated but reheat before using it as a topping. Chopped toasted pecans are a delicious addition.

**Mrs. Ray Lowell Peacock, Jr. (Margaret Anne McGowan)**
**Gainesville**

# CARAMEL SAUCE FOR ICE CREAM

1 cup brown sugar
½ cup white sugar
½ cup half-and-half cream

½ cup white Karo syrup
¼ cup butter
cashew nuts

Cook to soft ball stage white and brown sugars and syrup. Add butter and cream and fold in. Add cashew nuts and serve warm over ice cream.

**Mrs. Charles Smith Hogg (Fred Singer Turpin)**
**Americus**

# SHERRY SAUCE

4 egg yolks, well-beaten
1 cup sugar
½ pint cream, whipped

1 cup sherry
1 teaspoon flour

Add sugar, flour and wine to well-beaten egg yolks. Cook to a soft custard in double boiler, stirring constantly. Cool. Add sherry. May be frozen in two containers or, if to be used a day or two later, keep in refrigerator. Add ½ pint whipped cream before serving.

Good over warmed left-over pound cake, minced meat pies, or warmed or cold fruit cake.

**Mrs. Sam McArthur Duggan (Virginia Carlton)**
**Moultrie**

## STRAWBERRIES CARDINAL

1½ quarts fresh strawberries
¼ to ⅓ cup sugar
10 ounces frozen raspberries,
   thawed
mint sprigs

2 teaspoons sugar
1 teaspoon orange liqueur
1 teaspoon fresh lemon juice
½ pint whipped cream

Wash, cap and place in a serving bowl the strawberries. Sprinkle with ½ to ⅓ cup sugar, depending on tartness of the berries. Cover and chill for several hours. In an electric blender blend raspberries with their syrup at high speed until puréed and slightly frothy. Strain to remove seeds. Stir in the lemon juice, orange liqueur and 2 teaspoons sugar. Cover and chill. Just before serving ladle sauce over the berries in a serving bowl to coat them lightly. Garnish with mint sprigs, or top with slightly sugared whipped cream. The sauce will keep a long time in the refrigerator in a tightly covered jar.

**Mrs. Wesley Turnell Hanson, Jr. (Marie McHatton)**
**Rochester, New York**


## HAMILTON PUDDING

2 coconuts and the milk of each
½ pound sugar
1 cup citron, slivered
½ cup good brandy
4 tablespoons sugar

1 tablespoon butter
4 eggs
1 cup raisins, chopped
1 teaspoon lemon juice

Choose coconuts with a good amount of milk. This can be determined by shaking the nut. Pierce the eyes of the nuts and drain the milk into a cup. Set the nuts in a very hot oven for about ten minutes; the smaller the nut the less time it will take for the heat to penetrate and draw the meat away from the shell. Crack the nuts and shave off the brown rind. Grate the coconuts on a fine grater, do not shred. Put the coconut meat and the milk—about a cupful—in a pan with the sugar and boil until clear. Let cool. Add the citron, raisins, the butter, and the beaten egg yolks to the coconut and lastly the brandy, very slowly. Turn into a buttered baking dish and bake at 350 degrees until nicely browned. Cool. Beat the egg whites very stiff and beat in the 4 tablespoons sugar and the lemon juice. Return to the oven and bake at 325 degrees until the meringue is puffed and browned. Serve hot. Serves ten or twelve.

This was my family's traditional Thanksgiving dinner dessert.

**Mrs. David Robert Cumming (Elizabeth Hamilton Hall)**
**Athens**

# MINT AND MAGNOLIA

3 cups macaroons, crushed
½ cup sugar
1 cup half-and-half cream
1 teaspoon fresh lemon juice
pinch of salt
3 cups whipping cream

1 cup crème de menthe
cup of fresh mint
12 whole macaroons
12 magnolia petals or small
  magnolia leaves

Whip the cream. Combine macaroon crumbs, sugar, half-and-half cream, lemon juice and salt in large bowl. Fold in whipped cream. Gradually fold in crème de menthe. Spoon into individual small compotes or small crystal bowls that can be subjected to freezing temperature. Place in freezer about fifteen minutes before serving. Remove from freezer and let set at room temperature. Allow to partially thaw. Garnish with fresh mint. Place compote or bowl in dessert plate to serve. Add a whole macaroon placed on a magnolia blossom petal or small magnolia leaf to achieve mint and magnolia aroma.

**Mrs. W. Graham Ponder (Adelaide Wallace)**
**Madison**

# TANGERINES ORIENTALES

12 tangerines (shells only, use
  scooped out sections
  otherwise)

½ gallon vanilla ice-cream
2 cans (6 ounces) frozen
  concentrated tangerine juice

Wash and dry tangerines. Cut a thin slice (¼ to ½ inch thick) from stem end of each to form top of cup, being sure to keep both parts of each tangerine together. With a rounded spoon scoop out the pulp and membrane of tops and bottoms, being careful not to tear the outer skin. Set shells aside. Slightly soften ice-cream and frozen tangerine juice, then quickly, but thoroughly, mix together with electric beater. After mixing, return ice-cream to freezer for ½ to 1 hour. Fill tangerine shells with stiffened ice-cream, mounding slightly to fit tops. Put tops on and return to freezer to freeze hard. Ten to fifteen minutes before serving, remove from freezer, garnish with citrus (or ivy) leaves. 12 servings of 1 tangerine each.

This is a pretty, light dessert to follow a large dinner, such as Thanksgiving or Christmas.)

**Mrs. Albert Sidney Britt, Jr. (Annie McIntosh)**
**Savannah**

# CHOCOLATE PECAN PIE

½ cup butter or margarine
1 cup sugar
1 tablespoon corn meal
2 whole eggs

1 tablespoon vinegar
1 teaspoon vanilla
1 cup chopped pecans
½ cup chocolate morsels

Melt butter. Add sugar and corn meal. Mix well. Add beaten eggs. Mix thoroughly. Add nuts, vinegar, chocolate morsels and vanilla. Pour into unbaked pie shell. Bake at 325 degrees for 40 to 50 minutes.

**Mrs. E. P. McCollum (Louise Sewell)**
**Thomasville**


# COCONUT PIE

3 eggs
6 tablespoons margarine
¼ cup buttermilk
1 cup sugar

1 teaspoon vanilla
6 ounces coconut, grated fresh or
   frozen
pinch of salt

Beat eggs slightly. Add sugar and buttermilk. Add melted margarine and coconut. Add salt and vanilla. Bake in uncooked pie crust in 350 degree oven for 10 minutes. Reduce oven to 300 degrees and cook about 40 minutes more.

**Mrs. Erskine Lee Carter (Martha Virginia Eldridge)**
**Americus**


# FRENCH SILK PIE

½ cup butter
¾ cup sugar
3 eggs
1 teaspoon vanilla

2 squares dark chocolate
graham cracker pie shell
whipped cream, if desired

Cream butter and sugar. Add eggs one at a time, beating 2 minutes by the clock after each addition. Melt chocolate in *slightly* buttered double boiler and add to mixture. Add vanilla. Pour into graham cracker pie crust and let stand in refrigerator for 24 hours. Add a dollop of whipped cream on each slice.

**Mrs. W. H. Zimmerman (Frances Barrett)**
**Columbus**

# PECAN PIE

1 cup light corn syrup
1 cup dark brown sugar
½ teaspoon salt
⅓ cup melted butter

1 teaspoon vanilla
3 whole eggs, slightly beaten
1 heaping cup shelled pecans

Combine syrup, sugar, salt, butter, vanilla and mix well. Add slightly beaten eggs. Pour into 9-inch unbaked pie shell. Sprinkle pecans over all. Bake in pre-heated 350 degree oven for approximately 45 minutes. When cool, whipped cream or ice cream topping may be added.

**Mrs. George B. Hightower (Emily Anderson)**
**Atlanta**

# MISSISSIPPI PECAN PIE

1 cup cane syrup
½ cup sugar
3 tablespoons butter, melted

3 eggs
1 cup pecans, chopped
grated rind ½ lemon

Cook sugar, syrup and butter while eggs are being beaten. Beat eggs in syrup slowly, add nuts. Pour in unbaked pastry. Bake in moderate oven until firm. Serve with whipped cream.

**Mrs. Allen Daughtry (Rebecca Hearn)**
**Milledgeville**

# PECAN TASSIES

3 ounces cream cheese
½ cup butter or margarine
1 cup sifted flour
1 egg
¾ cup brown sugar

1 tablespoon soft butter or
   margarine
1 teaspoon vanilla
dash salt
⅔ cup coarsely broken pecans

For cheese pastry, let cream cheese and ½ cup butter soften at room temperature. Blend. Stir in flour. Chill slightly about 1 hour. Shape in 2-dozen 1-inch balls. Place in tiny ungreased 1¾ inch-muffin cups. Press dough against bottom and sides of cups. In the pecan filling, beat together egg, sugar, 1 tablespoon butter, vanilla and salt just until smooth. Divide half the pecans among pastry lined cups. Add egg mixture and top with remaining pecans. Bake in slow oven of 325 degrees for 25 or 30 minutes or until filling is set. Cool. Remove from pan.

**Mrs. Idus Brown Small, Jr. (Lena McMath)**
**Americus**

# GRAPE PIE

1 quart thick-skinned grapes,
  black or scuppernong
1 scant cup sugar
1½ tablespoons lemon juice

2 frozen 9-inch pie crusts
1 teaspoon flour
1 teaspoon butter or margarine
¼ teaspoon salt

Wash and pulp grapes. Cook pulps alone about 10 minutes until they can be pressed through a sieve to remove seeds. Add this liquid to the hulls with just enough water to cook covered until hulls are tender, about 30 minutes. Add sugar, salt and flour blended together and lemon juice and butter. Put mixture into uncooked pie shell. Cover with second pie shell. Prick top shell and dot it with butter then sprinkle with a tiny bit of sugar. Bake at 450 degrees for 10 minutes. Reduce heat to 350 degrees and bake 20 mintues or till nicely browned. Serve warm with slices of cheese or ice cream. Serves 6.

**Mrs. Edward B. Dawson (Elizabeth Lott)**
**Milledgeville**

# GERMANE'S BRETONNE BLUEBERRY PIE

4 cups blueberries
¾ cup sugar, granulated
½ cup water
2 tablespoons cornstarch
1 tablespoon butter
2 tablespoons Cointreau

¼ cup slivered toasted almonds
1 9-inch baked pie shell or tart
  shells
1 cup whipped cream
3 tablespoons confectioners' sugar
¼ teaspoon almond extract

Bring slowly to a boil, 1 cup blueberries, granulated sugar and water. Cook until soft, about 10 minutes, then put through a sieve or blender. Add 2 tablespoons cornstarch that has been dissolved in a smidgen of cold water. Cook all this until thick. Stir in 1 tablespoon butter. Cool mixture, then add 2 tablespoons Cointreau or other orange liqueur, ¼ cup slivered almonds and 3 cups *uncooked* blueberries. Put in a 9-inch baked pie shell or baked tart shells. Serve with 1 cup whipped cream sweetened with 3 tablespoons confectioners' sugar and ¼ teaspoon almond extract.

**Mrs. Joseph Harrison (Louise Lynah)**
**Savannah**

## STRAWBERRY PIE

1 quart fresh strawberries
1 cup sugar
3 tablespoons cornstarch
pinch salt

½ pint whipping cream, sweetened
    to taste
1 baked pie crust

Cook half of the berries with the sugar, cornstarch, and salt. When thickened, remove from stove and cool. Put in cooled baked pie shell and add other half of the berries. Cover with whipped cream and chill.

**Mrs. Alexander Graham Little, Jr. (Roline Adair)**
**Valdosta**

## LEMON PIE
*(My Grandmother's original recipe)*

1 cup sugar
2 tablespoons flour
4 eggs
juice of 2 lemons

1 cup boiling water
¼ teaspoon salt
¼ cup margarine

Mix flour, sugar, and boiling water. Add egg yolks and lemon juice, margarine and salt. Cook in double boiler until thick. Cool, put in cooked pie shell, top with meringue. Then run back into oven and brown.

**Mrs. Wightman Warren (Dorothy Wightman)**
**Albany**

## LIME CHIFFON PIE

3 eggs, separated
¼ cup lime juice (Key limes, if
    available)
3 tablespoons hot water

1 cup sugar
few grains salt
graham cracker pie crust

Beat egg yolks until light in color, add lime juice, hot water and ½ cup sugar. Cook in double boiler, stirring until thick. Beat egg whites stiff adding ½ cup sugar. Fold into lime mixture and pour into baked pie shell. Brown lightly in a 325 degree oven. Serve chilled. Top with whipped cream.

**Mrs. Silas Mason Hearne (Louise Scott)**
**Marathon, Florida**

## SWEET POTATO PIE

2 cups sweet potato, cooked,
  mashed
1 tablespoon nutmeg, freshly
  grated
½ teaspoon cinnamon
1 cup sugar
1 teaspoon vanilla or maple
  flavoring

1 cup milk
1 tablespoon butter
1 teaspoon salt
½ cup chopped pecans
2 eggs

Mix potatoes and sugar, sifted with the salt, nutmeg and cinnamon. Add butter and blend. Add eggs one at a time, beating after each addition until well blended. Stir in milk and flavoring. Pour into an unbaked pie shell. Bake in 325 degree oven for thirty minutes. Remove from oven and top with pecans. Return to oven and continue baking for fifteen minutes more, or until well set.

**Mrs. John A. Hunnicutt III (Grace Holden)**
**Athens**

## ORANGE CHIFFON PIE

½ cup sugar
½ teaspoon salt
1 envelope gelatin, unflavored
1 cup fresh orange juice
1 cup diced orange sections
  (about 2 large oranges)

4 eggs
grated rind of 1 lemon
grated rind of 1 orange
⅓ cup sugar
whipped cream, if desired
2 baked pie shells

Dissolve the gelatin in ⅓ cup orange juice. Put the slightly beaten egg yolks, ½ cup sugar, salt and the remaining juice in a double boiler and cook until thickened, stirring constantly. Stir in the gelatin and the grated peel. Place this mixture in a large bowl and chill over ice until it is about to congeal. Then fold in the stiffly beaten egg white to which has been added the remaining ⅓ cup sugar. Finally, add the chopped orange sections from which all membrane has been removed. Chill until it begins to congeal again, then pour into the baked pie shells. Place in refrigerator until firm, then serve with a *very* thin topping of whipped cream flavored with a little sugar and some additional grated rind.

**Mrs. Francis Norman (Virginia Illges)**
**Columbus**

# MATTIE'S GLORIFIED APPLE PIE

1 9-inch pie shell baked 10
  minutes in 350 degree oven
  and brushed with egg yolk
1 cup apple, diced
2 eggs, beaten well
1 cup sugar, if apples are sweet
  (1½ cups, if sour)

½ cup melted butter
½ teaspoon cinnamon
½ teaspoon allspice
½ teaspoon allspice

Mix all ingredients and pour into pie shell. Bake at 350 degrees for 25 to 30 minutes until well done and brown.

**Mrs. Thomas Clay (Anita Lippitt)**
**Savannah**

# SHERRY CREAM PIE

1½ cups crushed vanilla wafers
¼ cup butter or margarine,
  melted
½ teaspoon almond flavoring
1 envelope plain gelatin
¼ cup milk

3 eggs, separated
⅝ cup sugar
1 cup milk
pinch of salt
½ cup sherry
½ pint whipping cream

Crush wafers very fine. Save some to sprinkle on top. Mix well with melted butter to which has been added almond flavoring. Pat firmly into 10 inch pie pan. Chill 1 hour. Soften gelatin in ¼ cup cold milk. Put 3 egg yolks in double boiler and beat slightly. Add sugar and 1 cup of milk. Cook over hot water until custard coats the spoon. Remove from stove and add gelatin and salt. Add sherry very slowly. Put in refrigerator to thicken. Beat egg whites and the cream. When custard is slightly thick, fold in egg whites and cream. Fill crust with custard and sprinkle with crumbs. Refrigerate at least 8 hours before serving. 8 servings.

**Mrs. William F. Barron (Mary Sue Jones)**
**Rome**

# VIRGINIA CHESS PIE

4 eggs
½ cup butter, melted
3 cups white sugar

1 cup evaporated milk
1 tablespoon vanilla

Add eggs to milk. Beat thoroughly. Add sugar. Beat well. Pour melted butter slowly into mixture, mixing well. Add vanilla. Pour mixture into two 9-inch pie shells or sixteen tart shells. Preheat oven to 400 degrees. Bake for ten minutes at 400 degress then reduce temperature to 300 degrees and bake about 50 more minutes or until golden brown. Delicious served hot with small scoop of vanilla ice cream on top.

**Mrs. William Gallatin Baker (Emily H. Plummer)**
**Atlanta**

# DATE NUT PIE

2 cups boiling water
¾ cup sugar
1 tablespoon cornstarch
¼ teaspoon salt

8 ounces pitted dates, chopped
1 cup pecans, chopped
1 baked 9-inch pie shell
whipped cream

Mix sugar, salt and cornstarch and stir in gradually to boiling water. When mixture begins to thicken put in dates and cook to a pulp. Add chopped pecans and pour into the baked pie shell. Serve with whipped cream.

**Mrs. William H. Cox (Mary Bellinger)**
**Waycross**

# MACAROON PIE

12 chopped dates
12 soda crackers, rolled to fine
    crumbs
1 cup sugar

3 egg whites
½ cup chopped pecans
1 teaspoon almond extract

Beat egg whites, add dry ingredients. Bake in greased aluminum pie pan at 350 degrees for 30 minutes. Serves 6.

**Mrs. Calder W. Payne (Eugenia Coleman)**
**Macon**

## COFFEE SUNDAE PIE

18 chocolate wafers (Oreos are
  good to use)
⅓ cup melted butter or
  margarine
2 squares baking chocolate

1 tablespoon butter or margarine
½ cup sugar
¾ cup evaporated milk
1 quart coffee ice cream

Crush chocolate wafers and add melted butter. Press into a 9 inch pie plate and chill. Melt the chocolate and 1 tablespoon of butter together, then add ½ cup sugar and ¾ cup evaporated milk. Cook and stir until thick; cool. Fill chilled pie shell with coffee ice cream. Put in freezer and when cold spread the chocolate mixture over the ice cream and return to the freezer. Serves 6.

**Mrs. James H. Lawrence (Virginia Sheppard)**
**Waycross**

## BUTTERSCOTCH ICE CREAM PIE

½ gallon vanilla ice cream
1 graham cracker crust,
  thawed

1 jar Butterscotch Sauce
6 Butterfinger candy bars (crushed
  fine)

Pour a thin layer of butterscotch sauce in bottom of crust. Layer softened ice cream and crushed butterfingers two times, ending with butterfingers. Freeze. To serve, pour sauce over each slice.

**Mrs. M. Felton Hatcher, Jr. (Beth Hall)**
**Fort Valley**

## HEATH BAR PIE

1⅔ cups honey graham cracker
    crumbs '
¼ cup granulated sugar
¼ cup butter
2 packages instant vanilla
    pudding

2 cups milk
1 quart butter pecan ice cream
6 Heath candy bars, crumbled
1 carton Cool Whip

To make graham cracker crust, roll crackers and mix with butter and sugar. Bake 8 minutes and cool. Mix 2 packages vanilla instant pudding with milk, ice cream and 3 crumbled Heath Bars. Pour into crust. Spread Cool Whip on top with 3 crumbled Heath Bars. Refrigerate until chilled thoroughly. Serves 6 to 8. Will keep in freezer.

**Mrs. Vance Watt (Mercer Pendleton)**
**Thomasville**

## CHOCOLATE PIE

¼ cup butter
2 egg yolks, well beaten
4 tablespoons flour
½ salt spoon salt

1 cup sugar
3 tablespoons cocoa
1 cup water, hot but not boiling
1 cooked pie shell

Cream together the butter and sugar. Add the egg yolks. Mix cocoa and flour together and add to the butter mixture. Add salt and hot water. Cook in a double boiler until thick. Cool. Pour into cooked pie shell and top with whipped cream or a meringue made with the egg whites of the eggs.

**Mrs. Thomas Walter Rogers (Mary Emma Gee)**
**Athens**

## CHOCOLATE CHESS PIE

1 square unsweetened
    chocolate
½ cup butter
2 eggs
1 cup sugar

dash salt
1 teaspoon vanilla
½ cup pecans, coarsely chopped
unbaked frozen 9-inch pie crust

Melt chocolate and butter together. Beat eggs and sugar. Pour over melted chocolate and butter. Add salt and vanilla. Place pecans in partially thawed pastry. Pour custard over pecans and bake at 350 degrees for 25-30 minutes.

**Mrs. John F. Shackelford (Lucy Eason)**
**Albany**

## PEPPERMINT ICE CREAM

60 sticks peppermint candy       2 quarts milk
  (3½" long)                     1 pint whipping cream
1 large can evaporated milk

Use Old Fashion Peppermint Pure Sugar Sticks of candy. Soak in 1 quart milk overnight or until dissolved. Add 1 pint whipping cream, 1 can evaporated milk, and remaining quart of milk. Freeze. Serves 8 to 10.

**Mrs. Charles McKinnon (Ann Gravely)**
**Thomasville**

# OLD FASHIONED CARAMEL ICE CREAM

2 cups sugar                      2 tablespoons flour or cornstarch
½ to 1 cup boiling water          1 pint whipping cream
4 eggs, slightly beaten           1 6-ounce can evaporated milk
½ cup sugar                       2 teaspoons vanilla
1 quart milk                      ½ teaspoon salt

Melt 2 cups sugar over low to medium heat. Stir to keep from burning. Add boiling water and continue cooking until dissolved. Set aside. Scald milk. Combine ½ cup sugar, flour or cornstarch and salt. Add enough hot milk to sugar-flour mixture to make a thin paste and stir into hot milk. Cook over low heat, stirring constantly, until thickened. Add hot mixture gradually to beaten eggs and cook again, stirring constantly, no more than 2 minutes. Combine custard and caramel syrup. Chill. When ready to churn, add whipping cream, evaporated milk and additional milk if needed. Freeze. For gallon churn.

**Mrs. Alvin M. Ratliff (Frances Lott)**
**Blackshear**

## COCONUT ICE CREAM

1½ quarts half and half cream
2 cups milk
1½ cups sugar
⅛ teaspoon salt
5 eggs plus 5 egg yolks

2 tablespoons cornstarch
1 pint whipping cream
1 tablespoon vanilla
2 cups grated coconut

In a heavy 4 quart saucepan, heat the half and half cream, milk, sugar, and salt, stirring until the sugar dissolves. In a separate bowl, beat the eggs, egg yolks and cornstarch. Beat in a little of the hot cream, then add the egg mixture to the saucepan, stirring constantly. Cook over low heat for 10 minutes. Cool. Whip whipping cream and add with the vanilla to egg custard. Pour into an ice cream freezer, and freeze according to manufacturer's instructions. Churn until mixture thickens. Add coconut and continue until firm. Makes 1 gallon.

**Mrs. John Leitch (Anne Douglas)**
**Savannah**

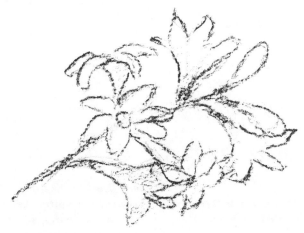

## PEACH ICE CREAM

1½ quarts peaches, after
    slicing
1½ quarts half-and-half cream
¼ teaspoon almond extract

sugar to taste, (make it a bit
sweeter than desired as the cold
will make it taste less sweet.)

Put all in blender and purée. Put in ice cream freezer. Ice and pack well. Turn until the dasher stops.

**Mrs. L. Neill Bickerstaff (Sara Bussey)**
**Columbus**

## COFFEE ICE CREAM PIE

¼ cup margarine
1 package chocolate chips
Rice Krispies, as needed

coffee ice cream
Bakers chocolate

Melt margarine and chocolate chips. Fold in enough Rice Krispies to make a crust and pat into a pie pan. Fill crust with coffee ice cream and add shredded Baker's chocolate over top. Keep in freezer and put in refrigerator when you sit down to dinner. It will be soft enough to slice for dessert.
**Mrs. Lucius Smith (Mary Cooper)**
**Rome**

## BUTTERMILK PIE

3 eggs
⅔ cup buttermilk
2 cups sugar
1 tablespoon flour

½ cup melted butter (or
   margarine)
1 teaspoon vanilla
2 9-inch pastry shells

Preheat oven to 375 degrees. Beat eggs until smooth. Add buttermilk and mix well. Add sugar, butter and vanilla. Mix to blend. Pour in shells and bake one hour.
**Mrs. Cullen Hoffman (Anne W. Chancellor)**
**Columbus**

## SCUPPERNONG GRAPE ICE CREAM

4 to 6 cups grape juice*          ¾ cup to 4 cups whole milk
1 quart whipping cream          dash of lemon juice
2 to 2½ cups sugar

Combine all ingredients and freeze in hand or electric ice cream churn. While the 4 cups of juice produces a mild refreshing flavor, it is even better with additional juice. The variation in amount of sugar depends on the sweetness of the grapes, and needs to be done by tasting. Since homemade ice cream seems to lose some of its sweetness during the churning process, it is necessary to have it slightly sweeter than tastes good before freezing it. Add milk to within 2 inches of top of churn.

*About 3-4 pounds of grapes are necessary for this amount of juice. Grapes should be washed and may be mashed by hand in a flat container with high sides, such as a turkey roaster, then strained. Another way is to use a large cone shaped colander on a metal tripod, with a long, two-inch wide wooden pestle. Juice may be frozen, without any sugar or water, and will keep indefinitely.

**Mrs. S. William Clark (Susan Lott)**
**Waycross**

## LEMON-LIME ICE CREAM

2 eggs                              ½ teaspoon grated lemon rind
½ cup sugar                     ½ teaspoon grated lime rind
½ cup light corn syrup      3 tablespoons lemon juice
1½ cups milk                     3 tablespoons lime juice
½ cup half and half cream  green vegetable coloring

Beat eggs, gradually add sugar, beating constantly. Add corn syrup, milk, cream, lemon rind, lime rind and juices. Tint pale green. Pour into freezing tray. Freeze to mush, place in chilled bowl and beat until smooth. Return to tray and freeze until firm. Delicious served with melon balls or in cantaloupe slices. Serves 4-6.

**Mrs. Porter Wilkins Carswell (Elizabeth McMaster)**
**Augusta**

## GRAND MARNIER ICE CREAM TORTE

1⅓ cups sugar, sifted
4 egg whites at room
  temperature
¼ teaspoon salt
¾ teaspoon baking powder
1 teaspoon vanilla

1 pint vanilla ice cream
1 cup chocolate syrup
1 tablespoon Grand Marnier
1 teaspoon vinegar
1 teaspoon water

Combine egg whites, baking powder, salt, vanilla, vinegar, and water. With electric beater mix at high speed until egg whites are stiff. Add sifted sugar, a tablespoon at a time continuing to beat. Heap the meringue into lightly greased pans. Bake in a very slow oven 250 degrees for 1 hour or longer. When cool spread light layer of whipped cream over meringues and refrigerate several hours or overnight. When ready to serve put a layer of ice cream on one meringue and top with second meringue. Pour Grand Marnier and chocolate sauce over meringues in decorative way. Serves 6 to 8.

**Mrs. James Anderson (Mary Neel)**
**Thomasville**

## DAIQUIRI ICE

1 6-ounce can frozen
  concentrate for lemonade
3 cups crushed ice
⅔ to ¾ cup superfine
  confectioners' sugar

2 egg whites
¼ cup light rum

Place all ingredients in blender. Blend at high speed until mixture is snowy, about 45 seconds. Freeze 2 or more hours until firm. Makes 3 cups, 4 to 6 servings.

**Mrs. Shelby Myrick Jr. (Alice Barrow)**
**Savannah**

# FRESH FRUIT SOUP

A lovely summer dessert served in a sherbet dish or punch cup with crisp cookies on the side.

**1½ pounds fresh plums, halved
  and pitted (about 9)
3 cups water
¾ cup sugar
dash of salt**

**1½ cups seedless grapes
1½ cups fresh pineapple chunks
1½ cups fresh peaches sliced, or
  strawberries
Burgundy or vodka if desired**

Boil plums, water, sugar and salt for 10 minutes or until plums are tender. Pour plums and juices in blender or food processor and whirl until smooth. Pour into 3 quart serving bowl. Chill. At serving time add fruit and wine or vodka to taste. Makes 2 quarts. Serves 8.

**Mrs. Thomas Clay (Anita Lippitt)
Savannah**

# WINE JELLY

**2½ envelopes plain gelatin
1 cup boiling water
¼ cup lemon juice
¼ cup brandy
½ cup dry sherry**

**½ cup cold water
1¼ cups fresh orange juice
1 cup sugar
¼ cup Kirsch
whipped cream**

Soak gelatin in cold water. Dissolve in boiling water. Add sugar and stir until dissolved. Add everything else. Put directly into sherbet cups or small compotes. Chill. Just before serving, top with whipped cream. Serves 6 to 8.

**Mrs. Frank Sheffield (Quenelle Harrold)
Atlanta**

# WINE JELLY

**4 packages plain gelatin
3½ cups sugar
3 lemons
4 cups boiling water**

**3 cups sherry
¼ cup rum
2 cups cold water**

Put gelatin in large bowl. Add 2 cups cold water and let stand a few minutes. Add 4 cups boiling water and 3½ cups sugar. Stir until entirely dissolved. Add juice of 3 lemons. Mix well. Add sherry and rum. Put into jars and keep in refrigerator. Serve with or without cream. Serves 16.

**Mrs. Charles H. Watt (Julie Rogers)
Thomasville**

# Cakes, Cookies and Candies

Mary F. Passalacque

## GRANDMA GIBBS' DARK FRUIT CAKE

2 pounds raisins
½ pound candied cherries,
  sliced
½ pound candied pineapple,
  sliced
½ pound citron, slivered
1 pound figs, cut in bits
1 pound butter or margarine
1 pound dark brown sugar or
  light brown or granulated
  may be used
1 cup molasses
4 cups flour

6 eggs
1 wine glass of sherry or brandy or
  about ⅓ cup, any desired fruit
  juice
1½ teaspoons nutmeg, freshly
  grated
3 teaspoons cloves
3 teaspoons cinnamon
3 teaspoons baking powder
1½ pounds nut meats, almonds,
  pecans, black walnuts or brazil
  nuts or mixed nuts, broken

Cream butter and sugar. Add beaten eggs. Sift flour before measuring, then take out 1 cup of the flour for dusting the fruit. Sift the rest of the flour with the other spices and dry ingredients. Add the flour mixture and the fruits and nuts alternately with the molasses and wine to the egg and butter mixture. Mix well by hand. Paper line and grease a tube cake pan. Bake in a slow oven, 300 degrees, approximately 5 hours or until done. This will make about 6½ pounds of cake.

**Mrs. James M. Treadwell, Jr. (Lynn Walker)**
**Madison**

## CHRISTMAS CAKE

1½ cups butter
2 cups sugar
6 eggs, well beaten
4 cups all purpose flour
½ pound candied red cherries,
  chopped
½ pound candied green
  cherries, chopped

½ pound candied pineapple,
  chopped
¼ teaspoon salt
2 teaspoons baking powder
1 cup whiskey
2 teaspoons vanilla
1 pound pecans, chopped

Cream butter and sugar. Add well beaten eggs and mix thoroughly. Dredge red cherries, green cherries and pineapple in ½ cup of the flour. Sift remaining flour (3½ cups) with salt and baking powder. Slowly add flour to creamed mixture, then add whiskey and vanilla. Add pecans and mix well. Line 2 loaf pans with foil. Fill pans about two thirds full. Place in preheated 300 degree oven. Bake 1 hour and 15 minutes or until done, depending on size of loaf pan. (Freezes well.)

**Mrs. Converse Ferrell (Jane Lumpkin)**
**Valdosta**

# JAPANESE FRUIT CAKE

| | |
|---|---|
| 1 cup butter | 2 teaspoons baking powder |
| 2 cups sugar | 1 teaspoon vanilla |
| 3½ cups flour | 1 scant cup water or milk |
| 5 eggs | |

Cream butter and sugar until fluffy. Add eggs one at a time, beating well after each addition. Add flour to which baking powder has been added alternately with water until well mixed. Stir in vanilla.

Divide batter into parts. To one part add:

| | |
|---|---|
| 1 teaspoon cinnamon | ¼ pound raisins |
| 1 teaspoon allspice | ½ cup pecans, chopped |
| ½ teaspoon cloves | |

Bake in two layers, one white, one spiced, at about 325 degrees for about 20 minutes or until straw comes out clean.

FILLING

| | |
|---|---|
| juice of 2 lemons | 2 cups sugar |
| grated rind of one lemon | 1 cup boiling water |
| 1 good sized coconut, grated | 1 tablespoon cornstarch |
| ½ cup cold water | |

Put all ingredients, except cornstarch, in saucepan. When mixture begins to boil, add cornstarch which has been dissolved in ½ cup cold water. Continue to cook, stirring constantly, until mixture drops in a lump from spoon. Cook and spread between layers and on top.

**Mrs. James R. Buchanan (Elizabeth Smith)**
**Americus**

# FIG CAKE

| | |
|---|---|
| 2 cups flour | 1 teaspoon nutmeg |
| 1½ cups sugar | 1 cup nuts, chopped |
| 1 teaspoon salt | 1 cup cooking oil |
| 1 teaspoon soda | 3 eggs |
| 1 teaspoon ground cloves | 1 cup buttermilk |
| 1 teaspoon cinnamon | 1 cup fig preserves, chopped |

Sift dry ingredients. Add oil and eggs. Beat well. Add buttermilk, figs, and nuts. Beat well. Pour into bundt pan. Bake in 325-degree oven for 45 minutes to 1 hour.

**Mrs. John Tyler Mauldin (Anne Scott Harman)**
**Atlanta**

# APPLE CAKE

1¼ cups cooking oil
3 eggs
3 cups fresh apples, diced
1 teaspoon soda
2 cups sugar

1 cup chopped pecans
3 cups flour
1 teaspoon salt
1 teaspoon vanilla

Beat eggs well, add oil and sugar, mix well and add apples. Sift flour, measure again and sift three times with the soda and salt. Stir flour mixture into egg mixture, blending well. Add pecans and vanilla. Pour into pan and put into cold oven and turn heat to 325 degrees. Cook until done. Frost with caramel icing.

**Mrs. Charles M. Woolfolk (Eleanor Bussey)**
**Columbus**

# BLENDER DELIGHT CHEESECAKE

CRUST

1½ cups graham cracker
　crumbs
⅓ cup brown sugar

½ teaspoon cinnamon
⅓ cup melted butter

Mix above ingredients to form pie crust in deep 10″ pie pan.

FILLING

8 ounces cream cheese
1½ cups creamed cottage
　cheese, softened
2 eggs, beaten

1½ cups sugar
½ teaspoon vanilla
1 cup sour cream

Put eggs, sugar, cottage cheese, softened cream cheese, broken into small pieces, and vanilla into blender. Mix until of a smooth consistency. Pour into pie crust. Bake in 350 degree oven thirty minutes or until set. Spread sour cream over pie while hot. Cool and chill. Yield: 8-10 servings.

**Mrs. Jack Cutts Smith (Rhett Jenkins)**
**Moultrie**

# ANGEL GINGERBREAD

1 egg
½ cup sugar
½ cup molasses
½ cup salad oil
1½ cups flour
½ teaspoon nutmeg, freshly
  grated

½ teaspoon powdered cinnamon
½ teaspoon salt
1 teaspoon soda
½ teaspoon powdered ginger
½ cup water, boiling

Beat egg, add sugar, molasses and oil. Sift dry ingredients together. Add and stir well. Add boiling water. Bake in greased and floured 9x12-inch pan or pyrex dish at 350 degrees for 30 minutes. If you like it thicker, use an 8-inch square pan.
**Mrs. Walter Burt, Jr. (Helen Higginbotham)**
**Albany**

# ITALIAN CREAM CAKE

½ cup margarine
½ cup shortening
2 cups sugar
5 eggs, separated
2 cups flour

1 teaspoon soda
1 cup buttermilk
1 teaspoon vanilla
¾ cup coconut, grated
1 cup nuts, chopped

Cream margarine, shortening and sugar until light and fluffy. Add egg yolks. Mix well. Sift flour and soda together. Add to creamed mixture alternately with buttermilk, beginning and ending with dry ingredients. Add vanilla, coconut and nuts. Fold in stiffly beaten egg whites. Pour into three 9-inch greased and floured cake pans. Bake in 350 degree oven for 30 to 35 minutes or until done. Fill and frost with icing. *Note:* Cuts better if made a day ahead.

ICING

¼ cup margarine
8 ounces cream cheese
1 pound confectioners' sugar,
  sifted

1 teaspoon vanilla

Cream margarine and cream cheese together; add sugar and vanilla. Mix well. (If too stiff, add milk, 1 teaspoon at a time.) Garnish with pecans, grated coconut or candied fruit.
**Mrs. William Hanger (Sudie Clark)**
**Atlanta**

# CARROT CAKE

| | |
|---|---|
| 4 eggs | 1 teaspoon cinnamon |
| 2 cups sugar | 1 teaspoon vanilla |
| 1½ cups vegetable oil | 3 drops black walnut flavoring |
| 2 cups self-rising flour | 1 cup grated carrots |

Combine eggs, sugar and oil. Add remaining ingredients. Mix well and bake in a 10-inch tube pan which has been greased and floured for 1½ hours in a 350-degree oven.

GLAZE

| | |
|---|---|
| 1 cup sugar | 1 teaspoon soda |
| ½ cup buttermilk | 1 teaspoon corn syrup |

Cook until bubbly. Pour over cake while cake is still warm. Let set in pan several hours or overnight.

**Mrs. Charles Thomas Huggins (Sada Mason)**
**Augusta**

# ORANGE, NUT, DATE CAKE

| | |
|---|---|
| 1 cup sugar | 1 cup pecans, chopped |
| ½ cup butter | 1 cup dates, chopped |
| 2 eggs | ⅔ cup sour milk |
| grated rind of one orange | 1 teaspoon soda |
| 2 cups plain flour | ¼ teaspoon salt |

Cream butter, flour and sugar; add beaten eggs, one at a time, then dates, nuts and rind. Sift soda and salt with flour; mix into above mixture alternately with milk. Bake at 300 degrees.

GLAZE

| | |
|---|---|
| juice one orange | ½ cup sugar |

Blend juice and sugar well. Pour this over cake while hot. Let stand until juice is absorbed.

**Mrs. Mercer Sherman (Ernestine Walker)**
**Albany**

# LUSCIOUS BANANA CAKE

2 cups sugar
2 eggs
3 cups flour, plain
1½ teaspoons baking powder
1⅛ cup buttermilk
¾ cup butter

½ teaspoon vanilla
1½ teaspoons baking soda
½ teaspoon salt
1½ cups mashed bananas—not too
  mushy

Cream butter, add sugar gradually. Beat in eggs, one at a time. Sift together dry ingredients and add alternately with buttermilk. Add vanilla and bananas. Bake in three greased and floured layer cake pans, at 350 degrees until done. Fill and frost with following frosting.

ICING

½ cup butter or margarine
3 ounces cream cheese,
  softened
1 pound confectioners' sugar

1 teaspoon vanilla
2 tablespoons milk
⅔ cup nuts, chopped
pinch of salt

Cream together butter and cream cheese. Add the box of sugar, vanilla and nuts. Add more milk to make spreadable, if necessary.
**Mrs. Joe Glenn Smith (Virginia Marie Converse)**
**Hahira**

# MRS. REYNOLDS FLOURNOY'S CHOCOLATE ICE BOX CAKE

¼ pound Baker's sweet
  chocolate
2½ teaspoons water
1 egg, separated

1 tablespoon confectioners' sugar
¼ cup nut meats
½ cup whipping cream, whipped
1 angel food cake

Melt chocolate in top of double boiler. Add 2½ teaspoons water and blend well. Remove from heat and add one egg yolk beaten until blended. Add 1 tablespoon confectioners' sugar and ¼ cup nut meats and blend well. Add cream which has been whipped, then fold in stiffly beaten egg white. Chill in Charlotte mold or bowl and decorate with whipped cream. *OR* slice angel food cake twice through the center and fill with the chocolate mixture. Then fill the center of the cake. Ice the cake with whipped cream sweetened with sugar and vanilla.
**Mrs. Jack M. Passailaigue (Mary Flournoy)**
**Columbus**

## ORANGE SLICE CAKE

2 cups coconut, grated
2 cups sugar
2 cups flour
2 cups pecans, chopped
1 cup butter
1 cup buttermilk

1 pound orange slices, chopped
½ pound dates
1 teaspoon soda
½ teaspoon salt
4 eggs
2 tablespoons orange peel

Cream sugar, butter and eggs. Mix soda, salt and 1 cup flour. Add to first mixture along with buttermilk. Add orange slices, dates, nuts, and coconut. Work in 1 cup flour. Bake in an angel food cake pan for 1 hour at 350 degrees. Remove from pan while hot and punch full of holes. Pour half of glaze over cake and save the rest to serve over it.

ICING

2 cups powdered sugar
1 cup orange juice

1 tablespoon grated orange peel

Mix together and pour half over cake while it is hot. Save other half to serve with it.

**Mrs. Montague Graham Clark, Jr. (Elizabeth Hoyt)**
**Point Lookout, Missouri**

## BLACKBERRY JAM CAKE

1 cup shortening
2 cups sugar
4 egg yolks, beaten
1 teaspoon vanilla
3 cups sifted flour
1 teaspoon soda
2 teaspoons cinnamon

1 teaspoon nutmeg
1 teaspoon cloves
1 teaspoon allspice
1 cup buttermilk
1 cup blackberry jam (seedless)
4 egg whites, beaten

Cream shortening and sugar together until light. Add beaten egg yolks and vanilla. Beat until thoroughly blended. Sift dry ingredients together and add alternately with buttermilk. Stir in blackberry jam. Fold in egg whites beaten stiff but not dry. Pour batter into large tube pan or bundt pan lightly greased. Bake at 325 degrees for 30 minutes; increase heat to 350 degrees and continue baking for about 45 minutes or until cake tester comes out dry and free of batter. Set pan on wire rack and allow cake to cool 20 minutes before removing from pan.

**Mrs. Banks Haley, Jr. (Eloise Thackston)**
**Albany**

# PINEAPPLE CAKE

¼ pound butter
1 cup sugar
2 eggs
1½ cups unsifted flour
3 teaspoons baking powder

⅛ teaspoon salt
¾ teaspoon vanilla
6 tablespoons pineapple juice
¼ cup evaporated or fresh milk

Cream butter and sugar well. Add eggs and beat well. Sift flour with baking powder and alternate adding flour, milk and pineapple juice to creamed mixture. Bake in two greased and floured 8-inch cake pans at 350 degrees. This makes a thin batter.

ICING

2 tablespoons butter
pinch of salt
⅔ pound confectioners' sugar

juice of ½ lemon
4 to 6 tablespoons pineapple juice

Melt butter. Add salt, sugar and lemon juice. Add pineapple juice until icing is right consistency for spreading. This is an original recipe of Mrs. Eustace Sirmans.

**Mrs. Thomas Starnes, Jr. (Edith Sirmans)**
**Jacksonville, Florida**

# WINDSOR FORGE SPONGE CAKE

2 cups sugar
8 eggs, separated

2 cups flour

Beat egg whites until stiff. Beat in 1 tablespoon of sugar at a time until 8 tablespoonfuls have been beaten into whites. Set aside. Beat egg yolks and remaining sugar until thick. Fold whites into yolk mixture. Gradually sift flour over this, folding after each several sifts. Grease and flour a 10″ Turk's head pan (tube pan). Pour batter into pan. Bake 1 hour in 325 degree oven. Invert pan over wire rack and cool in pan. To serve, slice cake and eat "as is." Delicious with fresh fruit in season or with fresh fruit ice cream. Serves 12 generously.

**Mrs. Francis Willson Daily (Alice Lincoln Hunt)**
**Savannah**

(A family recipe dating back to the days of the great Pennsylvania Iron Masters of the 18th century.)

# MARBLE CAKE

2 sticks butter
1½ cups sugar
4 eggs, separated
½ cup milk

2 cups self-rising flour
1 teaspoon vanilla
¼ cup chocolate syrup

Cream butter and sugar. Add yolks, one at a time, beating after each addition. Add vanilla to milk. Sift flour. Add flour alternately with milk. Beat egg whites until they form soft peaks. Fold into batter. Remove ⅓ of the batter to small bowl and mix in the chocolate syrup. Grease and flour tube pan. Fill with ½ of the batter. Add chocolate batter and swirl with a spoon. Add remaining batter. Bake in preheated oven 300 degrees for 1 hour. Cool and ice with Seven Minute White Icing.

**Mrs. John Ely Simpson (Marjorie McKinnon)**
**Savannah**

# MADDOX WHITE FRUIT CAKE

¾ pound margarine
3 cups sugar
5 cups plain flour, sifted
2 teaspoons baking powder
12 egg whites, unbeaten
1 pound crystallized cherries,
   chopped
1 pound crystallized
   pineapple, chopped

1 cup orange juice
1 tablespoon vanilla flavoring
1 tablespoon lemon flavoring
½ pound citron, chopped
1 pound white raisins
½ pound pecans, chopped
1 large coconut, grated, or frozen
   grated coconut

Combine fruit and nuts with last cup of flour, then with the cake mixture. Put into *two* tube cake pans lined on the bottom with brown paper and greased well. Cook at 325 degrees for about an hour and a half, or until cake pulls away from sides of cake pan. If the cakes are brown on top at the end of an hour, cover them lightly with aluminum foil for the remainder of the cooking time.

Note: These cakes will keep for several weeks in a cake tin or can be frozen.

**Mrs. William E. Johnson (Nancy Hale)**
**Rome**

# FRESCA CAKE

1½ cups butter, softened
3 cups sugar
5 eggs
3 cups plain flour (sifted after
    measuring)

2 tablespoons lemon extract
¾ cup Fresca

Cream sugar and butter. Add eggs, one at a time, mixing well. Add flour and Fresca (alternating). Add lemon extract. Pour into bundt pan that has been greased and floured. Bake at 325 degrees for 1 hour and 15 minutes.

**Mrs. James Wimberly (Helen Boardman)**
**Atlanta**

# BEA MASSENGALE'S DEVIL'S FOOD CAKE WITH SEAFOAM ICING

1 cup butter
2 whole eggs
3 ounces unsweetened
    chocolate, melted
1 teaspoon soda
¾ cup sour milk or
    buttermilk

2 cups sugar
4 eggs, separated
2½ cups cake flour
1 pinch salt
1 teaspoon vanilla

Cream butter and sugar together thoroughly. Add 2 whole eggs and 4 egg yolks. Beat until light and fluffy. (Set whites aside for icing.) Add unsweetened chocolate. Sift together flour, soda and salt. Add dry ingredients alternating with sour milk or buttermilk. Bake in layer pans at 350 degrees for 25 to 30 minutes. This makes a 3-layer cake.

SEAFOAM ICING

1 pound brown sugar
1 cup water
1 teaspoon vanilla

1 cup white sugar
4 egg whites

Mix sugars and water. Bring to a boil until it spins a good thread. Beat egg whites until stiff. Add boiling syrup a little at a time. Beat until dull on top and thickened. Add vanilla. Do not make on a warm, wet day.

**Mrs. Thomas Maxwell Blanchard (Anne Harper)**
**Augusta**

# BEST EVER CHOCOLATE CAKE

2½ cups sugar
1 cup shortening or margarine
2 eggs
2½ cups packed flour
½ cup cocoa

½ teaspoon salt
1 cup buttermilk
1 cup boiling water
2 scant teaspoons soda

Cream sugar and shortening together and add eggs one at a time. Sift flour three times with cocoa. Add salt. Add buttermilk. Add soda and water and add to above ingredients. Grease and flour a 9x13x2-inch pan. Bake at 300 degrees for 90 minutes. Test for doneness. Cool and ice with your favorite icing.

**Mrs. John Driver (Mary Frances Calhoun)**
**Columbus**

# AUNT MARY'S COCOA POUND CAKE

1½ cups butter or margarine
3 cups sugar
5 eggs
3½ cups flour
1 cup milk

½ teaspoon salt
1 teaspoon baking powder
1 teaspoon vanilla
4 tablespoons cocoa

Cream butter and sugar. Add eggs one at a time, beating thoroughly after each addition. Mix together flour, salt, baking powder, vanilla, cocoa and add alternating with milk. Pour batter into a greased bundt or angel food pan. Bake 1½ hours at 300 degrees. Let cool for several minutes, remove from pan and ice with chocolate glaze.

CHOCOLATE GLAZE

2 tablespoons butter or
  margarine
1 square unsweetened
  chocolate

2 tablespoons water, boiling
1 cup confectioners' sugar, sifted

Melt butter and chocolate. Combine with rest of ingredients. Beat until smooth. Glaze may be thin but will thicken as it cools.

**Mrs. James G. Hardee III (Mary Cunningham)**
**Savannah**

# POUND CAKE

2½ cups sugar
4 cups all-purpose flour
½ teaspoon baking powder
1 cup butter

½ cup Crisco
5 large eggs
1 teaspoon vanilla
1 scant cup water

Put sugar in blender, ½ cup at a time to pulverize. Cream butter and Crisco, add pulverized sugar. Sift flour, measure, add baking powder and sift again. Add eggs one at a time to sugar mixture beating after each addition for 2 minutes. Add flour and water alternately, beginning and ending with flour. Then add vanilla. When adding flour turn mixer to lowest speed. Bake at 350 degrees for 1 hour and 15 minutes or a little longer if necessary. May be baked in 2 greased loaf pans or 1 tube pan.

**Mrs. Lonnie Dunlap Ferguson (Georgia Boykin)**
**Thomasville**

# COCONUT POUND CAKE

1½ cups butter
2½ cups sugar
3 cups plain flour
2 teaspoons coconut flavoring
5 eggs

1 cup milk
1 teaspoon baking powder
¼ teaspoon salt
1 cup coconut, grated, fresh or
    tinned

Mix butter and sugar ten minutes at high speed. Add eggs one at a time. Sift flour, salt, baking powder, together. Add milk alternately with flour mixture. Add flavoring. Fold coconut in last. Pour into a large greased and floured tube pan. Place in a cold oven. Bake at 300 degrees for 1½ hours.

SAUCE

1 cup sugar
1 cup water

¼ cup white corn syrup
2 teaspoons coconut flavoring

Bring to a boil and pour over cake in pan while cake is still hot. Let cake stand in pan until cool.

**Mrs. John Archie Cauble (Florence Horkan)**
**Moultrie**

# CHOCOLATE POUND CAKE

| | |
|---|---|
| 1 cup butter | ¼ teaspoon salt |
| ½ cup Crisco | 4 heaping tablespoons cocoa |
| 3 cups sugar | 5 eggs |
| 3 cups plain flour | 1 cup milk |
| ½ teaspoon baking powder | 1 tablespoon vanilla |

Cream sugar, butter and shortening, add eggs one at a time, beating after each addition. Sift flour, baking powder, salt and cocoa. Add this alternately to creamed mixture with milk and vanilla. Bake at 300 degrees for 1½ hours to 2 hours.

**Mrs. Wightman Warren (Dorothy Wightman)**
**Albany**

# LEMON SQUARES

CRUST

| | |
|---|---|
| 2 cups flour | ½ cup confectioners' sugar |
| 1 cup soft butter | pinch salt |

Mix together thoroughly and pack into a 12x7½ greased, floured pan. Bring crust up on sides. Cook about twenty minutes in 350° oven. Remove from oven and quickly put in following mixture:

FILLING

| | |
|---|---|
| 4 eggs | 4 tablespoons lemon juice |
| 2 cups sugar added gradually | grated rind of two lemons |

Beat eggs slightly with fork. (Don't overbeat.) Add other ingredients and mix well. Pour over first mixture. Bake 25 minutes at 350 degrees. When cool but not cold, cut in squares. Have filling prepared before time to take crust from oven.

**Mrs. James Gainer Balling (Jeannette Martin Jones)**
**Uniontown, Pennsylvania**

## NUT SQUARES

| | |
|---|---|
| 1 heaping cup nuts, broken | ¼ teaspoon salt |
| 1 cup brown sugar | ¼ teaspoon soda |
| 1 large egg | 1 teaspoon almond flavoring |
| 5 rounded tablespoons flour | |

Beat egg, add sugar. Mix flour, salt, soda and sift into egg and sugar mixture. Add almond flavoring. Pour into well-greased 8-inch square pan. Bake in 350 degree oven for 20 minutes. Sprinkle with confectioners' sugar. Do not cut until cold. Makes 16 square cookies.

**Mrs. J. Mack Barnes (Betty Newton)**
**Jekyll Island**

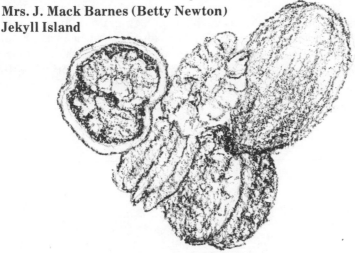

## LADYFINGERS

| | |
|---|---|
| ½ cup egg whites (4 eggs) | 1 teaspoon vanilla |
| ¼ teaspoon cream of tartar | 1¼ cups cake flour, sifted |
| 10 tablespoons sugar | ½ teaspoon baking powder |
| 2 egg yolks | confectioners' sugar |
| ⅛ teaspoon salt | |

Beat egg whites to foam. Add cream of tartar. Gradually add 5 tablespoons sugar. Beat until mixture is very stiff. Beat egg yolks, salt, and vanilla until light. Gradually add other 5 tablespoons sugar. Beat until thick. Fold egg yolk mixture into egg whites. Fold in flour sifted with baking powder. Form 3-inch fingers on well greased cookie sheet. Bake at 350 degrees for 12 minutes. Sift confectioners' sugar over ladyfingers as soon as taken from oven. Remove from sheet immediately. Makes 3 dozen.

**Mrs. Lee Hudson (Frances Davenport)**
**Americus**

## ROUND TABLE ROSETTES

1 cup plain flour, sifted
½ cup evaporated milk
½ cup water
½ teaspoon salt

1 teaspoon sugar
1 unbeaten egg
oil for deep frying
onion salt or confectioners' sugar

Mix together milk, water, salt, sugar and egg. Stir slowly into flour and beat until smooth. Heat oil to 365 degrees, using an electric frying pan if possible. Dip rosette iron into hot oil for about 10 seconds, draining excess oil as you remove. Immediately, dip heated iron into batter to not more than three-fourths its height. Plunge into hot oil and cook about two minutes until desired brownness is reached. Remove from iron and drain well on paper towels. Sprinkle lightly with onion salt. Store, when cool, in an air-tight tin. Will keep ten days or more when properly stored. Makes about 2½ dozen. For sweet wafer-type rosettes, omit onion salt and sprinkle with confectioners' sugar instead.

**Mrs. Walter Edward Lee, Jr. (Betty Monroe)**
**Waycross**

## SNICKER DOODLES

1 cup margarine (or butter)
1½ cups brown sugar
½ teaspoon salt
2 eggs, separated
1 cup sour milk
2 cups flour
1 teaspoon soda

½ teaspoon cloves
½ teaspoon nutmeg
1 teaspoon cinnamon
1 cup raisins
1 cup nuts
grated rind of 1 lemon

Beat margarine (or butter) and egg yolks until light and fluffy. Add lemon rind. Alternate milk with dry ingredients which have been sifted together. Add beaten egg whites and then fold in raisins and nuts which have been lightly dusted with flour. Bake in medium size cup cake tins at 375-400 degrees for 20-25 minutes. Serve warm. Makes around 18-24 depending on size of tins.

**Mrs. John Zantzinger Speer (Frances Carter Tanham)**
**Augusta**

# BUTTERSCOTCH DROPS

12 ounces butterscotch
morsels
2 tablespoons peanut butter,
plain or crunchy

½ to 1 cup almonds, slivered and
toasted
2 cups crisp cornflakes
½ teaspoon vanilla

Melt the butterscotch drops in a double boiler. Add the peanut butter and stir well. Add cornflakes, toasted nuts, and vanilla. Drop by teaspoonfuls on a greased cookie sheet and refrigerate until firm. Makes four to six dozen depending on size. They freeze well.

**Mrs. Frank Chipman Dudley, Sr. (Patsy Brannen Woodruff)
Athens**

# CHOCOLATE GLAZED ÉCLAIRS

½ cup butter
¼ teaspoon salt
1 cup all-purpose flour
4 eggs
1 3-ounce package vanilla
pudding mix

¼ teaspoon almond extract
1 cup whipped cream
1 cup water

Preheat oven to 375 degrees and grease a large cookie sheet. In a 3-quart saucepan over high heat, heat 1 cup water, butter and salt until butter melts and mixture boils. Reduce heat to low. With a wooden spoon vigorously stir in flour until mixture forms a ball and leaves the side of pan. Remove from heat immediately and let cool a minute or two. Vigorously beat eggs into mixture until thoroughly blended. Then drop by ¼ cup full onto cookie sheet 2 inches apart and in rows 6 inches apart. Spread each mound of dough into 1 5-inch by ¾-inch rectangle, rounding the corners. Bake 40 minutes or until lightly brown. Cut a slit in the side of each shell and bake 10 minutes longer. Cool shells on wire rack.

PUDDING: Prepare pudding mix as label says—but add almond extract. Cover surface with wax paper and chill. Fold in whipped cream. Slit about ⅓ from top of each shell and fill bottom of shells with filling. Replace tops and spread with chocolate glaze. Refrigerate until ready to serve. Makes 10 layered eclairs.

CHOCOLATE GLAZE: In a small saucepan over low heat melt 2 squares of semi-sweet chocolate. Add 2 tablespoons of butter or margarine. Stirring constantly. Stir in 1 cup confectioners' sugar and add 3 tablespoons of milk. Beat until smooth.

**Mrs. Martin Cooper (Margaret Philips)
Thomasville**

# DATE BARS

2 eggs, well beaten
½ teaspoon cinnamon
1 teaspoon baking powder
1 cup nuts, chopped
½ tablespoon vanilla

¾ cup brown sugar
6 tablespoons flour, sifted
1 tablespoon orange rind, grated
1 cup dates, cut in bits
confectioners' sugar

Combine beaten eggs with sugar, cinnamon, orange rind, vanilla, flour and baking powder. Add nuts and dates. Bake in a greased 8x8 inch pan which has a depth of two inches, in a 325 degree oven for about forty minutes. Cut in strips about two inches by one inch and sprinkle with powdered sugar. Makes about eighteen bars.

**Mrs. Edgeworth Lamkin (Sarah Gerdine)**
**Athens**

# LACE WAFERS

1 egg
2 cups brown sugar
2 cups quick oatmeal

1 tablespoon vanilla extract
¾ cup butter
¼ teaspoon salt

Cream butter and sugar. Add beaten egg, salt and flavoring. Beat well and add oatmeal. Mix thoroughly. Drop from teaspoon on greased aluminum foil on cookie tins, 12 to a tin. Cook 10 minutes at 300 degrees. Remove when slightly cool.

**Mrs. John C. Symmes (Jane H. Campbell)**
**Madison**

# SAND TARTS

2 cups flour
1 cup melted butter
1 teaspoon vanilla
3 tablespoons sugar

1 tablespoon water
1 cup chopped pecans
1 cup confectioners' sugar

Mix flour and granulated sugar. Add melted butter, water and mix. Stir in vanilla and pecans. Roll dough into balls by the teaspoonful. Place on ungreased cookie sheet one inch apart. Bake at 275 degrees about 1½ hours. Roll in confectioners' sugar while warm. Makes 45-50 cookies.

**Mrs. Joe Britt Ehresman (Kay Weeks)**
**Brunswick**

# DROP COOKIES

1 cup butter
1 cup sugar
2 cups flour
2 teaspoons baking powder
2 teaspoons salt
4 egg yolks

2 tablespoons fresh lemon juice
1 tablespoon milk (if needed to
   make dough workable)
1 teaspoon grated lemon rind
1½ cups black walnuts, half of the
   nuts may be pecans

Cream butter, add sugar gradually, then egg yolks and beat well. Add sifted dry ingredients, add the lemon juice and rind and lastly nut meats. Drop by teaspoon portions on ungreased cookie sheet about two inches apart. The mixture is consistency of a very soft dough and spreads out in cooking. Bake in 300 degree oven for approximately six minutes. They burn easily. Remove from oven, cool three or four minutes. Slip a very thin spatula under each cookie. Place on wire rack to cool. Break very easily and must be handled very quickly while still warm.

**Mrs. Edwin W. Allen, Sr. (Catherine Tait)**
**Milledgeville**

# PEANUT BUTTER MELT-AWAYS

1 cup butter
1½ cups peanut butter
3 cups confectioners' sugar

1 ounce paraffin
6 ounces German's sweet
   chocolate

Mix butter, peanut butter, and sugar. Pinch off pieces and roll into small balls. Refrigerate on wax paper. Melt paraffin and chocolate together in top of double boiler over hot, not boiling water. Dip each ball into hot chocolate mixture to coat the outside. (Work quickly, using a fork or toothpick.) Place on wax paper and refrigerate. Do not let balls touch one another. Yield: 4-5 dozen.

**Mrs. Joe Uhler (Margaret Bybee Anderson)**
**Milledgeville**

## DISAPPEARING MARSHMALLOW BROWNIES

½ cup butterscotch pieces
¼ cup butter
¾ cup all purpose flour
⅓ cup brown sugar, firmly
   packed
1 teasooon baking powder
¼ teaspoon salt

1 egg
½ teaspoon vanilla
1 cup miniature marshmallows
6 ounces semi-sweet chocolate
   pieces
¼ cup chopped nuts

Grease bottom and sides of a 9-inch square pan. Heat oven to 350 degrees. In a 3 quart heavy sauce pan, over medium heat, melt butterscotch pieces with butter, stirring constantly. Remove from heat. Cool to lukewarm. Add flour, brown sugar, baking powder, salt, egg and vanilla. Mix well. Fold in marshmallows, chocolate pieces and nuts. Spread in prepared pan. Bake at 350 degrees for 20-25 minutes. Do not over bake. Center will be jiggly but becomes firm on cooling.

**Mrs. N. A. Hardin (Margaret Fatio L'Engle)**
**Forsyth**

## BROWN SUGAR BROWNIES

1 pound butter
1 cup light brown sugar
1 cup chopped nuts

4 cups flour
2 teaspoons vanilla

Cream butter and sugar. Add flour, one cup at a time. Stir in nuts and vanilla. Place in a 16x11-inch pan and pat down. Mark off squares and place ¼ nut on each. Bake at 350 degrees for 30 minutes. Sprinkle with granulated sugar. Let cool in pan. Cut through into squares.

**Mrs. Joseph Elliott Bright (Marion Converse)**
**Valdosta**

## MAGGIE'S CHOCOLATE CHIP COOKIES

6 ounces chocolate chips
1 cup flour
½ cup corn oil
½ cup chopped nuts
½ teaspoon baking soda

1 egg
½ cup sugar
½ cup brown sugar
1 teaspoon vanilla
1 teaspoon salt

Combine egg, oil and vanilla in a bowl. Add flour, salt and soda. Add chocolate chips and nuts. Spoon, drop on an ungreased cookie sheet. Bake approximately 6 minutes in 375-degree oven.

**Mrs. Louis LeGarde Battey (Mary Mell)**
**Augusta**

# CHOCOLATE THINSIES

2 ounces unsweetened
  chocolate
½ cup butter, melted
1 cup sugar
grated nuts

½ cup flour
¼ teaspoon salt
2 eggs
1 teaspoon vanilla

Into top of double boiler put 2 squares of chocolate and melt over hot water. Add the melted butter, sugar, flour, salt. Beat well. Add well-beaten eggs and vanilla. Spread with spatula very thinly on greased cookie sheet. Sprinkle thickly with grated nuts. Bake in 400 degree oven for 10 minutes. Cut while hot.

**Mrs. Howell Hollis (Janet Bowers)**
**Columbus**

# CHOCOLATE DELIGHTS

1¼ cups flour
½ cup butter
1 egg yolk
2 tablespoons water
1 teaspoon sugar
1 teaspoon baking powder

2 cups chocolate morsels
2 eggs
¾ cup sugar
6 tablespoons melted butter
2 teaspoons vanilla
2 cups nuts, chopped

Beat butter, egg yolk and water together. Sift and stir in flour and 1 teaspoon sugar and baking powder. Press into greased pan, 13x9x2-inch. Bake in 350 degree oven for 10 minutes. Remove from oven and sprinkle crust with chocolate morsels. Return to oven for 1 minute. Remove and spread chocolate on top. Beat 2 eggs until thick. Add ¾ cup sugar, 6 tablespoons melted butter, vanilla and nuts. Spread over top and bake for 30 to 35 minutes in 350 degree oven. When cooled, cut into 1½-inch squares. Makes about 4 dozen.

**Mrs. Barry Lee Frazier (Nancy Kennon)**
**Atlanta**

## EGGNOG FUDGE

2 cups sugar
1 cup eggnog
1 tablespoon light corn syrup
4 tablespoons butter or
  margarine

1 teaspoon vanilla
½ cup chopped walnuts
2 tablespoons semisweet chocolate
  pieces

Butter sides of heavy 3-quart saucepan. In prepared pan, combine sugar, eggnog, and corn syrup. Cook over medium heat, stirring constantly until sugar dissolves and mixture comes to a boil. Cook to soft ball stage (238 degrees F.) stirring only as necessary. Immediately remove from heat and cool to lukewarm (110 degrees F.) without stirring. Add the 2 tablespoons butter and the vanilla. Beat vigorously till fudge becomes very thick and starts to lose its gloss. Quickly stir in nuts. Spread in buttered 8x4x2-inch pan. In glass 1-cup measure, combine chocolate pieces and remaining 2 tablespoons of butter. Set cup in saucepan filled with 1-inch water; heat till melted. Drizzle over top of fudge; score in squares while warm. Cut when cool and firm. Makes 1 pound.

**Mrs. Montague Graham Clark, Jr. (Elizabeth Hoyt)**
**Point Lookout, Missouri**

## MARSHMALLOW FUDGE

½ cup butter or margarine
⅛ teaspoon salt
1 6-ounce can evaporated milk
  (⅔ cup)
2¼ cups sugar
1 8-ounce package
  marshmallows

1 6-ounce package chocolate chips
1 square semisweet chocolate cut
  in pieces
1 teaspoon vanilla
½ cup chopped nuts

Combine butter, salt, evaporated milk and sugar in 2 quart heavy saucepan. Stir and bring to a boil; then continue cooking at a steady low boil 8½ minutes, stirring constantly. Meanwhile, combine marshmallows, chocolate chips, chocolate and vanilla. Pour hot candy over mixture and blend with electric mixer. Add nuts. Pour into buttered 9-inch square pan; cool. Cut in 1-inch squares. Makes 81 pieces, or about 2½ pounds.

**Mrs. Leon Belk (Marsha Blackmar)**
**Columbus**

# SPICED PECANS

1 egg white
1 pound pecans
½ cup sugar

½ teaspoon cinnamon
½ teaspoon salt
1 teaspoon water

Beat 1 egg white with 1 teaspoon water and add one pound pecans; mix well until pecans are well-coated. Mix ½ cup sugar with ½ teaspoon cinnamon and ½ teaspoon salt. Pour mixture over nuts; mix well. Put nuts on greased cookie sheet; bake in 200 degree oven for 1 hour stirring nuts every 15 minutes.

Mrs. Charles Iverson Bryans (Louise K. Rowland)
Augusta

# LOUISE HICKY'S PRALINES

3 cups sugar
3 cups shelled pecans
butter ("size of large egg")
milk "enough to cover dry
    ingredients", approximately
    1½ cups "half and half milk
    is best"

¼ teaspoon salt
¼ teaspoon soda
1 to 1½ teaspoons vanilla

(The above is just the way Louise gave the recipe.) Put dry ingredients (sugar, salt and soda) into a rather tall heavy 10 cup boiler. Add milk. Cook one minute on high then lower to medium heat and cook until mixture begins to color slightly. Drop in butter (3½ to 4 tablespoons) when mixture is hot enough to melt the butter. Cook until a small amount of mixture dropped into cold water makes a soft ball between fingers. Remove from heat. *Immediately* add vanilla and nuts and beat well. Much depends upon the beating. If not beaten sufficiently, mixture will be too thin. Drop by spoonfuls on greased marble.

Mrs. Daniel Hicky (Louise McHenry)
Madison

# KISSES

4 egg whites
pinch of salt
1 cup granulated sugar

½ teaspoon vanilla
1 cup coarsely chopped nuts

Add salt to egg whites. Beat until stiff. Beat in sugar and vanilla. Stir in nuts. Drop by teaspoonfuls on cookie sheet. Bake at 300 degrees for 25 minutes. Yield 40-50 kisses.

**Mrs. Evan Thomas Mathis (Lois McMath)**
**Americus**

# FUDGE CANDY

½ cup margarine
1 pound confectioners' sugar
½ cup cocoa
1 tablespoon vanilla

4 tablespoons evaporated milk
¼ teaspoon salt
2 cups nuts, chopped

Measure all ingredients except nuts into glass mixing bowl. Place bowl in pan containing one inch simmering water. Stir over low heat until smooth. Stir in nuts, pour into buttered pan. Let cool. Cut into small squares. Yields two pounds of candy.

**Mrs. Bert D. Schwartz (Edith Wasden)**
**Macon**

# LEMON CHEESE FILLING

6 eggs
1½ cups sugar

4 tablespoons butter
3 lemons, juiced

Beat eggs. Add sugar and butter and juice of lemons. Put on low fire or in double boiler and boil until very thick stirring. Ice cake with plain white boiled icing.

**Mrs. Lee T. Newton (Catherine Hardin) (original from Annie Susan Callaway—my grandmother)**
**Forsyth**

# CARAMEL ICING

3 cups light brown sugar          ¾ cup butter
¾ cup evaporated milk             ½ teaspoon vanilla

Put in heavy saucepan and cook over moderate heat to soft ball stage (275 degrees), approximately 25 minutes. Remove from heat and allow to cool. Add vanilla and beat to spreading consistency.

**Mrs. Charles M. Woolfolk (Eleanor Bussey)**
**Columbus**

# CARAMEL ICING

2 cups sugar                      pinch salt
½ cup milk                        ½ cup sugar
½ cup evaporated milk             ½ cup butter

Put into large boiler 2 cups sugar, milk, salt. Heat to boil. At same time melt in heavy pan the remaining sugar until caramel color. Pour into boiling sugar and milk, add butter and cook until soft-ball stage. Cool. Beat until creamy.

**Mrs. George Arthur Horkan (Martha Oliff)**
**Moultrie**

# CHOCOLATE ICING

1½ squares melted chocolate       1 tablespoon lemon juice
¼ cup butter                      1½ cups confectioners' sugar
pinch of salt                     1 cup chopped nuts
1 egg, beaten                     1 tablespoon vanilla

Melt chocolate squares and butter in top of double boiler. Cream melted chocolate, butter and salt together. Cool chocolate mixture and add beaten egg. Add remaining ingredients, except nuts, mixing thoroughly. Stir in nuts.

**Mrs. Jack L. Stephenson (Winifred Harriss)**
**Atlanta**

# GRAPEFRUIT CANDY

3 grapefruit, peels only          2½ cups sugar
1 tablespoon salt

Remove membrane of segments of thick skinned grapefruit from peel. Soak the peel in a crock of water with salt, overnight. Drain off the water. Put in pot, cover with cold water and bring to a gentle boil for about two hours. During this time, change the water 3 times and repeat the process. In separate pot bring to boil 1½ cups of sugar and ½ cup water. Slice peel in strips, add to sugar syrup and boil slowly until the syrup boils away (about 15 mintues). Roll fruit strips in 1 cup of sugar while warm. Let stand until cool.

**Mrs. Noble Jones (Lynn Hargreaves)**
**Savannah**

# DATE LOAF CANDY
*Old Recipe of my Grandmother Cowan's*

2 cups sugar                      2 cups shelled pecans
1 cup milk                        1 pound dates, cut in bits
2 tablespoons butter

Cook sugar and milk until temperature on candy thermometer registers 250 degrees. Add butter and dates. Stir until mixed and add nuts. Cool until stiff enough to roll into 3 long rolls. Wrap in damp napkins or wax paper. Chill in refrigerator and slice as thin as possible. Will keep well for weeks.

**Mrs. Thomas Clay (Anita Lippitt)**
**Savannah**

# Pickles, Preserves and Jellies

PEACH PRESERVE

PEPPER JELLY

Ball

Mary F. Passailaigue

# WATERMELON RIND PICKLE

The following are the approximate proportions for one small melon.

1 Stone Mountain watermelon, small
1 cup slaked lime to 1 gallon water
2 tablespoons alum to 1 gallon water

3 pounds sugar
3 drops oil of cinnamon
1 pint cider vinegar
3 drops oil of cloves
6 drops oil of allspice

Pare off all green rind from the melon very carefully, after having scraped out all the pink meat. Cut in thin two-inch squares, about one-inch thick. Soak overnight covered by lime water. Stir occasionally. Next morning, drain and rinse and place in the weak solution of alum water sufficient to cover. Soak two hours. Drain and rinse thoroughly. Put in cold water and let come to a boil. Boil for one hour. Drain and plunge in ice water. Boil water to cover and, after draining the rinds, put in boiling water and cook until tender enough to be pierced with a straw; this usually means hard cooking for about an hour. Drain and pour over the rinds, in the same pan, a syrup made from the sugar, the oil of cloves, cinnamon and allspice and vinegar. (Good vinegar is very hard to find. It should be apple cider vinegar and tested for roughness by taste.) Cook in this syrup for about twenty minutes more. Too much cooking in vinegar, as well as too long soaking in alum, will toughen the pickle. Place rind and hot syrup in sterilized jars immediately and seal.

**Mrs. Andrew Cobb Erwin (Camilla McWhorter)**
**Athens**

# ARTICHOKE RELISH

6 bell peppers, cut up
3 quarts artichokes, sliced
1 quart onions, cut up
3 pounds white cabbage, cut up
½ gallon vinegar
1 jar mustard

¾ cup flour
3 pounds sugar
1 tablespoon turmeric
1 tablespoon black pepper
1 tablespoon mustard seed

Soak peppers, onions and cabbage overnight in 2 cups salt and 1 gallon water. Next morning, strain vegetables. Make paste of sugar, flour, turmeric, black pepper and mustard seed; add vinegar. Let cook 10 minutes; then add vegetables and cook 8 minutes longer. Add artichokes and let cook long enough to get hot through (2 to 3 mintues). Put in sterilized jars.

**Mrs. John Carroll Hagler (Susan Barrett)**
**Augusta**

# BREAD AND BUTTER PICKLES

4 quarts cucumbers, sliced
6 medium onions, cut in pieces
⅓ cup salt
5 cups sugar

3 cups vinegar
1½ teaspoons turmeric
1½ teaspoons celery seed
2 tablespoons mustard seed

Cover cucumbers, onions, and salt with ice. Let stand for 3 hours. Drain. Mix remaining ingredients in pan and bring to boil. Add drained cucumbers. Heat thoroughly, but do not boil. Pack while hot in sterilized jars.

**Mrs. James Wimberly (Helen Boardman)**
**Atlanta**

# BOO'S PEACH PICKLE

7 pounds of peaches, unpeeled
3½ pounds sugar

1 quart white vinegar
1 tea cup whole allspice

Bring sugar and vinegar to a boil with whole allspice tied in a bag (preferrably a clean piece of linen) to a side of pot. Boil 15 minutes. Put in a few peaches at a time, not boiling too hard, and let them stay in until tender. Test with a broom straw. When you feel the straw touch the seed, put in a sterilized jar and fill to top with juice. Seal. One seed in the juice makes it a pretty color. Try to get cling stone peaches, they are best, or later in the season, New Jersey peaches are good. They should be firm.

**Mrs. Robert Reid, Jr. (Helen Fuller)**
**Savannah**
Recipe of my mother, Mrs. Paul Hamilton Fuller (Beulah)

# SQUASH PICKLE

18 medium-size yellow squash
   sliced thin
2 tablespoons salt
2 bell peppers, chopped
2 onions, chopped
1 4-ounce jar pimentos

2 cups vinegar
1 teaspoon turmeric
2 teaspoons celery seed
2 teaspoons flour
2 teaspoons mustard seed
3 cups sugar

Sprinkle salt over sliced squash and cover with ice cubes. Let stand 2 hours or more and drain. Mix bell peppers, onions, pimentos, turmeric, celery seed, flour, mustard seed, sugar and vinegar. Bring to a boil. Add drained squash. Bring to a good boil again. Pack in sterile jars and seal. Makes 6 pints.

**Mrs. Edward L. Floyd, Jr. (Martha Ball)**
**Atlanta**

# SPICED PEACHES
*(Yield–12 to 14 Peach Halves)*

| | |
|---|---|
| 2 29-ounce cans peach halves | 2 teaspoons whole cloves |
| 1 cup white vinegar | 1⅓ cups sugar |
| 4 sticks cinnamon | |

Drain peaches reserving liquid. To liquid add all ingredients except peaches. Bring to a boil and simmer five minutes. Add peaches. Remove from heat and let cool. Refrigerate in covered container.

**Mrs. Floyd T. Taylor, Jr. (Annie Lee Wilson)**
**Brunswick**


# PICKLED FIGS

| | |
|---|---|
| soda | 7 cups sugar |
| 5 pounds of figs with stems | 1½ sticks cinnamon |
| 1 pint of vinegar | 1 tablespoon cloves |

Put handful of soda on figs. Cover with boiling water. Let stand 10 minutes. Wash thoroughly. Combine vinegar, sugar, and spices and bring to full rolling boil for 15 minutes. Add fruit. Bring to rolling boil again for 20 minutes. Place in sterilized jars and seal. Makes 5 to 6 pints.

**Mrs. Jim Porter Watkins (Joyce Ferrell)**
**Albany**


# GREEN TOMATO PICKLE

| | |
|---|---|
| 1 peck green tomatoes, sliced | ¼ box of mustard seeds |
| 1 quart of sliced onions | ½ ounce of whole cloves |
| 1 cup of salt | 1 ounce of celery seeds |
| 6 large green peppers | apple vinegar |
| 2½ pounds of sugar | |

Place tomatoes and onions in a large bowl. Sprinkle with salt and let stand overnight. Next day drain and rinse in cold water. Add sugar and cover with apple vinegar. Add mustard seed to the mixture. In a small cheesecloth bag put whole cloves and celery seed. Let bag float in mixture. Simmer two hours. Makes 5 pints.

**Mrs. James Sloan Budd, Jr. (Katharine Bowdré)**
**Atlanta**

# PEAR RELISH

| | |
|---|---|
| 1 peck pears | 1 tablespoon salt |
| 6 large green bell peppers | 1 tablespoon celery seed |
| 6 large red bell peppers | 3 cups sugar |
| 6 medium onions | 5 cups cider vinegar |
| 4 hot red peppers | |

Grind first five ingredients in food chopper. Add salt, celery seed, sugar and vinegar and boil for 30 minutes. Pour in sterilized jars and seal. Makes about 20 pints. Delicious served on vegetables.

**Mrs. Joe Glenn Smith (Virginia Marie Converse)**
Hahira

# RELISH

| | |
|---|---|
| 4 quarts cabbage, shredded | ½ ounce celery seed |
| 2 quarts green tomatoes | ½ ounce turmeric |
| 6 green peppers | 2 pounds sugar |
| 6 large onions | ½ cup salt |
| 2 ounces white mustard seed | 2 quarts vinegar |
| ½ teaspoon ground red pepper | |

Mix all ingredients together and cook for 20 minutes after coming to a boil.

**Mrs. Irwin L. Potts (Catherine Battle)**
Savannah

# ARTICHOKE RELISH

| | |
|---|---|
| 4 quarts Jerusalem artichokes, sliced thin before measuring | 2 tablespoons salt |
| | 2½ tablespoons dry mustard |
| 4 quarts mixture of cabbage, celery, green pepper, cut fine | 2 tablespoons French's prepared mustard |
| 2 quarts white vinegar | 2 cups flour |
| 4 cups sugar | turmeric, 1 tablespoon or more for color desired |
| 1 tablespoon cinnamon | |

Mix artichokes, cabbage, green pepper, celery, vinegar, sugar, cinnamon, salt, prepared mustard, dry mustard. Bring to a full boil. Let simmer 15 minutes. Make a flour paste by adding flour to water. Add a little at a time until thickened. Add turmeric. Again bring to a boil. Simmer 5 minutes. Pack in sterile jars.

**Mrs. Carl Linton Meadows (Comer Varnedoe)**
Savannah

## ARTICHOKE PICKLE

1 peck of artichokes
1 quart small white onions
1 gallon vinegar
3 pounds brown sugar
½ pound dry mustard
2 ounces white mustard seed

1 ounce celery seed
2 ounces whole black pepper
1 teaspoon salt
1 tablespoon whole cloves
1 tablespoon whole allspice
1 tablespoon turmeric

Scrub artichokes with small brush until white. Soak in strong brine for 24 hours. Rinse well. Put artichokes in sterilized jars. Add peeled onions. Mix mustard and turmeric with 1 cup of vinegar. Add remaining spices to rest of vinegar. Heat to boiling point, stirring occasionally. Add to cold vinegar. spice mixture slowly. Pour mixture over artichokes and onions in jars. Seal tightly. Allow to stand for 2 months to ripen before using. Yield: 8 quarts

**Mrs. J. Righton Robertson (Catherine Beard)**
**Augusta**

## CHOW-CHOW PICKLES

4 quarts green tomatoes
1½ dozen green bell peppers
4 medium white cabbages

2 pounds white onions
2 dozen dill pickles (not Kosher)
1 cup salt

Make brine of 1 cup salt and 1 gallon water. Cut vegetables in fairly large (bite-size) pieces and let soak overnight.

Next morning drain.

SAUCE

7½ cups sugar
1½ tablespoons turmeric
2½ cups flour
3 quarts white vinegar

1½ tablespoons dry mustard
1½ tablespoons celery seed
1½ tablespoons black pepper

Combine above ingredients and rub out all lumps. Add 3 quarts white vinegar and cook until thick as cream. Add vegetables that had been soaking in brine. Cook 5 to 10 minutes (until bell pepper is done). Stir well from bottom of pot and pack in jars and seal. Makes about 14 quarts.

**Mrs. Randolph Brooks (Polly Chisholm)**
**Savannah**

# CAULIFLOWER CABBAGE PICKLES

| | |
|---|---|
| 1 large cabbage | 4 tablespoons mustard seeds |
| 1 large cauliflower | 2 tablespoons turmeric |
| 3 or 4 white onions | ¾ cup sugar |
| 2 cups vinegar | stalk of celery |
| 1 cup water | salt to taste (1 tablespoon to begin) |

Chop cabbage, cauliflower, celery, and onion. Mix in a large pot. Mix vinegar, sugar, water, and pour over vegetables. Add mustard seeds, turmeric, salt, and mix together. Cook to a boil, lower heat and cook until tender but still crisp. Do not over salt. The desired taste can best be tested while hot. Fill sterilized jars while standing in hot water. Good with roast beef and vegetables.

**Mrs. George Wilmer Williams (Minnie Keller Roberts)**
**Savannah**

# PICKLED SHRIMP—SEA ISLAND

DRESSING

| | |
|---|---|
| 1½ cups Wesson Oil | ½ teaspoon Tabasco |
| ¾ cup vinegar | 4 pounds cooked shrimp |
| 1½ teaspoons salt | 8 small white onions, sliced thin |
| 1½ teaspoons mustard | |

Into a dish that has a cover, place a layer of shrimp, then a layer of onions. Bring dressing to a boil and pour over shrimp and onions. Cool. Cover dish and let stand in refrigerator overnight. Place on large platter with parsley to serve. This dressing can be strained and re-used, but all seasoning must be re-placed in it.

**Mrs. Joseph Thomas Warren (Rebecca Baldwin Jackson)**
**Americus**

## GRANDMA'S BLACKBERRY JELLY

**2 quarts or 4 quarts firm berries      sugar**

Remove all trash, such as stems, leaves, etc. Wash through at least two waters. Put in large preserving kettle and cover with water. Bring to boil and cook until berries are perfectly tender. Strain through a cotton cloth (like a flour sack opened into a square) into pan. The measure is ¾ cup sugar to 1 cup juice. But 3 cups sugar to 4 cups juice is the same. Put back in kettle and bring to a boil. Rinse cloth and strain again. This removes a lot of scum that comes up when boiling. Cook until the jelly boils thick, coming up in big thick bubbles. Watch closely to keep from boiling over. Either turn down the heat a little or slip the kettle a little. Test by using a spoon to drop a small amount onto a saucer. When drop remains firm, pour into heated jelly glasses. When cold, pour over each glass a thin covering of paraffin.

Remarks: Be sure the fruit isn't too ripe. Lots of red blackberries will help. This furnishes the pectin that makes the juice jelly. So if fruit is very ripe, use the juice of a large lemon or a box of Sure-Jell, which can be had at any grocery store. A two or three gallon kettle is best to use, even then you'd better watch to keep from boiling over. Two quarts makes 6 or 8 glasses, depending on size. This was my Grandmother's recipe—1800's, given me by my Mother, Mrs. H. H. Glover.

**Mrs. William B. McMath (Henryetta Glover)**
**Americus**

# Herbal Hints

Mary F. Passailaigue

# HERBAL HINTS

*To add different flavors to your salads or wherever vinegar is called for, the following herb and flower vinegar can easily be made.*

*TARRAGON:* Place either fresh or dried tarragon in a glass jar or bottle. Fill with white wine vinegar, let stand about six weeks. Basil, dill, mint, rosemary can be made in the above manner.

*ELDERFLOWER:* Place elderflower after being washed and dried in a glass bottle or jar. Fill with white wine vinegar, let stand ten days. Strain and bottle.

*ROSE PETAL:* 2 cups of white wine vinegar
        ½ cup of sugar
        1 quart of rose petals
Bring sugar and vinegar to a boil in an enamel pan. Add rose petals, cover and let stand overnight. Next day, strain and bottle.

*HERB BUTTERS:* Cream any one or combination of your favorite herbs with either butter or margarine. Use to make sandwiches or to put on cooked vegetables or meats.

*FRIED PARSLEY:* Take sprigs of fresh parsley. Heat butter or oil in a pan or skillet. Stir-fry for a few minutes until crisp. Do not overcook or it will be brown and bitter. Serve as an unusual garnish.

*ROSEMARY BISCUITS:* Add chopped fresh or dried rosemary with a little grated orange peel and a small amount of orange juice and sugar to your biscuit dough. Nice for tea.

*ROSEMARY CHICKEN:* Place chicken breasts on squares of aluminum foil. Salt and pepper the breast. Place a generous pat of butter on top. Sprinkle with fresh or dried rosemary leaves. Fold aluminum foil over chicken so it is completely sealed. Place on broiler or in pan and cook in a 350° oven 30 to 45 minuts. If not brown enough, unwrap and place under broiler for a few minutes.
    Rosemary adds a wonderful flavor to a leg of lamb.

*DILL SHRIMP:* 2 pounds shrimp
        1 stick butter or margarine
        1 tablespoon (or more if desired) fresh or dried dill weed
Clean shrimp. Melt butter in saucepan, add dill, stir-fry shrimp in butter until pink (5 to 10 minutes). Do not overcook. Serve with saffron rice.

*ROSE PETAL JELLY:* 2 cups apple juice
1 quart prepared rose petals
3½ cups sugar
1½ tablespoons lemon juice
2 tablespoons rose water
½ bottle Certo

Cook rose petals and apple juice five minutes. Remove from heat and let stand for 30 minutes. Strain. Add sugar, lemon juice and rose water. Bring to a boil, stirring constantly. Add Certo, bring to a boil and boil for one minute. Remove from heat and pour into sterilized glasses. Seal.

To add a different flavor to your favorite custard, add ½ teaspoon of rose water instead of vanilla.

*ELDERFLOWER FRITTERS:* Break flower heads into small clusters. Wash thoroughly. Make a tempura batter:
1 can beer (12 ounces)
1 cup flour
Salt to taste

Blend above ingredients and let stand 2 hours. Dip clusters into batter and fry in 375° oil.

Rose petals, tuberoses, squash blossoms or buds, day lily buds, may be made into fritters with the above recipe.

*GARDENIA PETALS:* To the above tempura recipe add 2 teaspoons sugar. Dip into batter and fry in 375 oil. Serve with powdered sugar.

*CANDIED ROSE PETALS:* Take the petals of roses. Cut off the white heel. Whip the whites of eggs until frothy. With a small brush cover the petal with the egg white, and holding it with tweezers, dip into granulated sugar. Place on waxed paper and dry.

Leaves of mint, carnations and whole violets may be candied in the above manner.

*BROILED TOMATOES WITH DILL:* Wash firm tomatoes. Cut in half and place on broiler. Sprinkle halves with garlic salt and black pepper. Sprinkle with fresh or dried dill weed. Cover with bread crumbs. Dot with butter or margarine. Sprinkle with fresh or dried parsley. Cook in a 350° oven for 30 to 45 minutes.

To remove white blush marks from furniture where water has marred the finish—use equal parts of turpentine, boiled linseed oil and paint thinner. (All may be purchased at a paint store). After mixing these three ingredients rub with a lint-free cloth and the spots disappear.

When unmolding a congealed salad always sprinkle a few drops of water on the serving plate. It will be easy to move the salad around to position it correctly.

Club soda will shine stainless steel in a jiffy.

To keep cottage cheese—store carton upside down. It will keep twice as long.

Garlic cloves will never dry out if you store them in a bottle of cooking oil. After the garlic cloves are used up you can use the garlic flavored oil for dressing.

When using green shrimp with 21-25 count per pound buy ⅓ pound per person.

To keep egg yolks from crumbling when slicing hard cooked eggs, dip the knife into water before each cut.

Use greased muffin tins as molds when baking stuffed green peppers.

Breaded meats tend to stick to the pan and lose their coating if they are fried. To prevent this bread the meat ahead of time and let it stand on waxed paper at least 20 minutes before frying.

Before opening a package of bacon roll it into a long tube. This loosens the slices and keeps them from sticking together.

Do *not* wash strawberries before storing. Wash before eating but store unwashed in colander covered lightly over top with foil or plastic wrap.

Egg whites may be frozen for future use. Freeze them in an ice tray, one egg white per compartment. When frozen remove from tray and store the blocks in a plastic bag. Take out the number needed each time and thaw them in the refrigerator—*never* at room temperature or they won't beat.

# Cook's Guide

## COOKING TERMS

**Boil**—Cooking in water, or liquid at boiling temperature. Bubbles will rise continually and break on the surface.

**Broil**—Cooking uncovered by direct heat, placing rack under the source of heat.

**Pan-boil**—Cooking in lightly greased pan on top of stove. Pour fat off as it accumulates so food does not fry.

**Baste**—Moistening food while cooking by pouring melted fat, drippings or other liquid over it.

**Cream**—Mashing or mixing food together until creamy.

**Pan-fry**—Cooking in small amount of fat in fry pan.

**Knead**—Pressing, stretching and folding dough mixture to make it smooth. Bread dough will become elastic.

**Parboil**—Boiling until partly cooked.

**Scald**—Heating liquid to just below boiling point.

**Simmer**—Cooking in liquid just below boiling point. Bubbles will form slowly and break below surface.

**Stew**—Boiling or simmering in small amount of liquid.

**Braise**—Cooking slowly in fat and little moisture in closed pot.

## CAKE TROUBLESHOOTING

| PROBLEM | POSSIBLE CAUSE |
| --- | --- |
| Cake is bready and solid. | Too much flour used |
| Cake falls | Insufficient quantity of flour or rising ingredients OR excess temperature OR moving cake in the oven before the cell walls have become firm by the heat after the cake has risen. |
| Uneven surface | Too much heat used |
| Crusting over the top before mixture has risen to full height | Too much heat used |
| Bursting at weakest point | Too much heat used |

# COOKING FOR 25

| | |
|---|---|
| BEEF | 10 pounds |
| HAM | 10 pounds |
| PORK | 10 pounds |
| HAMBURGER | 8½-9 pounds |
| WIENERS | 6-7 pounds |
| MEAT LOAF | 6 pounds |
| POTATOES | 8½ pounds |
| VEGETABLES | 1 No. 10 can |
| BAKED BEANS | 1¼ gallons |
| CABBAGE FOR SLAW | 5 pounds |
| BREAD | 3 loaves |
| ROLLS | 50 |
| PIE | 5 |
| CAKES | 2 |
| ICE CREAM | 1 gallon |
| PICKLES | ½ quart |
| OLIVES | ⅜ pound |
| FRUIT SALAD | 5 quarts |
| POTATO SALAD | 3 quarts |
| VEGETABLE SALAD | 5 quarts |
| LETTUCE | 5 heads |
| SALAD DRESSING | ¾ quart |
| MILK | 1½ gallons |
| COFFEE | ¾ pound |
| SUGAR | ¾ pound |
| CREAM | ¾ quart |

To serve 50 people, multiply by 2
To serve 100 people, multiply by 4

# Index

Mary F. Passailaigue

**Index**   **293**

Spinach I, 144
" II, 144
" Supreme, 144
" & Artichoke, 145
Squash and Corn, 140
Squash, 140
Squash, Emily Neel's, 140
Sweet Potato, 147
Swiss Bean, 158
Cauliflower Cabbage Pickle, 281
" Supreme, 157
Caviar Dip, 17
" Egg Mold, 16
" Mousse, 17
Charlotte, Chocolate, 227
Charlotte, Margarita, 224
Charlotte, Orange, 223
Charlotte Russe, Lemon, 222
CHEESE:
And Rice Dish, 164
" Shrimp Casserole, 79
Bacon Roll-ups, Hot, 37
Ball, Chutney, 23
Ball, Left Over, 20
Ball, Pineapple, 24
Biscuit, 20
Blue Velvet Mousse, 19
Boursin, 18
Bread, Pimento, 212
Cake, Blender Delight, 252
Casserole, 173
Cookies, 21
Dainties, 22
Fondue, Classical, 173
Grits, Garlic, 158
Hors' d'Oeuvres, Hot, 19
Onion Spread for Crackers, 21
Puffs, 23
Puffs, Baked, 23
Rings, 22
Soufflé I, 171
Soufflé II, 172
" , Freezer, 172
" , Quick, 173
Soup, Canadian, 50
Spread, Georgia Ramble Pimento, 212
Straws, 21
Wafers, 22
Welsh Rarebit, 170
Cherry Fruit Salad, 194
Cherry Mold, 221
Chess Pie, Chocolate, 242
Chess Pie, Virginia, 240
CHICKEN:
And Artichoke Casserole, 119

And Avocado with Curried Rice, 117
Baked in Buttermilk, 124
Bordeaux, 123
Breast with Artichoke Hearts, 118
Camoose Creek, 116
Casserole, 121
Chowder, 52
Company, 127
Country Captain, 114
Croquettes, Miss Maggie's, 127
Curry Crêpes, 129
Deviled, 128
French Herbed Casserole, 122
Hash, 125
Hot Luncheon Dish, 120
Japanese Casserole, 121
Layered Casserole, 115
Lemoned Baked, 117
Lemon with Wine, 116
Livers Divine, 130
Livers Hugo, 130
Liver Pâté, 31
Luncheon Casserole, 120
Mold, 185
Noodle Casserole for Company, 118
Oven Barbecued, 126
Party Casserole, 124
" Spaghetti for Eighteen
People, 115
Phillipine, 116
Pilau, 128
Poulet de Normandie, 122
Pressed, 121
and Rice Casserole, 128
And Rice, 129
Ritz, 126
Salad, 184
" , Baked, 126
" , Grandmother Hamilton's, 184
Sauterne, 123
Soup, Corn and Chinese, 51
Sour Cream, Maggie's, 125
Chili, 99
" Con Carne, 100
" Sauce, Midwinter, 175
Chinese Barbecued Spareribs, 110
" Chicken and Corn Soup, 51
" Rice, 164
" Vegetable Salad, 181
Chipped Beef Appetizer, 32
CHOCOLATE:
" Angel Torte, 225
" Cake, Best Ever, 260
" " , Devil's Food, 259
" Charlotte, 227

Georgia Heritage
329 Abercorn Street
Savannah, Georgia 31401

Please send me _____ copies of Georgia Heritage, at $7.95 plus
$1.25 handling.        New Price $8.95 Plus $1.50 Handling

Enclosed is my check or money order for $_____

NAME _____

ADDRESS _____

CITY _____STATE_____ ZIP CODE_____

Georgia Residents please add 4% sales tax

------------------------------------------------------------

Georgia Heritage
329 Abercorn Street
Savannah, Georgia 31401

Please send me _____ copies of Georgia Heritage, at $7.95 plus
$1.25 handling.

                    New Price $8.95 Plus $1.50 Handling

Enclosed is my check or money order for $_____

NAME _____

ADDRESS _____

CITY _____STATE_____ ZIP CODE_____

Georgia Residents please add 4% sales tax

------------------------------------------------------------

Georgia Heritage Prints
329 Abercorn Street
Savannah, GA 31401

Please send me _____ sets of watercolor prints at $5.00 each
plus $1.00 postage and handling per set.

Enclosed is my check or money order for $_____.

NAME _____

ADDRESS _____

CITY _____ STATE _____ ZIP CODE _____

Georgia Residents please add 4% sales tax.

Re-OrderAdditionalCopies

UNAVAILABLE